*Learning from
Real World Cases*

Lessons
in Leading
Change

D. D. Warrick & Jens Mueller

R🌑S
RossiSmith
ACADEMIC PUBLISHING

"There is nothing so practical as a good case study" is how Kurt Lewin might have introduced Warrick and Mueller's insightful book about leading change. Jam packed with rich cases that immerse the reader in the complex and uncertain world of organization change, this book is an invaluable guide for learning how to lead change.
– Thomas G. Cummings, PhD – Professor and Chair of the Department of Management
   and Organization, USC, Co-Author with Christopher Worley of Organization Development
   and Change (9th ed.) and Dynamic Strategy-Making with Larry Greiner

Warrick and Mueller's book of cases on leading change presents us with an outstanding collection of stories about the challenges and successes of change efforts on the ground in real organizational settings. This truly global collection of cases from experts in the field brings you closer to what change really means on an individual, group, and organizational level and how best to maximize your results. This book is one you must have for leading change and practicing organization development.
– Allan H. Church, PhD – Vice President, Global Talent Development, PepsiCo, Co-Author with
   Janine Waclawski of Organization Development: A Data-Driven Approach to Organizational Change

This book is a must read for those interested in successfully leading change. The fundamentals of leading change at the individual, group, and organizational level are illustrated by a diverse range of case studies. These exciting and well written cases inspire and instruct – highly recommended for leaders and students of leadership and change.
– Virginia E. Schein, PhD – Professor Emeritus of Management and Psychology,
   Gettysburg College, Co-Author with Larry Greiner of Power and Organization Development:
   Mobilizing Power to Implement Change

Outstanding book! When it comes to the topics of Change and Leadership there are theories and then there is reality. Warrick and Mueller walk us through real-life examples, which to me, is the most powerful way for people to take away something tangible that will benefit and improve their own organizations.
– President and CEO – Broadmoor Hotel (Five Star Hotel, Spa, and Golf Course)

Reading a book by Don Warrick is always an exceptional investment in knowledge. This book with Jens Mueller takes us into a world that we need to more fully understand – the world of leading change. This work of Warrick and Mueller moves us in a very meaningful way toward that goal. Read it! Student, executive, professor – read it if you want a better understanding of the most crucial role of leadership today – the role of leading change.
– Peter F. Sorensen, PhD – Director, PhD & Masters Programs In Organization Development, Benedictine
   University, Co-Author with Therese Yaeger of Strategic Organization: Managing Change For Success
   and Co-Author with David Cooperrider, Diana Whitney, and Therese Yaeger of Appreciative Inquiry:
   Rethinking Human Organization Toward A Positive Theory Of Change

All professionals who aspire to lead must become masters of change. Lessons in Leading Change offers the opportunity to learn through others who have led change. As a practitioner, I found the book relevant, useful, and inspirational.
– Karen Gardner – Director of Human Resources, Sandia National Laboratories

This is a superior collection of cases by many of the leading change agents in the world. The cases give the reader a real world feel for how to effectively lead change. It is a very important read for business students and leaders of all types of organizations.
– Robert A. Zawacki, PhD – Professor Emeritus of Management and International Business,
   Univ. of Colorado at Colorado Springs, Former Leadership Course Director, U.S. Air Force Academy,
   Co-Author with Wendell French and Cecil Bell of Organization Development and Transformation

Leading change is at the center of real value creation. This book is superb preparation for that most difficult challenge of successfully leading change.
– Robert E. Quinn, PhD – Margaret Elliott Tracy Collegiate Professor Of OB and HRD, Univ. of Michigan,
   Author of Change the World: How Ordinary People Can Achieve Extraordinary Results and Deep Change:
   Discovering the Leader Within

In these times of unprecedented change and transformation in the Healthcare industry, much of the change will be mismanaged with far reaching consequences because leaders don't understand how to effectively lead change. Lessons in Leading Change is an outstanding resource for preparing Healthcare leaders to lead change in the new world of integrated, coordinated, and collaborative healthcare delivery.
– Deborah L. Chandler – CEO, Colorado Springs Health Partners

Learning from Real World Cases
LESSONS IN
LEADING CHANGE

D.D. Warrick & Jens Mueller

ROSSISMITH
ACADEMIC PUBLISHING

National Library of New Zealand Cataloguing-in-Publication Data

Warrick, D. D.
Lessons in leading change : learning from real world cases /
D.D. Warrick, Jens Mueller. (Read to lead casebook series)
Includes index.
ISBN 978-0986459-70-2
1. Organizational change.. 2. Leadership—Case studies. I. Title.
II. Mueller, Jens, 1956- Ill. Series.
658.406—dc 23

©2012 RossiSmith Academic Publications Ltd., Oxford, UK
www.rossismith.com

Production and Distribution: Triaxis Ltd., New Zealand,
www.publicationsales.com
Design and layout: TYPE + *grafik*, B Janitz

It is my privilege to dedicate this book to one of the best and most inspiring leaders and change agents that I know, my dear wife Anna.
Anna continuously invests in the lives of others and persists as a self-less leader and friend in good times and bad and while suffering from many health problems and other challenges that would discourage all but the most courageous.
My admiration for her grows daily!

– D.D. Warrick

TABLE OF CONTENTS

Learning from Real World Cases,
LESSONS IN LEADING CHANGE

CHAPTER ONE:
Inspiring Cases On What Can Be Accomplished With Effective Change Leadership

Arienne McCracken & Susan Albers Mohrman

Gus Kious, president and medical director of Huron Hospital, used a focus on sustainability to turn the struggling inner-city hospital into a high-performing organization. At the hospital, he worked to change mental models, develop his employees, and empower teams for decision making. As he and his hospital faced ongoing turmoil stemming from the shifting strategies of the larger healthcare system in which Huron operated, Kious remained committed to his values and to the people whose efforts made the difference in his hospital's transformation.

David W. Stewart

Leading change at the community level requires creating a collaborative vision among constituents with often competing interests and with little or no formal authority. The financial crisis of the first decade of the 21st century required a city, Riverside California, to rethink its vision of itself and its future. This case describes how the City was reinvented into an award winning city.

Neha Gupta

The case highlights the role of leadership in engaging employees to sustain the supremacy of the ageing public-sector bank amidst competition from customer-oriented, sophisticated, tech-savvy private banks.

CHAPTER TWO:
The Significant Consequences Of
Ineffective Change Leadership

CHAPTER THREE:
The Fundamentals Of Effectively Leading Change

CHAPTER FOUR:
Leading Individual Change

CHAPTER FIVE:
Leading Group Change

CHAPTER SIX:
Leading Organization Change

FOREWORD

Studying and applying this book could be a career changer!
There are several reasons why we are confident in making such a
bold statement. First, next to leadership skills, skills in leading change
may very well be the most important skills you can acquire that will
determine your future success. We live in times of dynamic, non-stop,
unpredictable change and yet few leaders have ever been trained how
to lead change. Consequently, as you may have seen in numerous
studies on change, close to 70% or more of organization changes fail
altogether or fail to achieve the desired results. Failed change can
have far reaching short and long term consequences. Even when you
do the right things the wrong way they are likely to fail. You will see
cases in this book where excellent leaders damaged or even lost their
careers because they didn't understand and apply basic fundamentals
of effectively leading change. Skills in leading change will clearly set
you apart and significantly enhance your value.

There is another reason why we are confident this book can be a
career changer. Just gaining knowledge about change isn't enough to
make one skilled at leading change. *This book is designed to present
brief and highly interesting real world cases involving real world
leaders and to provide practical and applied discussion opportunities
and summaries of Key Lessons In Leading Change. In other words
it is designed for leaders and students to learn and internalize the
fundamentals of successfully leading change.* The principles and
patterns of what it takes to make changes with a high probability of
success will become abundantly clear.

There is a third reason we believe the book will have an impact
on your career. The cases should motivate you to see what is
possible when leaders are skilled at leading change and to encourage
you to realize the significant differences you can make if you are
willing to be a change leader. You will see cases where ordinary
individuals, some high in the organization hierarchy and some near
the bottom, have been able to make changes in people, teams, whole
organizations, processes, systems, and even whole countries.

To help you see what is possible when you are skilled at leading
change and keep your interest at a high level, we have tried to collect
cases about a wide variety of subjects related to change that are not
your typical academic cases. **The cases are written by authors
from around the world, many of whom who are internationally**

recognized experts. We think you will enjoy reading their profiles ad learning about the wealth of experience they bring to the cases.

As you begin to read this book we would encourage you to think about the structure of the book as a way of organizing your thinking about leading change. The book begins with inspiring cases on what can be accomplished with skilled change leadership. Hopefully this will encourage readers to recognize the importance of change leadership and to realize that skills in change leadership can help them accomplish far more than they may have thought possible. The book then focuses on cases that portray *the significant consequences that can occur when leaders do not understand the fundamentals of effectively leading change.* If leaders are not motivated to develop skills in leading change by inspirational cases they will surely be motivated by wanting to avoid the potential consequences of mismanaged change. The remainder of the book then presents cases on the *fundamentals of leading change followed by cases on leading individual change, then group change, and finally leading organization change.* We chose the last case in the book to be a capstone to the strong appeal for leaders to develop skills in leading change as you will read about a young staff worker in the Ministry of Education in Columbia who used skills in leading change to transform a country!

Chapter 1 begins with **Inspiring Cases On What Can Be Accomplished With Effective Change Leadership**. In this chapter you will read stories of a hospital President and Medical Director who took a struggling, money losing inner-city hospital and developed it into a profitable, high performance organization. One of the most inspiring cases is about how the Dean of the College of Business at the University of California at Riverside partnered with the Mayor of Riverside to organize community leaders to seize the destiny of the city when it was hit by the housing crisis and a 14% unemployment rate in the surrounding area and in two years turned it into an award winning city that was ranked number 3 among "can do" cities by *Newsweek* and was named by the state of California as its first Emerald City for its accomplishments. You will also see how a bank President in India was able to turn around the largest public sector bank in India by using skills in change leadership to build commitment to transforming the bank at the top and then engage over 200,000 employees and 16 branches in the change process.

Finally, you will read about how leaders of a bank in the Kingdom of Bahrain were able to successfully acquire and integrate another bank and become one of the leading banks in Bahrain and about how change leadership was used to design and build a world class Army Hospital. As is the process in all of the cases in the book, each case concludes with rich opportunities for discussing the case and key lessons that can be learned about change leadership.

Chapter 2 addresses **The Significant Consequences Of Ineffective Change Leadership**. Leaders are seldom trained in change leadership so they are often unaware of the serious consequences that can occur when change is mismanaged. This chapter begins with a case on the world of *pseudo change* where leaders think they are changing things when they are not or they are addressing symptoms rather than the real issues or worst yet, because of poorly planned change, the cure is far worse than the disease. Then there is a fascinating case that occurred at Brandeis University where an excellent university President and his board made a decision to implement a change and because of a lack of understanding of the fundamentals of change and how to build support for change, had a backlash that made national news and alienated many of their stakeholders. Next is a case where a well respected COO of a large metropolitan hospital system implemented a new Electronic Medical Records system in a well intended but flawed way that caused a major uproar among the physicians and medical staff. In the next case you will see an opportunity for redemption after a CEO implemented change the wrong way, learned from his mistakes through the coaching of his HR Director, and then took a much more effective and successful approach to change. You will also have an opportunity to learn from cases on how not to do strategic planning and the mistakes leaders can make in initiating change when they are out of touch with those they lead and again don't understand effective change leadership.

Chapter 3 provides cases on **The Fundamentals Of Effectively Leading Change**. Throughout this book you will begin to see fundamentals *of successful change leadership such as having a keen awareness of present realities and future ideals, having a clear and compelling vision, leader involvement in helping lead the changes, engaging key stakeholders in the change process, having a sound change plan and being willing to make needed adjustments, and planned follow through to make sure the change is sustained.*

The first case in this chapter points out the importance of self-awareness in leading change. Change leaders who are unaware of the impact they are having and the example they are setting will not understand their influence on the change process and the probability of the change succeeding. Then there are cases on applying change fundamentals to developing a top leadership team into a high performing team and applying sound change fundamentals to transforming a deep South University into a leader in preparing students for a new internationally influenced organization world. What was accomplished in this Southern University by a visionary President who was a skilled change leader is quite amazing! This chapter concludes with a case that gives the reader an opportunity to explore how to use change leadership to merge two companies and a case on the importance of being able to communicate changes in a way that influences the heart as well as the mind. Engaging both the heart (emotions) and the mind (logic and reason) is important to successful change leadership.

Chapter 4 is titled **Leading Individual Change**. It is the first of three chapters on leading individual change, then group change, and finally organization change. The first case helps readers think through what change leaders need to do to help change weary employees transition through yet more changes. The next case shows how a private hospital in Dhaka Bangladesh used effective feedback and positive employee recognition to successfully change the way customer service department employees interacted with patients, doctors, nurses, and other hospital staff to improve the customer care experience. Then a case is presented that shows how efforts were made to re-engage teachers and the community in helping change the culture of a high school that had a history of success but was starting to decline on many levels and was losing the favor of the local community. The last case in this chapter addresses a situation where a collaborative relationship needed to be developed between a manager in a manufacturing enterprise and a long time vendor where the relationship could possibly be damaged because of some quality issues with the vendor. Skilled change leaders use a positive approach to building relationships, resolving issues, and turning difficulties into opportunities rather than an in your face or win/lose approach.

FOREWORD

Chapter 5 is titled **Leading Group Change**. This chapter begins with a case that points out that while everyone believes in teamwork and it is clear that teamwork is one of the keys to gaining competitive advantage, few organizations do anything to build teamwork and high performance teams. The payoffs can be substantial when there is teamwork at the top, within teams, between teams, and outside the organization with important stakeholders. The case provides guidelines on how to build high performance teams and applies the guidelines to helping change a dysfunctional top leadership team into a high performing team. In the second case, we are introduced to the lavish, hi-tech, continuously changing movie industry and how the HR Director in a major file studio transformed the HR function. The next case takes the reader to China and an interesting case where nine doctoral students and two professors from a US college worked with a visionary HR Director in a Chinese company to help develop a high impact department. The following case is also an international case. It involves building a leadership community with 250 leaders spread across seventeen countries in the Asia Pacific in Unilever Food's Asia division. The goal is to help the leaders understand the simple proposition that *"none of us is as smart as all of us"* and to learn to share ideas and work together as a team with common interests. It should be pointed out that large group changes have the potential to result in significant payoffs and to accelerate the change process but that they require a high level of experienced expertise to guide the process. The final case in this chapter on changing groups involves using a concept called *"complexity theory"* to manage change in diverse groups that have difficulty working together.

Chapter 6 concludes the progression of learning to be a change leader with individuals, groups, and whole organizations. The chapter is titled **Leading Organization Change**. Leading organization change requires the same change fundamentals used in working with individuals and groups but involves more complexity and greater payoffs and greater risks. It is more likely to require the involvement of external expertise although you will see a case where an individual at a fairly low level in a large organization leads changes that impact a whole country. The first case invites readers to use what they have learned about leading change to help plan a merger of three sports medicine organizations. Then the reader is introduced to a concept called *"appreciative inquiry"* that is used to change a school district. Next readers are taken to Italy and the luxury Apparel and Fashion Industry and are engaged in a case involving the turnaround of a well established company that was losing business and market share and needed to be transformed. The next case involves applying a process called *"whole system transformation"* to transforming the Information and Communication Technology function in a global manufacturing organization with 55,000 employees worldwide. The final case and the one we especially like and chose as the capstone to the book shows how a person at any level of an organization who has skills in leading change can use these skills to influence significant changes. In this captivating case, a young staff worker in the Ministry of Education in Columbia uses *"transformational leadership"* to involve, engage, and empower leaders, teachers, and communities to transform the elementary educational system in Columbia where the average number of primary education years in Columbia averaged 3.8 years in urban areas and 1.7 years in rural areas. Her efforts and the process for educational reform that she helped developed not only impacted her whole country but now are used in countries throughout Latin America and Asia.

While this book has required a substantial effort to put together, it has been a labor of love as working with the accomplished authors and seeing the need for a book of real world cases on leading change has been a tremendous motivator. We are convinced that the lessons provided in this book can transform careers and lives as few leaders are trained in how to lead change and effectively led change can result in significant payoffs to organizations, the people in them, and the people impacted by them. In conclusion, we want to thank the many authors who made this book possible and those involved in the production of the book.

D.D. Warrick and Jens Mueller

BIOGRAPHY *D. D. Warrick*

Dr. Warrick is an award winning educator, consultant and author who specializes in developing high impact leaders, high performance teams and organizations, and successfully managing change. He is a Professor of Management and Organization Change at the University of Colorado at Colorado Springs where he holds the title of President's Teaching Scholar and has received the Chancellor's Award, the university's highest award, as well as the Outstanding University Teacher of the Year Award, and many teaching awards in the College of Business. Dr. Warrick is also the President of the Warrick Agency and has been a consultant to many large companies such as Allied Signal, British Petroleum, Dow Corning, Harley-Davidson, Hewlett Packard, IBM, and Whirlpool, as well as smaller and mid-sized companies, public agencies, and numerous colleges and universities. He has received many awards for his contributions including being named the Outstanding Organization Development Practitioner of the Year, the Outstanding Human Resources Professional of the Year, and the Outstanding Educator of the Year in Organization Behavior. He has also received numerous awards from the Academy of Management and was recently named the Best Professor in Organisational Development by the World HRD Congress.

Dr. Warrick received his BBA and MBA degrees from the University of Oklahoma and doctorate from the University of Southern California.

D. D. Warrick
Professor of Management and Organization Change and
President's Teaching Scholar
Graduate School of Business
Email: ddwarrick@aol.com

BIOGRAPHY *Jens Mueller*

Jens Mueller is Associate Professor for Entrepreneurship and Strategy at the Waikato Management School at the University of Waikato in Hamilton, New Zealand, Triple Crown accredited business school and the No 1 Research-Led Business School in New Zealand. Based on his research work and more than 20 years of Chair/CEO experience in global industries, Jens assists leaders of many organizations worldwide to create effective strategies for sustainable growth. Jens sits on several boards of companies and teaches MBA courses at several prestigious universities internationally. He is a prolific author and a very engaging presenter, frequently invited to work with the leadership teams of government departments, non-profit entities and commercial enterprises. His details are at **www.muellerjens.com**

Jens Mueller
Associate Professor of Entrepreneurship and Strategy
Waikato Management School
University of Waikato
Hamilton, New Zealand
Email: m@usainfo.net

CHAPTER ONE

1

Huron Hospital: Leading With Sustainability To Create A High Performing System

Arienne McCracken
Susan Albers Mohrman

Center for Effective Organizations, Marshall School of Business
University of Southern California

Major Focus Of The Case

Gus Kious arrived at Huron Hospital and set out to turn this struggling inner-city hospital into a high-performance system. Starting in the late 1950's, participative management has been documented as leading to higher organizational effectiveness and outcomes, as people "are motivated by a sense of involvement and commitment" (Lawler, 1986, p. x). The presence or absence of the following key characteristics at lower levels in the organization reveals how participative a workplace actually is: 1) power/decision making, 2) information flowing both downwards and up, 3) rewards, 4) knowledge of the organization and skills/training. A fifth characteristic is how much of the organization is actually involved. Kious explicitly had the development of a high-performing organization in mind as he took the reins at his hospital in 2004.

In a twist on earlier high-performance transitions, Kious used a focus on sustainability as a lever to change the mindset of people and stimulate a focus on high performance. A commonly cited definition of sustainability comes from the UN Brundtland Commission's 1987 report, which called for "meeting the needs of the present without compromising the needs of future generations" (UN General Assembly, 1987). Current thinking fleshes out this definition by specifying the so-called triple bottom line of sustainable ecological, economic, and social outcomes. Although there is no standardized "recipe" for a sustainable organization, there is a core realization that sustainability requires a complex and systemic approach, since "all boundaries are permeable" (Mohrman & Worley, 2010).

What do high-performance systems and sustainability initiatives mean to a leader's role? In this case, we introduce a leader, Gus Kious, who took the reins of a poorly performing hospital and describe his actions and successes. We also touch upon the issue of the shifting strategies of the larger health care system in which Kious operates, which may eventually lead to Kious' hospital being repurposed or shut down – a casualty, ironically, of the national search for sustainable health care delivery approaches. This leads us to a recognition that in today's world of rapid and dynamic change, globalization, and resource shortages, effective leadership may look far different than it did in the past.

Gus Kious, Huron Hospital, and the Cleveland Clinic

The man was drowning, and he didn't know if he was going to make it. He had been swimming off the coast of South Africa when a riptide suddenly dragged him away from shore. Terrified, he frantically fought against the current without much success. The man understood that he was indeed beginning to drown and felt a myriad of things at the same time: he was aware that his energy was almost used up, and he was pessimistic about getting out alive. As a physician, the man had seen death and was accepting of it. But at the same time, he somehow knew that it wasn't yet his time, and in his mind he saw what he had to do. With the last bit of energy he had, he reoriented the direction of his movement and made it to shore.

Gus Kious had cause to remember that day in his past when he took on the role of president and medical director of Huron Hospital in 2004. Huron is a 211-bed acute care teaching hospital located in East Cleveland, Ohio and is one of the regional hospitals in the Cleveland Clinic system.

The non-profit Cleveland Clinic is an internationally recognized hospital system. Its accolades include being cited as an exemplar of health care by President Obama during his fight to pass the health care reform bill in 2009. It was lauded in a *Newsweek* article as being the future of healthcare and a model of effectiveness both in the realm of curing and in its method of doing business (Adler & Interlandi, 2009), and is currently ranked #4 in the *U.S. News & World Report* "Honor Roll" of best American hospitals (Comarow, 2009). The Clinic, which was founded in 1921 by four doctors, now employs 2000 physicians and scientists and system wide sees 4.2 million patient visits per year. Centered in Northeast Ohio, the Cleveland Clinic system has or manages facilities in Canada, Las Vegas, Florida, and Abu Dhabi. The main campus building of the Cleveland Clinic is a gracious, ergonomic, art- and light-filled structure with handsome patient rooms and a state-of-the-art nether level filled with robots that move supplies throughout the main campus.

The laurel wreathes heaped upon the Clinic may seem fairly incongruous when taking a cursory glance at Huron Hospital. Huron is clearly an old, small facility in East Cleveland, the poorest part of a struggling city in the heart of the so-called Rust Belt, that part of the U.S. that was the erstwhile manufacturing center of the country but is now mostly known for its weak economic base and depopulation. Huron Hospital has for many years been a major provider of charity care and thus a money loser for the Clinic system. In addition, when Kious became head of the hospital, it was also struggling with quality issues, long lengths of stay, and employee morale.

Kious at Huron

Kious set out first to get to know people at every level in the hospital. He made it a habit to take long walks throughout the facility. Staff, patients, and family members saw the big, amiable, bald guy in the hall, and he talked to them. You want to talk to him – he's just that kind of person. "Never better!" he'd reply when asked, "How are you, Dr. Kious?"

The walk arounds were a sign that Huron would no longer operate as a stratified and siloed organization. Now, Huron people speak to everyone else, no matter the function, the department, the title, or the level. Tommy Anastasio, a manager in facilities engineering, mentioned that now it's "easier to get your point across. [Michael] O'Connell is my VP. I can come up and talk to him any time."

Gus had clear objectives in his mind as he began his tenure as president of the hospital. First was the goal of developing the hospital into a high-performing organization. Kious also wanted the hospital to become a valued referral center (especially for chronic diseases), in order to attract a broader population of patients. He was strongly committed to identifying, developing and promoting talent. These goals coalesced into one overarching goal: to become a sustainable hospital: financially, strategically, and environmentally (Kious, 2009).

Kious began to associate the feelings and attitudes prevalent among hospital employees with how he had felt during his near-death experience so many years earlier. The mounting despair and frustration against something seemingly unconquerable was obvious to him. And yet again, he somehow knew that it wasn't time for the hospital to give up the fight. His Huron people had talents, and the hospital would need them all to make a turnaround. He worked primarily with the existing staff, although he did fire a few people, including doctors who did not want to "get it right." What needed to change was, rather, his people's mental models as to what was possible. As Senge (1990, p. 8) has written, mental models are "deeply held internal images of how the world works, images that limit us to familiar ways of thinking and acting." Extremely powerful, outmoded mental models need to be exposed to daylight so that real change can be effected.

Kious first challenged the old mental models in place at Huron by steadily developing the talents of his employees. Katie McGhee, director of case management and co-chair of the Operations Council, says that he taught her to talk to physicians, not always an easy thing to do. Kious says, "My promise to my people is that I will help develop them if they sign on to make Huron a great place – and I see it as success if they move on and are promoted." Kious held voluntary monthly one hour education session aimed at helping staff and physicians "learn the business." The first ten minutes of every management council meeting were spent on learning something new to the group. Kious created a process for what he called "charettes" – intense participative design processes using full knowledge of the system being redesigned. A very large bulletin board made information accessible to all staff, physicians, and any patients, family, or other community members who walked by. It contained all the relevant information about the community being served, the challenges being faced by the hospital, and all current operating statistics and accomplishments of the system. Passersby could post questions and ask for more information, and initiate and participate in design projects.

Sustainability Enters the Picture

Sustainability came into Gus' awareness through the consciousness raising of his daughter-in-law. Their talks began to merge in Gus' thoughts with the latest accoutrement to his walk arounds: the "Kious bag" – a trash bag Gus would fill with expired or old medicines, supplies, and equipment. The Kious bag was a tangible symbol of the unnecessary waste that the hospital was generating.

Gus soon saw that issues of sustainability, especially "green" or environmental issues, found fertile ground in all levels of the Huron staff. Kious provided several managers with opportunities to be trained in leadership for sustainability by the local group E4S (Entrepreneurs for Sustainability). These leaders in turn set up a "Green Team" to shepherd improvements into how the hospital operated. The Huron employees who constituted the Green Team quickly became personally committed to environmental sustainability and rapidly involved many others in the initiatives. Kious challenged his staff to eliminate 50% of the hospital's solid waste within four years. It was a very ambitious goal, and they achieved a 37% reduction. The Green Team introduced many more environmental improvements into the hospital, such as focusing on energy efficiency, reduction of toxicity, the elimination and consolidation of the myriad of redundant printers and other electronic equipment that were scattered in offices throughout the hospital, and the introduction of a community garden and of organic foods into the patients' menus.

The green aspect of sustainability proved to be a springboard for Huron's overall collective vision. It instilled the value of using resources carefully and with an eye to reducing waste and leveraging resources. This value began to permeate all decisions. For example, the lab team initiated a sharing process with another Cleveland Clinic hospital, whereby each would do analyses for each other during very busy periods, thereby removing the necessity to increase the staff in either lab. Green sustainability unleashed a positive energy and pride that spilled over into other areas – it was a truly powerful reshaper of mental models. It also provided a vehicle to start to break down barriers with the community, which had been mainly distrustful of large institutions.

Teams Making Decisions

Kious is a strong advocate for management by teams, and he pushed decision making down to middle managers in his hospital. The Operations Council, which is composed of approximately 25 middle managers from all functions, has decision-making rights over day-to-day operations and accountability for the hospital's bottom line. The Green Team works closely with the Operations Council and with other leadership groups, all of whom are collectively accountable for making progress toward the goals and achieving excellence in all aspects of hospital functioning. Together they have identified the various elements of sustainability and established goals, initiatives, and measurement systems that ensure that there is continual focus on ecological, financial and patient and employee outcomes.

Front-line workers meet as a team every morning to coordinate patient information, care, and check-ins and check-outs. This team includes floor nurses, admissions staff, orderlies, and others who see to it that people are treated and discharged in the most efficient way possible.

A residents' group meets with the head doctor daily to discuss cases and treatments. These teams share information and learning with each other while striving to effect the best care. Greater integration both within the hospital and with surrounding community agencies has led to greater financial sustainability, as patient stays that had been the longest in the system now are among the shortest.

Where does Kious fit into decision making? He has stated that he and his executive team: 1) exist to remove barriers for the Operations Council; and 2) have decision rights only over policy and strategy. Kious has clearly pushed decision making very far down into the organization.

Fitting into the Clinic System

All of Huron's efforts didn't go unnoticed by the rest of the Cleveland Clinic system. Many of their pioneering efforts have now been implemented across the hospital system. For example, the Clinic's main campus now offers a farmers' market. Huron was the pilot for the networked printer concept, which is now a commonplace in the hospital system. Tommy Anastasio in facilities engineering noted that he gets asked all the time, "How much would it cost us if we went green? – Call Tom – Huron already did it. Ask him." Kious reports with pride that a number of Huron's managers have served on Clinic-wide councils, many have received system wide visibility, and some have been promoted into positions throughout the Cleveland Clinic System.

Huron Hospital had a positive EBIDA (earnings before interest, depreciation, and amortization) four quarters in a row for the first time in 2007-2008, is steadily becoming a referral center for chronic illness throughout Cleveland, and has greatly increased patient satisfaction metrics. In June, 2010, the hospital broke ground for an outpatient community health center focusing on chronic illness. However, even with Huron's high-performing culture, willingness to pilot, and dedication to excellence, Kious says, only half joking, "We're in the red, so word is always out that they're out to get us and close us down."

The vast transformation being undertaken in American healthcare at present must be kept in mind as a looming presence and constraint on all healthcare systems and actors. The Cleveland Clinic as a system is steering through unknown waters at the same time that Kious and his hospital are remaking themselves into a high-performing organization, but the two efforts are not always meshing. The Clinic, as a fee-for-service health care institution, is in the midst of a system-wide transformation to create sustainable healthcare delivery and position itself for the future by greatly increasing its efficiency and the leverage of resources to provide more affordable, high quality health care. It thinks about volume and numbers of procedures and the quality and reach of care across the greater system. Simply put, Huron's mission may not be in alignment with the Clinic system's strategy – a strategy formed for broader scope and leverage, with less focus on local communities and sub-populations. The recession that began in 2008 has negatively impacted Huron's case load and made it more difficult to achieve financial viability even with its new-found efficiencies. The 2009 Cleveland Clinic annual report writes about "cost measured against need" and the "progressive alignment of Cleveland Clinic's many parts into a fully integrated healthcare delivery network." Delos Cosgrove, the CEO of the Cleveland Clinic, said in an interview in *Newsweek*, that "The days of the stand-alone hospital being able to be all things to all people I think is gone – it winds up being a duplication of effort and duplication of cost, and it doesn't engender high quality." (Interlandi, 2009). Thus, Huron Hospital's future status is uncertain. At least in its current form, it may not be able to significantly contribute to the overall sustainability and effectiveness of the larger Cleveland Clinic system.

Leading During Difficulty

Gus Kious continues to be proud of and fight for Huron, but he is keenly aware of the uncertainties of the situation. He speaks thoughtfully about the latest developments in healthcare in general and in the Cleveland Clinic in particular, and he recognizes that decisions will come from his Cleveland Clinic bosses. But come what may, whether facing a recession, or a system-wide transition that may fundamentally change Huron Hospital as it is currently configured, Kious grows, supports, and promotes the talented people who do him proud every day. He now says that it's not the hospital per se that is important, but the people, and their opportunities to use their talents to provide high quality health care. And he worries for both the community and the Clinic because if Huron were to be closed, it could send a bad message about the Clinic and its intentions to the community, since Huron's patients are mainly economically disadvantaged and African-American.

Gus' approach to leadership has changed. Always a spiritual and philosophical man, Kious clearly is drawing upon a deeply held belief system as he exudes a stillness and receptivity in his commitment to leading in a time of greater difficulty without letting fear or reaction rule him.

Whatever the changes to come, unknown or inexorable, he will strive to remain true to his values. He is not the "heroic" fighter of old. At this point in time, Kious feels it is important for him to model and promote these values:

- **Know who you are as a spirit**
- **Be true to your values**
- **Speak with truth and from the center, without being reactionary**
- **Be present and give feedback**
- **"Doing" periodically, but "being" always**

Huron's staff remain motivated and committed, although aware that change may come. Perhaps Kious' experiences show that in today's world, developing people and building commitment and capabilities to support the principles of excellence and service is the most lasting contribution to a sustainable future. Building a particular high-performing institution may be best understood as one of an ongoing shifting of journeys and venues in which that happens.

References

Adler, J., & Interlandi, J. (2009, December). The hospital that could cure health care. Newsweek.

Cleveland Clinic. (2009). The future of healthcare: 2009 annual report. Retrieved July 11, 2010, from http://my.clevelandclinic.org/about/cleveland_clinic_annual_reports.aspx

Comarow, A (2009). America's best hospitals: The 2009-2010 honor roll. U.S. News & World Report. Retrieved July 11, 2010 from http://health.usnews.com/health-news/best-hospitals/articles/2009/07/15/americas-best-hospitals-the-2009-2010-honor-roll.html

Interlandi, J. (2009, August 7). Cleveland Clinic CEO speaks on health-care reform: "We may end up making the problem substantially worse." Newsweek. Retrieved July 11, 2010, from http://www.newsweek.com/blogs/the-human-condition/2009/08/07/cleveland-clinic-ceo-speaks-on-health-care-reform-we-may-end-up-making-the-problem-substantially-worse.html

Kious, A. G. (2009, October). Creating systemic sustainability in a resource-constrained setting. Presentation at the conference on "In Search of Sustainable High Quality Health Care: An International Exploration," Gothenburg, Sweden.

Lawler, E. E. (1986). High-involvement management. San Francisco: Jossey-Bass.

Mohrman, S. A., & Worley, C. G. (2010). The organizational sustainability journey: Introduction to the special issue. Organizational Dynamics, 39(4).

Senge, P. (1990). The fifth discipline: The art and practice of the learning organization. New York: Doubleday Currency.

United Nations General Assembly. (1987). Report of the World Commission on Environment and Development: Our common future. Transmitted to the General Assembly as an Annex to document A/42/427 - Development and international co-operation: Environment. Retrieved July 11, 2010, from http://www.un-documents.net/wced-ocf.htm.

Discussion

1. Building an exceptional organization only occurs when leaders are committed to building something special, provide the leadership necessary to accomplish great things, and are willing to make significant changes. Describe the vision Gus had for the hospital, the characteristics of Gus as a change leader, and indicators Gus was willing to make significant changes.

2. Change leaders often use an initiative or super goal as a lever to change the mindset of people and build a commitment to change. Gus used sustainability as a focus for change. Discuss your understanding of sustainability, how Gus defined sustainability, and what he actually did to achieve sustainability at the Huron Hospital.

3. Change leaders have a plan for making changes and doing things to prepare organizations for changes in thinking and acting. What were the change goals (objectives) Gus had and what were some things Gus did to change the way people think and act?

4. Gus used teams to make changes. Describe some of the teams he used and what they did to accomplish changes.

5. Building a healthy, high performance organization is a never ending process. You can never rely on past laurels to achieve future success. What are some of the challenges Gus faces in the future and what is he doing to prepare the hospital for the future? Can you think of other things he could be doing?

Key Lessons In Leading Change

1. Change leaders need to be committed to building something special, to being able to communicate a clear and understandable vision, and to having a sound plan for achieving and sustaining successful changes.

2. In any system, we can no longer assume stability; change is inevitable, and one's leadership should not be based on assumptions of permanence.

3. A leader has to implement change in several areas for a high-performing system to emerge. Per Lawler (1986), these include 1) power/decision making, 2) information flow, 3) rewards, 4) knowledge of the organization and skills/training, and 5) how much of the organization is actually involved.

4. Transformation requires changing mental models. Success stems from breaking away from the closed mindset of how things were done previously. Leaders play a key role in helping organizational members change mental models.

5. Coaching is one way that leaders can help people develop and become more effective. It relies on the establishment of trusting relationships, and of confidence by the coachees that the coach has knowledge and insight to impart that will help the coachees to achieve performances and goals and outcomes that they care about.

6. In an economy of scarcity, leaders have to learn to do more with less or with nothing and help the greater system do that as well. Helping the members of the system understand how they fit in the bigger system is an important part of coaching.

BIOGRAPHY

Arienne McCracken is program manager and research associate for the Sustainability Program at USC's Center for Effective Organizations (CEO) in the Marshall School of Business.
She lives in Los Angeles.

Arienne McCracken

Center for Effective Organizations

Marshall School of Business

University of Southern California

3415 South Figueroa Street, DCC 200, Los Angeles, CA 90089-0871, United States.
Tel: +1 213 740 9814.

Email: amccracken@marshall.usc.edu

Susan Albers Mohrman (Ph.D., Northwestern University) is senior research scientist at USC's Center for Effective Organizations (CEO) in the Marshall School of Business. She is co-author of *Self-Designing Organizations, Designing Team-Based Organizations,* and editor of *The Handbook of Collaborative Research* and *Useful Research: Advancing Theory and Practice.* She is co-faculty director of CEO's program in organization design and of its Sustainability Program, a program based on collaborative research and the creation of an international learning community involving practitioners and academics.
She lives in Altadena, California.

Susan Albers Mohrman

Center for Effective Organizations

Marshall School of Business

University of Southern California

3415 South Figueroa Street, DCC 200, Los Angeles, CA 90089-0871, United States.
Tel: +1 213 740 9814.

Email: smohrman@marshall.usc.edu

2

Seizing Our Destiny: Reinventing A City During An Economic Downturn

David W. Stewart

In 2008 Riverside, California found itself at the epicenter of the United States housing crisis. Unemployment in the city and surrounding region exceeded 14%. One in twelve houses were in foreclosure. An economic development model based on "cheap dirt," had dominated the city and the region for more than a decade. Residential and commercial construction, infrastructure, and related industries, such as mortgage origination, had been the growth industries on which the region had become dependent to the near exclusion of a more diversified economic base. There was a clear and obvious need for change and a new economic model for the City and the region. There was also a clear and obvious need for leadership that could create a new vision for the future and gain broad community for change and support for this vision.

This is a case study of the way a group of community leaders recreated the vision for economic redevelopment of the City of Riverside. It illustrates leadership within the context of a public/private sector partnership focused on changing the future of a city. It also demonstrates the power of ideas when embraced by a community grass roots movement. "Seizing Our Destiny" is the name that emerged to identify this movement. Begun in early 2009 and approved by the city council in late 2009 the movement has transformed a city. In 2011 the City of Riverside was named one of the seven most intelligent cities in the world by the Intelligent Community Forum and had become California's first Emerald City. In September of 2011 *Newsweek* ranked the City number 3 among "can do" cities. This case is the story of how Riverside, the City of Arts and Innovation, transformed itself through leadership at a grassroots level.

Background

From its beginning, Riverside has been a City of forward-thinking, creative and ingenious pioneers and innovators. In 1870 when John North looked at the rich land bordering the Santa Ana River, he was able to envision rolling hills of agriculture and a city destined to be the center of Inland Southern California. To make his dream a reality, North and other founders built in 1871 a canal that still brings a dedicated source of water, making Riverside one of the only cities in California approaching water independence. Early in the City's history, resident Eliza Tibbetts experimented with three Brazilian orange trees. They created the necessary ingredients that led to California's other "Gold Rush" – the citrus industry's rise from 1870-1940. By 1882 Riverside was home to more than half of the state's 500,000 citrus trees. Advances such as refrigerated railroad cars and innovative irrigation systems made Riverside the wealthiest city per capita nationally by 1895.

The end of World War II Riverside saw change in Inland Southern California as increasing urban sprawl in Southern California began to supplant the once prosperous agricultural region. This sprawl brought with it traffic, smog, and urban blight. The once idyllic City became a poster child for urban sprawl and smog. A study released by Smart Growth America in 2002 ranked the city number one in urban sprawl (Lyne 2002). Nevertheless, the combination of improving air quality in Southern California, improvements in infrastructure and the indomitable spirit of Riverside's citizens produced significant improvements in the quality of life of the City. In 2006 the City set about changing its economic trajectory and image by improving its infrastructure and quality of life through an investment of more than a billion and half dollars in "Riverside Renaissance," an initiative to improve traffic flow; replace aging water, sewer, and electric infrastructure; and expand and improve police, fire, parks, library, and other community facilities. This initiative focused on changing the physical environment of the City. It resulted in the completion more projects in five years than were completed in the previous 30 years and dramatically changed the physical character of the City for the better. But trouble loomed.

Proximity to the coastal counties of Southern California and the availability of relatively cheap land made Riverside and the surrounding area a Mecca for families seeking less expensive housing, as well as businesses needing office and warehouse space at lower cost. Thus, there was an explosion of growth in the City and region. Forty-two percent of all jobs created in California from 2000-2007 were created in the region.

Real estate developers scrambled to build homes and commercial space. The region was the fastest growing area in California. Then, it all stopped. Riverside became the epicenter of the housing crisis. Foreclosures ballooned. Commercial real estate vacancies soured. The economic engine that had fueled growth stalled. It was soon apparent that the "cheap dirt" model of economic development needed to change.

Even when it appeared successful by some measures, the rapid growth of the region had not always produced positive results. Even as the region grew quality of life suffered as the city and region worked to expand infrastructure and services. When growth stopped unemployment soared. It was a time of crisis and dismay. It was also a time that called for change and for leadership and a new vision for the City.

Changing the Vision

In late spring 2009 the Riverside City Workforce Advisory Panel (WAP) and the Council of Economic Development Advisors (CEDA) recognized the need for change and a new vision for the future of the city. Working together these two groups initiated a strategic visioning process for change with the goal of being forward-looking and highly inspirational. The two Riverside economic development groups were made up of leading area business persons and Mayor Ronald O. Loveridge. The Mayor asked David W. Stewart, Ph.D., Dean of the A. Gary Anderson School of Management at UC Riverside, to spearhead a fast-moving process to produce a plan for change, an "Agenda for the City" before the end of 2009. In order to provide a foundation for this effort a sub-committee of WAP-CEDA worked with Dean Stewart to create 10 bold and far-reaching aspirational statements titled "A Vision for Riverside" that served as a touchstone for the strategic visioning process and established the directions for change. On May 26, 2009, the City Council approved "A Vision for Riverside", with the intent to guide the City to a leading position in the region, country, and world (Table 1). Given the state of the economy the statements were audacious. The City Council also stipulated that significant community input should be a major component of data gathering in creating a plan for change and a vision for the future.

A Steering Committee that included twelve highly involved community leaders was formed to guide and oversee the community visioning process and development of a project that soon came to be known as the "Seizing Our Destiny Agenda." Over the next six months the steering committee oversaw an effort at community engagement and planning for change. In addition to hundreds of hours that the steering committee contributed to the effort the committee reached out to the diverse Riverside community for input. The driving questions were:

1. What do you want the city to be like in 10 years?
   What changes are necessary?
2. What makes you proud of your city? What should not be changed?
3. What would change and improve quality of life?

The committee conducted twelve focus groups and facilitated discussions with numerous community groups ranging in age, ethnicity, interests, and concerns. Leaders of the community participated in a vision lab designed to add depth and detail to ideas that surfaced in other venues. A community survey was carried out. Input was received from over a thousand people in the community. The goal of the steering committee was to create collective vision of the community that would guide change and the vision of the future. Another goal was to create a sense of collective contribution ro and ownership of change within the community at large.

Unlike many city-planning efforts the focus was not on infrastructure and improvement projects. Rather, the focus was on how to improve quality of life in the city:

> "Using modern economic development in this Agenda, we believe that by increasing the community's quality of life we will fuel intelligent growth, encourage innovation, position Riverside as the location of choice for diverse and dynamic people, and attract desirable businesses and jobs to the region. This is the way we will seize our destiny."

The committee quickly identified a travel metaphor to organize its thinking. It sought to identify characteristics of the city's future – the destination, the direction for change. It identified eleven routes for arriving at the destination. For each route several exemplary initiatives were identified to serve as examples of specific actions and changes that would move the City along a route toward the destination. These elements of the vision were organized into a map that communicated in a single page the vision and expected outcomes (Figure 1). The vision statement was considered and unanimously approved by the Riverside City Council in December of 2009.

Making it Happen

Creating a vision and plan for change is easy. The challenge for the steering committee was assuring that the vision would be realized and that the changes happened. The committee members also wanted the vision to be evergreen with the opportunity for incorporating new routes, new initiatives and ideas for change in the future. There was also the issue of creating an organizational structure that insured that the there was forward movement and positive change, as well as a sense of ownership by the larger community. The structure also needed to facilitate cooperation between community volunteers and city staff members. Implementation needed to be simultaneously organic and professionally managed. There was also a need for accountability and measurement of change both in activities and in outcomes.

The structure that emerged to guide implementation and updating of the vision and change process included the appointment of "route champions," 2-3 individuals from the community who were passionate about a route and the initiatives associated with it. These leaders of change, who volunteered their time, took responsibility for recruiting other volunteer members to a route committee that coordinated efforts and initiatives. To assure coordination with the City each route was assigned a senior staff person from the City, and each elected member of the City Council adopted one or more initiatives. A Web site was created for sharing efforts and successes. "Seizing Our Destiny" was the theme of numerous city events and became a part of the vocabulary of the City. Seizing our Destiny became the code words for a dramatic process of change.

By late 2011 change was well underway and numerous initiatives had been completed. These include launching an innovation economy initiative (Route 1, "Strong Innovative Economy that Builds Community"), obtaining a Communities Learning in Partnership grant from the Gates Foundation (Route 2, "Well Developed, Highly Sought After Workforce"), holding a Green Jobs Summit to discuss both short and long term green business (job) attraction strategies (Route 5, "Becoming a Green Machine"), the opening of a Broadway-style theater, the refurbished Fox Theater, where Gone with the Wind premiered decades earlier (Route 6, "Around the City, Around the Year, Around the Clock"), implementing a citywide Private Building Mural Program (Route 7, "Transforming Spaces into Places"), and the launch of a destination marketing campaign for the City (Route 11, ("Telling Our Story"). Indeed, in October of 2011, less than two years after the adoption of Seizing Our Destiny the City was tracking more than 40 initiatives and more than 150 specific activities related to these initiatives. The process of change was underway and the positive outcomes associated with change were already visible.

Although still suffering the effects of the housing bubble and the recent economic downturn Riverside was moving forward. It has a new energy and a new confidence. It's efforts at transformation and change were being noticed and celebrated: Riverside has been named the first Emerald City in California, one of the 21 most intelligent tech cities in the world (the Smart21 Communities Awards), among 13 of the U.S.'s "Most Livable Communities," and Number 3 among "Can Do Cities" by Newsweek. More importantly, residents and business owners in Riverside were excited by the changes in the City and what these changes suggested about the future of the City. Through a process of collective leadership and shared commitment to change the City had seized its destiny.

Table 1: **THE CITY OF RIVERSIDE ASPIRES TO BE...**

- A city of dynamism at the hub of the global economy where business is promoted and recognized as a powerful engine for both economic growth and for its contributions to the quality of life.

- A city of the future with deep historical roots that it celebrates and cherishes as a foundation for growth and future development.

- A city of international reach that celebrates, promotes, and seeks advantage in the diversity of its people.

- A city of inspiration that is the center of a vibrant arts and cultural community that contributes to the quality of life of its own residents and attracts visitors from the region and the world.

- A city of ideas that is a center of world-class education, drawing on its history, culture and location as a living laboratory for the development of minds, for fostering innovation, and for improving the quality of life.

- A city of innovation that encourages and promotes the development of new technologies and the industries and individual businesses that create and commercialize these technologies.

- A city of health that is home to leading institutions and industries that promote the health and welfare of its own residents and contributes to the well-being of all residents around the globe.

- A city of the earth that is committed to a clean and sustainable environment and creating solutions to global problems.

- A city of freedom to enjoy life in peace and safety.

- A city of community that includes a vibrant urban city center, exciting neighborhoods and a commitment to the responsible use and development of the extraordinary outdoor resources that surround us.

Figure 1

SEIZING OUR DESTINY:
The Agenda For Riverside's Innovative Future

Our Map – Where We Are
What makes our bold innovative future possible?

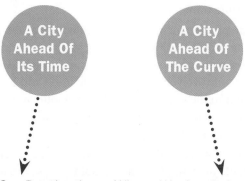

A City Ahead Of Its Time

A City Ahead Of The Curve

Our Destination – Where We Are Going
What will people believe about Riverside?

Outstanding Quality Of Life

Catalyst For Innovation

Location Of Choice

United City For Common Good

Our Strategic Routes – How We Will Get There
How will we achieve what we envision?

- Strong Innovative Economy That Builds Community
- Well Developed Highly Sought After Workforce
- Lifelong Learning For All

- Homes Of Next Century Health Care
- Becoming A Green Machine
- Around the City, Around the Year, Around the Clock
- Transforming Spaces into Places

- Big City Recreation With Hometown Feel
- Creatively Central
- Collaborating to Build Community
- Telling Our Story

Discussion

1. Discuss the proud history of the City of Riverside California and the crisis that created a sense of urgency for change.

2. Successful major changes don't happen by chance. Discuss how the change got organized, who the primary Change Leaders were, and your assumptions before and after reading the case about the possibility of a large city or organization being able to reinvent itself in a short time frame.

3. The change process included: (1) establishing a steering committee to guide the process; (2) a compelling vision statement; (3) an assessment of present realities and future ideals; and (4) widespread involvement to generate ideas and build commitment to the change; and (5) developing a travel metaphor to create a one page change model. Discuss what was done in each of these change process steps.

4. A critical part of successful change is following through on the commitments to change. In the part of the case titled "Making It Happen" what are some of the things the steering committee did to help implement and sustain the changes?

5. What were some of the accomplishments and awards achieved by the City of Riverside and what are some things you learned about leading change?

Key Lessons In Leading Change

1. Successful change requires visionary change leaders who carefully plan the change process, are willing to use a collaborative and inclusive process, find champions, and share leadership.

2. In planning changes, it is important to create an urgency for change, a compelling vision, a steering committee or change team to help guide the process for complex changes, a process for accessing present realities and future ideals, an understandable but adaptable change process, and a plan for successfully implementing and sustaining the changes.

3. Community transformation requires widespread involvement, rather than a traditional strategic planning committee of 10-12 people.

4. Transformational leaders are sponsors and facilitators of the planning process: they explain its importance, its benefits, and its outcomes in order to motivate the participation of others.

5. Setting audacious goals changes the way people think about the future.

6. The change plan and the written document that strategic planning produces is far less important than the process of planning.

References

Lyne, Jack (2002), "Urban Sprawl: New Smart Growth America Study Moves to Measure Elusive Location Factor," The Site Selector Online Insider, http://www.siteselection.com/ssinsider/snapshot/sf021028.htm, downloaded September 19, 2011.

Seizing Our Destiny, http://www.seizingourdestiny.com/default.aspx.

BIOGRAPHY

David W. Stewart, Ph.D. is Distinguished Professor of Management and Marketing in the School of Business Administration at the University of California, Riverside. From 2007 to 2011 he served as the Dean of UCR's School of Business Administration and the A. Gary Anderson Graduate School of Management. He has previously served as a member of the faculty of the Marshall School of Business at the University of Southern California where he held the Robert E. Brooker Chair in Marketing and served as deputy dean of the School for five years. He also served two terms as Chairman of the Department of Marketing in the Marshall School. Prior to moving to Southern California in 1986 he was senior associate dean and associate professor of marketing at the Owen Graduate School of Management, Vanderbilt University. Dr. Stewart is a past editor of both the Journal of Marketing and the Journal of the Academy of Marketing Science.

David W. Stewart, Ph.D.
Distinguished Professor of Management and Marketing
The School of Business Administration and
The A. Gary Anderson Graduate School of Management
900 University Avenue, Anderson Hall, University of California, Riverside, CA 92521
Telephone: 951.827.4237, Office Fax: 951.827.4998
E-mail: david.stewart@ucr.edu · www.agsm.ucr.edu

3

Transforming The State Bank Of India

Neha Gupta

Major Focus Of The Case

The transformation of the State Bank of India (SBI), India's largest public sector bank, under the stewardship of O.P. Bhatt, has been nothing short of a dream ride. The case highlights the role of leadership in engaging employees to sustain the supremacy of the ageing bank amidst competition from customer-oriented, sophisticated, tech-savvy private banks. The involvement of a mammoth workforce in articulating the vision of the organization was a remarkable feat accomplished by the leadership at SBI.

Introduction

State Bank of India, with roots tracing back to 1806, was the largest bank (by assets) in India with 60 percent of shares belonging to government. SBI was an opinion leader in the economic sphere of free India. But by 2006, the bank had become just another bank. Post-liberalization in 1990s, with the advent of private and foreign banks in India, the country's oldest bank with over 200,000 employees and 16,000 branches started losing its customers. Its unquestioned supremacy was threatened due to lack of customer orientation, outdated technology and inefficient business processes. These problems were compounded with the leadership pool that had become an ageing group. In the early 2000s, the private sector banks endowed with younger workforce, laced with superior technological capabilities provided higher quality of customer service which surpassed the public sector banks. With an ageing workforce and outdated technology, SBI figured low on the list of the rising segment of young and affluent Indians who were either salaried or self-employed. The frontline staff was losing its motivation as the number of customers dwindled every passing month. The bank's growth rate was slower compared to the competitors. SBI carried the legacy of being state owned and having outdated technology and no competitive spirit. Overall SBI, once a force to reckon with, was languishing in inertia.

Change of Guard

O.P. Bhatt, a lifetime SBI-insider, who joined the bank in 1972 as a probationary officer, was appointed as the Chairman in 2006. He was alarmed by the shrinking market share. He found that the bank's employees were not energized anymore. They had lost their pride and sense of belonging. Everybody, right from top to bottom was pulling the bank in different directions. The people weren't performing poorly as individuals; they just weren't aligned with a common goal. He felt that the entrenched mindset of employees, where customers were supposed to approach the bank as opposed to the bank being proactive in attracting customers, also inhibited the growth.

After assuming charge as Chairman, Bhatt started by talking to senior executives in small groups, trying to get them both worried and excited: worried about what had happened to the bank and excited about how they could undo the damage. During the second month, after gaining a critical mass who understood the problems at the top level, he invited 25 of the bank's senior leaders to a conclave. The agenda of the five-day conclave was to brainstorm and generate ideas to initiate the transformation process. The idea was to create an environment where people were free to voice their ideas, to criticize and to accept criticism, and in the end to build consensus and alignment. The discussion unanimously led to the view that altering the mindset of employees who had worked for decades in a non-competitive, almost monopolistic, closed economy was an imperative. Bhatt delivered his famous 'state of the nation' speech at the conclave to create awareness about change. The conclave concluded with a 14-point agenda that fell into three broad groups – i) issues related to business, ii) how to facilitate these businesses; and iii) focus on people to create alignment and enthusiasm.

Fostering Sense of Urgency

It was easy to create awareness in a small group of 25 but it was an uphill task to create a sense of urgency among 200,000 people in the bank. Nevertheless, it was important to create alignment to bring everyone on-board to avert the decline of the bank. A first step was to edit the state of the nation address into a presentation that the deputy managing directors could make to all 10,000 branch managers. There was some hesitation, but the deputy managing directors eventually made the presentation across the country in groups of up to 80 branch managers. People were astonished and touched by the management disclosing what happened at the conclave and openly sharing information with employees. This kind of openness was unheard of in the long illustrious history of SBI (Malone, 2009).

In addition, this was the first time the chief general managers had met with all the branch managers under them. For branch managers it signaled an entirely new approach, underlining the importance of individuals and the transformation process. It was also a great opportunity for the chief general managers to hear the issues from the front lines, establish rapport, and understand the pulse of the bank better (Malone, 2009).

The conclaves continued, bringing together senior managers and lower-level leaders. In groups of 50 to 100, Bhatt met with all the assistant general managers in closed-door, no-holds-barred conversations, where his primary role was to listen to their perceptions of the bank, its issues, and what they thought SBI should be doing (Malone, 2009).

'Parivartan' (Change) at SBI

A change program named 'Parivartan' (meaning 'transformation') was launched by Bhatt in 2007. The Chairman set a target of 100 days to reach out to 200,000 employees of the bank, right from clerks (junior level) to Scale-IV officers (senior level). The program aimed to bring about a mindset change through massive internal communication was steered by a team of top management and middle management employees, handpicked by Bhatt. The change team viewed communication as a tool to overcome the cognitive resistance arising from lack of information or ambiguity about rationale for change. The foremost step was creating a shared need for change through communication in the organization spanning all levels of employees across all branches. Subsequently, key employees at every level were identified and sent for a training program. The training equipped the selected employees with the theoretical frameworks and practical insights required for implementing the change plan. It enabled them to don the role of the messengers of change in their respective branches. Thus, the leadership found multiple mouthpieces to promote *parivartan* (change).

In July 2007, over 3,800 two-day *Parivartan* workshops were held at more than 100 locations throughout the country in 100 days to cover all employees. The workshops were conducted by more than 380 trainers including a few retired SBI employees who underwent a five-day *Parivartan* trainer's workshop. And to everyone's surprise and joy, the seemingly impossible target was met. Interestingly, after a long time, the organizational members were united by a collective enthusiasm to change the destiny of the bank. After establishing a sense of urgency among employees and building a powerful guiding coalition to facilitate change, the Chairman embarked on the path to co-create a new vision of SBI.

Articulating the New Vision

The vision statement, the fundamental element of an organization's identity is often vague in the minds of employees. SBI was no exception. It was difficult to find one person on SBI's payroll who could spell out the vision statement correctly. Nevertheless, employees were not ashamed of their ignorance because the vision of SBI was a complex, verbose statement, indistinct from several other organizations. Interestingly, it made no reference to *'customers'*.

Bhatt set upon the transformation journey by redefining the vision of SBI. As part of the transformation journey, the change team was directed to engage employees to sustain the momentum of change. The Chairman, along with the organizational members began a co-creation exercise to evolve the new vision statement for the bank. An external consultant in addition to internal change agents was appointed to facilitate the articulation of the vision.

Unlike the common practise of confining the task to the top management, SBI decided to engage 200,000 employees in deciding the future direction of the bank. The objective of involving employees in rearticulating the vision was to enable them to internalize it so that it could be implemented in letter as well as spirit. Even though it was a herculean task to involve the entire workforce, they didn't shy away from it. The guiding principle was to let every organizational member envision and shape SBI's destiny.

As a first step, the change facilitators were trained to initiate the process of envisioning. A series of five posters were created. They were sent to 16,000 offices one after another, for five consecutive weeks. The change team led by Chairman, ensured that every branch displayed the set of posters in places accessible exclusively to employees. The posters consisted of statements like: *"Today we are India's largest bank. How do we become India's best?"; "State Bank of India has got 140 million customers. How do you make each customer feel that s/he is the most important?"* After the posters were put up at bank, the change agents actively encouraged discussion among employees about the bank and its vision at tea time, lunch hour, social gatherings etc. The posters generated intrigue and triggered informal conversations amongst employees. They started thinking about it, talking about it, and debating about it. In the process, the employees unconsciously began pondering over the challenges encountered by the bank and ways to overcome them. Gradually, the demographically and geographically diverse workforce was entwined by a common thought – how to become the best bank.

In the sixth week, every employee received a letter from the Chairman with a questionnaire. The questionnaire had 10 multiple choice questions, each with three choices to select from. They were given 10 days to fill the questionnaire and send it back. The questions included: *"What is SBI's biggest challenge?"* *What can give SBI the winning edge?"*, *"What should SBI be famous for?"*, and so on. As for the vision statement, three choices had been offered:

   i) "My SBI - Improving life for all";

   ii) "My SBI - The bank of first choice"; and

   iii) a statement that focused more narrowly on the customers.

This last option won decisively with over 54% of the votes. It had maximum support among the blue collar staff, with uniform support across age groups (Chakrabarti, 2010). The whole process garnered a phenomenal response from 141,000 employees, which became the input for developing the final vision. The results were tabulated and then a random sample of 200 employees was selected to discuss the findings of the survey in an unstructured personal interview. The emergence of 'customer satisfaction' as the key idea in interviews was aligned with the winning option. As a result, the new vision *"My SBI, My customer first, My SBI: First in customer satisfaction"* was articulated where 90 percent of the employees were able to see their contribution (Bhatt, 2009).

SBI Reigns Supreme

The new vision statement, achieved through employee support including top management and persistent formal and informal communication set the ball rolling. It complemented other change initiatives – people-changes, technology-changes, process-changes, and business mix changes undertaken by bank. Rekindling employee pride, creating employee ownership of the organization and focusing the collective energy on customer service catalyzed the successful transformation of SBI (Chakrabarti, 2010). The story of SBI reigning supreme in markets is a testimony to the fact that engaging people not only helps in building employee ownership but in delivering superior performance. Firmly ensconced as India's flagship bank, SBI now aspires to be one of world's leading banks.

Discussion

1. Changing a bank with 200,000 employees, 16,000 branches, and 140 million customers sounds like an impossible task. However, Change Leaders with a sound change plan know that this can be done. Change usually starts with the recognition of compelling reasons for change. What were the signs that the bank needed transforming?

2. Chairman Bhatt began the change process shortly after taking office. Discuss some things he did to start the change process including what he did at the Change Conclave meeting of 25 Senior leaders.

3. Why are establishing a sense of urgency, building a powerful guiding coalition, and having a name for the change process (Parivartan) important to develop in the early stages of change?

4. Changing the mindset of those involved in change and affected by change and engaging people in the change process is critical to successful change. What are the advantages and disadvantages of engaging the entire workforce in the change process and what was the process used to engage all 200,000 employees?

5. If a change team (guiding coalition) is created it is important to have representative members and at least one person of significant influence. Who led the change team? How important is it for an influential leader to be involved? What are some guidelines that should be used in selecting members for a change team?

6. Vision statements are typically meaningless, similar to everyone else's and soon forgotten. However, a strong statement that is highly meaningful and motivating can be a strong force for change and can keep people focused. What was the process used to develop a vision statement and what are the advantages and disadvantages of the process used at SBI?

Key Lessons In Leading Change

1. Transforming organizations of all types and sizes can be done when leaders understand and are committed to the change and transformation process.

2. People are inherently averse to changes they don't understand and are not involved in. Engaging people in the change plan is critical because 'people support what they help build.'

3. In any change, the organization should address why before how i.e. 'why the change is needed' before 'how it will be implemented.' It helps overcoming the cognitive resistance (i.e. I don't get it) displayed by employees by providing the rationale for change.

4. Active involvement of an influential leader signifies the importance of the change initiative. Also, a leader seeking inputs from employees is a subtle form of ingratiation. It implies that the leadership values their opinion and helps in mobilizing employee support.

5. Communication is a key and determining factor in the success of a change initiative. In addition to mass communication through e-mails or memos, the organization should provide opportunities or create forums for face to face interaction.

6. The organization should equip employees with skills or capabilities required to effectively implement the change. Often employees are left to cope with changes on their own.

References

1. Adarsh, N. (2008). Parivartan for change in SBI staff mindset. Retrieved September 20, 2011, from HR Link.in: http://hrlink.in/news/parivartan-for-change-in-sbi-staff-mindset

2. Bhatt, O.P. (2009). Inaugural Key Note Address on "Transformation & Growth of SBI" at Global OD Summit, Indian School of Business, Hyderabad, August, 19-22, 2009.

3. Chakrabarti, R. (2010).Grits, Guts and Gumption- Driving Change in a State Owned Giant, New Delhi: Penguin Publishers.

4. Malone, R. (2009). Remaking a government-owned giant: An interview with the chairman of the State Bank of India . Retrieved September 27, 2011, from McKinsey Quarterly: http://mkqpreview1. qdweb.net/Asia_Pacific/Remaking_a_government- owned_giant_An_interview_with_the_ chairman_of_the_State_Bank_of_India_2249

BIOGRAPHY

Neha Gupta, Manager, Stakeholder Communications at the Indian School of Business (ISB), Hyderabad holds a MBA (HR) and B.E. (E&C).

With keen interest in organizational behavior, she has published several book chapters, case studies registered with Ivey, and articles in leading national HR journals and magazines like NHRDN Journal, Human Capital. She also conducts behavioral and soft skills training for IT professionals.

gupta.neha13@gmail.com

4

Leading Change:
A Case Study Of Al Salam Bank – Bahrain

Vijayalaxmi Moovala

Major Focus Of The Case

Al Salam Bank-Bahrain (ASBB) is a leading Islamic bank in the Kingdom of Bahrain which within three years of its establishment acquired a conventional bank in Bahrain and gained the benefits of acquisitive growth. It effectively integrated employees of both banks and fostered a positive team culture. This case provides insights into the leadership dynamics prevalent, human capital development practices, and change management strategies being implemented in the bank. Ethical leadership and strategic direction provided by the management during the change process, caused by both external and internal factors, are highlighted in the case. The case focuses on key aspects pertaining to marketing innovativeness and human capital management, which propelled ASBB as one of the leading Islamic banks in Bahrain.

Al Salam Bank-Bahrain (ASBB)

ASBB[1], a dynamic, diversified and differentiated Islamic bank, headquartered in the Kingdom of Bahrain[2] was incorporated in 2006 and started its commercial operations in the same year. In 2009, within 3 years of its operations, the Bank acquired Bahraini Saudi Bank (BSB), a conventional bank based in Bahrain, which became a controlled subsidiary of ASBB. ASBB focused on increasing its market share and retail branch network by providing a variety of Islamic financing solutions, investments, deposits, related products to its customers.

The noteworthy factor was that during the change process, caused by both external and internal factors, the bank emerged a winner due to the ethical approach, strategic leadership and futuristic outlook it adopted. The

---

1 www.alsalam-bahrain.com
2 An archipelago situated in the Gulf region.

advantages it reaped were due to acquisitive growth, change management strategies it implemented and the customer focus it had. Key mechanisms and best practices related to talent management, mentoring, and people orientation shaped ASBB into one of the leading Islamic banks in Bahrain.

Strategic Leadership and Core Values

The senior management of the bank led by the CEO, Yousif A. Taqi, comprised a team of high caliber visionaries who were ethical and personally credible. The CEO enjoyed a good reputation and personal credibility, which not only generated financial deposits/ business for the bank, but also earned the trust of customers. The 'pull approach' was evident in ASBB where this trust and credibility brought business to the bank.

The impact of the financial crisis which was felt in Bahrain was never a stumbling block, nor did it hinder the growth and progress of ASBB. It was one of the few banks in the country which during this period, made elaborate plans for business expansion and employee growth. At the peak of economic crisis, it initiated, negotiated and successfully completed the acquisition of BSB, a conventional bank of over 25 years standing.

ASBB leaders exhibited a judicious mix of business acumen and people orientation. During the process of integrating operations and employees of both banks, the senior management team spearheaded the change management processes on all fronts. They provided constant guidance and were, at all times, proactive, positive and patient. The core values espoused by the leaders were *integrity, ethical approach, transparency, trust, respect, equity, fairness, empowerment, employee engagement and customer focus.* The CEO's motto was: *'Good governance is the key to organizational success.'* He was instrumental in propagating the management concept that:

> 'The management team is the trustee of the bank, holding not only the money of the customers but also their trust and, that of the employees. Management should always have employees' and customers' interests at heart.'

Management Philosophy

The Bank's management team consisted of high-caliber internationally experienced professionals with proven expertise in key areas of banking and finance. They were committed to adopting internationally recognized banking standards, best practices and operated with transparency and trust. The key to ASBB's success was the priority it gave to a very critical body of stakeholders; the internal customers [employees], who in turn delivered their best service to external customers, thereby contributing to the bottom line/profit margin. In line with this thinking, the CEO and the senior management team took a humane approach while dealing with employees. They always put the employees' interests first and gave priority to them.

ASBB management was able to strike the right balance between people management and market orientation. They encouraged employees to contribute positively towards business development. They never missed an opportunity to tap business/ obtain deposits from customers and invest them in the right ventures. ASBB increased its market share through prefunding projects, thereby gaining the confidence of its counterparties. Keeping abreast with the technological advancements, the bank invested in world-class information technological infrastructure. The management continuously upgraded technology, as they believed that better customer service comes through cutting edge technology. With the acquisition, ASBB had the combined advantage of BSB's long standing reputation in the banking world and their modern business dynamism in the financial markets.

Excerpt from an interview[3] with the CFO, Mukundan Raghavachari:

"Islamic banking, in simple terms, is Ethical banking.
The corner stones of sustainable growth of the bank are ethics and quality. Long term focus is significant and it should never be compromised for short term gains. Employee welfare, development and contribution are of paramount importance for the growth and success of ASBB. Human capital is the driver/ enabler of financial capital/ wealth creation"

Rapid Growth

At a time when several organizations used the economic crisis as a 'credit crunch' to curtail business operations and downsize, ASBB expanded its operations and increased its employee strength. Within a short span of four years, the employee strength of ASBB more than doubled[4], and its branch outlets increased fivefold[5]. ASBB availed the opportunities that ensued from acquisition driven growth by reaping the benefits of its synergistic association with BSB. It efficaciously tapped the potential for its products in the Middle Eastern and North African region. The acquired bank and its branches were used as the retail/ commercial arm with the parent focusing on private banking, investments and treasury. The main objective was to

3 Interview conducted by the author on 28th December 2010 at ASBB headquarters in Bahrain.
4 From 120 in 2006 to 230 in 2010
5 From 2 in 2006 to 11 in 2010

expand ASBB's operations through three main synergies: cost, sales and functional. Sales synergies resulted in a better market reach, expanded customer base, and cross selling. Cost synergies gained were better pricing that came with volume increase. Functional synergies gained were the combined expertise of employees of both banks, which was effectively utilized to increase productivity and profitability.

Horizontal integration led to critical mass creation, volume expansion, bigger branch network/client base, a wide spectrum of financial products, and increased bank profitability. Taking advantage of a larger number of branches, ASBB assigned each branch with a specific business segment to handle, thus enabling a concentrated and specific marketing approach. Through advanced technological synergies, better customer service was provided.

All group processes were unified and ASBB operated as a holistic entity.

Change Management

During the first year of acquisition of BSB, the management of ASBB constituted a 'steering' committee, for planning and implementing the change management process. The 'steering' committee established 'integration' committees for each functional area/department to oversee the entire change management process. These committees consisting of members from both banks were entrusted with the task of preparing the change management plan. The plan was prepared and implemented with the consensus of both groups. Each 'integration' committee held weekly meetings to smoothen the change process.

The management used a 'bottom-up' approach rather than 'top-down' approach by identifying sponsors for each mega-process. They used a 'participative style' where employees were involved in the change process, rather than a 'coercive style' where the management enforces the process. Resistance to change was reduced and handled in an effective manner. The process of streamlining operations of both banks, and implementation of the change management framework was made possible through employees' contribution and each individual's involvement. Management of ASBB ensured that employees of the acquired bank, especially Bahrainis who were in jobs that became redundant, were not terminated. The bank took care to retrain and redeploy them to take over other suitable jobs by expanding the retail branch network.

On acquiring BSB, the first key initiative undertaken by the management of ASBB was to review and revise the compensation package of employees of the acquired bank. This helped build the trust of BSB employees and paved the way for their smooth transition into ASBB. On the social front, several get-togethers, staff parties were held to facilitate integration of employees of both banks. The senior managers of both banks actively involved themselves in helping employees get to know each other and cope with the change process.

Customer Focus

Excellent customer service and innovativeness in its marketing strategies was another key factor contributing to the bank's success. It was the first Islamic bank in Bahrain to introduce the smart card in 2007 and achieve RTGS[6] status soon after the Central Bank of Bahrain introduced it for its member banks. The acquisition helped ASBB in materialization of its plans for widespread geographical presence, business expansion and larger market share. It had established its first branch and 2 ATMs in May 2007 which soon resulted in an enlarged network of 11 branches and 24 ATMs[7]. Plans were afoot to project ASBB as a one-stop Islamic financial services centre in the Middle Eastern and North African region, within the next decade. It planned to have a wide spectrum of financial products in consumer finance. Its clientele was drawn from limited income customers to high net-worth individuals. It aimed to cater for all conceivable financial requirements and all foreseeable demands of its customers.

Talent Management/Succession Planning

ASBB believed that employees are its best assets. It upheld the truism that survival and growth of the bank is dependent on human capital development and its contribution. Through mechanisms like career development it provided the right impetus for enhancing the competency level/skills set of employees. The bank focused on management development programs and succession planning. Succession planning provided the right base for effectively developing leadership skills among potential successors and, ensured the availability and continuity of expertise in the bank.

In a strategic move towards human capital development and with a view to develop employee talent, the bank initiated a succession planning system termed 'future leaders' program. The bank identified twenty talented young Bahrainis as successors for eight key positions in the bank, namely, that of the *CEO, CFO, CRO, CTO, COO, Head of Legal, Head of Investment and Head of Banking*. These young Bahrainis were being groomed and trained to take over the mantle of leadership within the next decade or

6 'RTGS' stands for Real Time Gross Settlement.
7 Figures in December 2010

so. This succession planning system served the dual purpose of retaining talented young Bahrainis in the bank and contributed to the practice of developing home-bred management talent. These young *Bahraini leaders of tomorrow* were trained based on future job requirements and given the opportunity to succeed and grow in their careers. This talent management system endorsed ASBB's top management commitment towards human capital development and empowerment.

Mentoring System

ASBB took a holistic approach to people development. They provided ample opportunities for employees to build their capabilities and enhance their skills. Departmental heads played the role of mentors and whenever required, mentors from outside the department were assigned to facilitate the overall growth of these potential successors. The bank invested in training and developing these employees through different methods and techniques. It gave them the advantage and opportunity of job rotation to strengthen their professional base in the bank. In due course they would gain overall conceptual, technical, human and other requisite skills to take over the reins of leadership.

People Orientation

ASBB being a people-centric organization in the financial services industry gained success in the industry and market place through the support of its employees. The bank had a good work culture, and it empowered its employees. The managers examined various ways in which employee integration and engagement could be brought about. Employees were differentiated according to their commitment and contribution, and rewarded accordingly. This had a dual impact in ASBB; on one hand, it encouraged the high achievers to contribute more, and on the other, it became a motivating factor for other employees to get into the high achievers' league.

The CEO and his team of senior managers maintained an open door policy with the employees. They were accessible and went the extra mile to establish rapport and build a one-on-one relationship with each employee. 'Equal treatment' and 'equity principle' were very much in play in ASBB. It followed the principle of 'equal pay for equal work', where both expatriates and locals were given the same compensation package. Employees who separated from the bank were treated with utmost dignity and were given a fond farewell. The management believed that every single employee, both current and separated, were ambassadors of the bank. The word-of-mouth advertising done by these employees was as important to ASBB as that of the customers, to make or break the goodwill and reputation of the bank. In ASBB a "management that cares" concept was all encompassing. It was reflected in the environment of trust that the senior managers created, through their personal credibility and accessibility to employees. The senior managers took into account the overall well-being of employees, be it employee development, compensation, physical health or work-life balance.

Conclusion

The success of ASBB was mainly due to the personal integrity and business acumen of the senior management team and, committed teamwork of its employees. The management of ASBB through their credibility and ethical approach earned the trust of their stakeholders. They treated employees with respect by recognizing their personal worth and rewarding their professional contribution. The customers' business was managed ethically and their trust was maintained. The shareholders were assured of profitable operations and transparent governance. The society, at large, benefitted through the welfare measures undertaken by the bank. ASBB was recognized as an equal opportunity and equitable rewards employer in the banking industry of Bahrain. Meritocratic culture that prevailed in the bank helped attract and retain the best talent in the industry. ASBB was poised to scale great heights in the financial services industry of the Middle Eastern region, in general, and Bahrain, in particular.

Discussion

1. *'Leadership philosophy sets the tone for the success of any organization.'* To what extent is this statement true for Al Salam Bank – Bahrain?

2. Evaluate the effectiveness of the change management model used by *Al Salam Bank – Bahrain.*

3. Examine the succession planning concept in *Al Salam Bank – Bahrain.*

4. Assess the impact of rapid growth on the employees and customers of *Al Salam Bank – Bahrain.*

5. Analyze the factors that contributed to the Bank's success during changing times.

Key Lessons In Leading Change

1. Change is inevitable in all organizations. The essence of change is in managing it effectively. In *Al Salam Bank – Bahrain* the management used the most effective change management strategy, that is, the 'bottom-up' approach. Employees at all levels were actively involved in contributing to the change management process. The participative style used facilitated the smooth integration of employees of both the banks and streamlined the work processes, as well.

2. Customer focus is one of the key factors leading to an organization's success. In *Al Salam Bank – Bahrain*, the management was able to focus on the varied needs of its customers due to the innovativeness and commitment of its employees. Customer focus starts with meeting the expectations of employees who in turn cater for the external customers' needs.

3. Organizations that invest in their employees have better and long lasting returns. The key human capital management strategies of *Al Salam Bank – Bahrain* were the mentoring process and succession planning. Through these mechanisms the bank not only motivated their employees but also retained them. The motivation of employees helped the bank grow and prosper during the changing times.

4. Success of any organization can be attributed to the top management philosophy and approach, as in the case of *Al Salam Bank – Bahrain*. The management team was ethical in their employee and customer interactions. Customer-centric approach towards the internal and external customers paved the way for the progress of the bank.

BIOGRAPHY

Dr. Vijayalaxmi Moovala holds a Master's degree in Business Administration and a Doctorate in Business Management from India. She has a certificate in psychometric (occupational) testing: SHL [UK] and is a certified Master trainer of Neuro-Linguistic Psychology [USA]. Dr. Vijaya has over 20 years of experience in management training and consulting. She started her career as a Management Consultant and University faculty member teaching M.B.A. students. Her expertise is in the areas of *human capital development, applied managerial psychology, strategic and general management.* She has extensive experience in facilitating management training and development programs for supervisors and managers of different organizations in India, Kingdom of Bahrain and other Gulf countries. Dr. Vijaya has provided leadership and guidance to several human capital development projects. She is research oriented and has published several management articles in renowned journals. She believes in self-development and lifelong learning.

Dr. Vijayalaxmi Moovala
Program Manager
Center for Leadership & Management
Bahrain Institute of Banking & Finance
P.O. Box: 20525, Juffair
Kingdom of Bahrain
Mobile: +973-39263810
vijaya@bibf.com, mvijaya@hotmail.com

5

Building a State-of-the-Art, World Class Hospital

Jeanne D. Maes, Colonel Andrew W. Backus,
Willam A. Sorrentino Jr., James Moore &
Robert A. Shearer

This case is based on the Ft. Belvoir Community Hospital Lessons Learned Report, compiled for the Norfolk District, US Army Corps of Engineers by McDonough Bolyard Peck, Inc. (MBP). We specifically acknowledge Mr. Larry Anderson, MBP Senior Program Manager, the lead author of this report.

The case focuses on the challenge of building a state-of-the-art, world class medical facility for the U.S. military. This project had high visibility in both the US public and private sectors. The challenge was to design and build this facility within a four-year Congressionally-mandated window, something that usually takes between 6-8 years to complete.

From the project's inception, conditions were hardly favorable for a successful completion. The local construction industry was very busy with both private sector and Government projects, many materials (steel, cement) were experiencing record inflation and volatility and the availability of sufficient skilled labor was questionable. While the project experienced considerable cost growth, delivery was on time - the facility was outfitted and occupied by the government-mandated deadline. This case explains how the project's leaders were able to make this happen.

Introduction and Background

Construction of the recently completed Ft. Belvoir Community Hospital is serving as an interesting case study of how to successfully build a new, high-tech hospital in the federal sector. It was a mammoth undertaking.

The Ft. Belvoir Community Hospital

Base Realignment and Closure (BRAC) congressional legislation of 2005 required closure of Walter Reed Army Medical Center and structural realignment of military heath care in the National Capital Region (NCR). In a shift from having separate service-specific facilities for the Army, Navy, and Air Force, this realignment called for two primary hospital facilities in the NCR to serve military members and their families from all services: a renovated and upgraded Bethesda Naval Hospital (since renamed "Walter Reed National Military Medical Center") and the brand new Ft. Belvoir Community Hospital (FBCH).

Traditional construction metrics – schedule, scope, quality and cost – all provided significant challenges in the delivery of FBCH. Most challenging was the time constraint. New construction had to be complete so the old Walter Reed could close by September 15, 2011 to comply with BRAC law. This meant that the new FBCH facility progressed from a concept sketch on a napkin to a complete, functional medical center of 1.2 million square feet, 55 clinics housed in five different buildings, two parking garages and a utility plant in just 3 years and 10 months time. A project of this magnitude using traditional construction approaches takes at least twice this long.

Despite this aggressive schedule, there would be no shortcuts on the project scope and expectations of high quality facilities and medical equipment. A May 2009 Department of Defense report entitled "Achieving World Class, An Independent Review of the Design Plans for the Walter Reed

National Military Medical Center and the Fort Belvoir Community Hospital" (Kizer, McGowan, & Bowman, 2009) made this clear. Our Warriors and their Families would be served with a Congressionally-defined world class standard, and our nation's leaders from both the Department of Defense and Congress were watching closely to ensure that this standard was met. Of course, return on taxpayer investment was also a concern as the dollars invested from all sources for FBCH alone topped $1.2 billion.

Deliver an enormous world class health facility, do it in record time, under the highest scrutiny of our national leaders, while making sure every dollar invested was used judiciously – this was the challenge facing the Project Delivery Team, an integrated group representing over a dozen separate organizations, agencies, and companies. They delivered. FBCH opened for business on August 31, 2011, two weeks ahead of the BRAC deadline and less than four years from the architect's design concept napkin sketch. That day more than sixty patients were seen in the emergency room, the first person was admitted for inpatient care, the first surgery was conducted, and the first baby was delivered under the watchful care of FBCH staff consisting of Army, Navy, Air Force, Marines, and the Department of Defense civilian workforce.

The challenges of delivering FBCH and the dynamics of the integrated Project Delivery Team that completed this mission yielded numerous leadership lesson learned. While the team achieved ultimate success, it was not easy. A formal collection and analysis of these lessons learned is still ongoing as of this writing, but four of them stand out.

1. Get the Culture Right

To deliver FBCH in the compressed time allotted, the US Army Corps of Engineers used a fast-track delivery method it calls "Integrated Design Bid Build" or IDBB. This is an integrated project delivery method that required the design contractor and the construction contractor to each work under the leadership of the Corps of Engineers in an integrated fashion, rather than sequentially as in the traditional "Design-Bid-Build" model or together as a single entity as in the "Design-Build" method. This construct allowed the team to 'hyper fast-track' construction. In some cases, construction workers were waiting on site as design documents were completed and run out to them to commence building literally on-the-spot. Later in the project, other stakeholders such as furniture outfitters, information technology contractors, security and life safety specialists, and even medical equipment trainers all integrated with the construction effort to produce a working hospital in time to meet the BRAC deadline.

One venue where industry and the Corps of Engineers come together to share lessons is the Construction Industry Institute (CII). CII defines project "culture" as the degree to which (1) project leadership is defined, effective, and accountable; (2) communication within the team and with stakeholders is open and effective; and (3) the team fosters trust, honesty, and shared values. Under this definition, the FBCH project labored early as various partner and stakeholder cultures merged. That the Project Delivery Team worked through these difficulties and moved toward completing the project with considerable success is a credit to the grit and determination of those people who emerged – at every level of every organization – to get this job done. In retrospect, they would probably all say that it should not have been so difficult.

A factor which restrained progress in this regard was that the Integrated Program Office (IPO) was initially allowed to behave as multiple different "fiefdoms" rather than as a unified whole. Faced with the new IDBB delivery method and integration of multiple partners and stakeholders, senior leaders initially made assumptions based on traditional operating processes that did not pan out with the new approach. Strategic direction was inadequate to set a successful course for FBCH project delivery, and recognition that the unique challenges of this project required significant senior leader engagement and decision-making was slow. Early on, a number of organization-to-organization communication links were clearly strained as various team members strove to complete "their" missions without clear understanding of impacts to other team members and the mission as a whole.

Midway through the project, when it became clear that project delivery by the BRAC deadline was in jeopardy, senior leaders moved to "get the culture right." This entailed engagement with the very top (CEO) leadership of the organizations involved: initially the Corps of Engineers, design and construction contractors, and the client organization, then later other stakeholders organizations critical to hospital operations. Monthly Senior Executive Review Groups (SERGs) were established to review progress and strategic direction, and address any obstacles that threatened positive forward movement in the project. These forums also afforded senior leaders the opportunity to set priorities and adjust the logic-driven integrated master schedule to ensure the broad team had the best possible chance at success.

Once the top-level leaders were engaged and aligned, a positive culture trickled down to the program management and working levels. Program managers – call FBCH "Principles" – developed an integrated master schedule that each member personally signed. They then reviewed it monthly to hold each other accountable, adjust as problems arose, and remain centered on the overall team goal. The monthly meetings did not always go smoothly – there was often contentious discussion as individual goals and schedules conflicted, but the spirit of the team to achieve collective success always prevailed. Risk was taken, shared, and mitigated on hundreds of different issues and challenges associated with delivering this major medical facility. The team adopted a mantra: "August 2011 – Whatever It Takes!" The singular goal of opening the FBCH for medical care was clear to all and the driving force for the team.

2. Focus on The Basics: Processes, Resources and Client Needs

In addition to having a healthy culture, an effective project must execute its fundamental responsibilities prudently. For construction projects, there are three widely recognized project management imperatives: management of the schedule, management of the costs, and quality control/assurance. We add two more to round out our Project Management "Big Five": safety management, and transparent client communications/expectation management. In a number of important respects, the FBCH project strained to execute prudently, largely because of disconnects between the objective and the approach being taken to get there. The new IDBB project delivery method was no excuse for inadequate attention to project management fundamentals, but unfortunately that was the initial condition.

At the beginning of the project, the Corps of Engineers made major scope reductions to fit within the available funding. Later, the reduced scope was added back in with increased funding as the "world class" standard and intent was clearly defined. However, the Project Delivery Team had to cope with the consequences of these early decisions throughout the project's life. Coordination and associated impacts of this major change were not thoroughly communicated and understood. Project management basics such as an approved Project Management Plan (PMP), effective change management, and use of Earned Value Analysis were inadequate or incomplete. Another basic – client communications – was uneven. Early on, some senior members of the Project Delivery Team could not identify the specific "client" for the FBCH project among the multi-agency Department of Defense Health Affairs team. Everyone needed to be on the same page – and they weren't.

A central concern in this area is that the priority among safety, quality, scope, schedule and cost must be clear. Rather than a relative priority being established, there was much misunderstanding about how a ranking among them would work in practice. The stakeholders generally were not familiar with how the IDBB delivery method was supposed to work. In our formal lessons learned collection effort, some stakeholders reported that cost and schedule, by the evidence of what occurred, held a higher priority than quality on this project. This was at odds with the priority preferences of most stakeholders who earnestly sought a "world class" project. Had all of the stakeholders been exposed to how the IDBB method was supposed to work, and a sharper focus on project management fundamentals been emphasized, a better alignment of priorities could have been achieved.

3. Train Participants for their Roles, especially with Novel Processes

The FBCH used the Integrated Design Bid Build (IDBB) project delivery method. There is no question that this method enabled the team to achieve the compressed schedule required by the BRAC law. This project would not have successfully made that deadline if it had used traditional construction project delivery methods. However, IDBB was new to the team and it did not succeed in reaping the most sought-after benefits of this novel methodology. Many of the lessons learned in this regard delve into the complexities of the IDBB approach, which would be a full paper unto itself. With respect to leadership lessons, however, suffice it to say that when a team embarks on a mission using a new process or tool, it must train to be successful. Several aspects of the IDBB method such as "design-assist", achieving "production point", and finalizing the contractual firm-fixed-price (FFP) agreement were unnecessarily painful and in many cases conducted in a "learn-as-you-go" fashion. Taking the time on the front end to train on IDBB fundamentals would likely have resulted in the new methodology being used in a more optimal way, as well as serving to define roles and align the team before it embarked upon its mission.

4. Make Use of Valuable, Sophisticated Tools

Similarly, the same comment can be made concerning tools such as Earned Value Management and Schedule Analysis. The construction industry has valuable tools to measure performance and, by extension, keep stakeholders aligned. In large integrated projects like FBCH, it is critical that these tools are used and understood by both the Project Delivery Team and external stakeholders. If they are not used, or used in ways that do not engage important features, we will never know what they might have added.

The starkest example on the FBCH project was the use of Earned Value Management. This concept tracks production and cost against the base line of how the project was planned to be done. Leaders use this tool to provide a clear picture of project performance. As the FBCH project got underway, a decision was made to forgo use of Earned Value Management as a tool available to the team. Much later, as the project neared completion, available funds were dwindling, and the calendar clicked closer to the BRAC deadline, having an Earned Value Analysis would have been especially helpful as a common platform to engender confidence in the status of the project.

Conclusion

The Ft. Belvoir Community Hospital project was a significant success and, for many of the participants of the Project Delivery Team, a career highlight. Our team operated with a spirit of continuous improvement, and it is in that spirit we share our FBCH experience. These four lessons – getting the culture right, focusing on the fundamentals, training new processes, and using available tools – are not especially fresh new ideas. But, they become especially important in large, complex endeavors like construction of the FBCH where new delivery strategies, team integration and broad stakeholder participation are central components.

References

Kizer, K.W., McGowan, M., & Bowman, S. (May, 2009). Achieving world class, an independent review of the design plans for Walter Reed Military Medical Center and Ft. Belvoir Community Hospital. National Capital Region Base Realignment and Closure Health Systems Advisory Subcommittee of the Defense Health Board.

Key Lessons In Leading Change

1. Preparing for change is a critical part of the change process.

2. Engaging senior leaders can make or break change projects.

3. Get the culture right.

4. Focus on the basics in implementing changes: processes, resources, and client needs.

5. Train participants for their roles and especially for new behaviors, skills, and processes.

6. Make use of valuable tools.

7. Keep people focused, create opportunities and processes for open communications and problem solving, and celebrate successes.

Discussion

1. When faced with a significant challenge such as building a world class hospital in record time, what are some steps leaders can take to prepare those involved, considering some may have different objectives and processes, for change, success, and unity of purpose?

2. The overall vision for the project appeared to be to build a world class hospital in record time and the motto adopted for the project was "August 2011 – Whatever It takes!" Do you think it is important to take the time to have a vision or motto to provide focus for a major change? Discuss reasons for your position.

3. Why is it important to define, build, and reinforce a supportive culture in successfully accomplishing change? What was done in the case to build a supportive culture?

4. Why is it important to plan for significant senior leadership engagement and involvement in making significant changes? What was done in the case to engage and unite senior leaders?

5. A lesson learned during the project was the need to focus on the basics such as processes, resources, and client needs in implementing changes. What was done in the project to keep people focused on the basics?

6. Another lesson learned was the importance of training participants for their roles and especially where the roles require new behaviors, skills, or ways of doing things. Why is this aspect of change so important and what are some of the consequences when people are not properly trained?

7. A final lesson learned was the need to make use of valuable, sophisticated tools such as management tools, technology, and state-of-the-art processes. What can be done to discover and utilize these tools and best practices?

8. As various team members enter and leave change projects, what can be done to ensure continuity over the life of the project?

BIOGRAPHY

Jeanne D. Maes currently serves as Board President of the International Society of Organization Development and Peer Review Editor for The Organization Development Journal. She is Professor of Management in the Mitchell College of Business at the University of South Alabama. An experienced facilitator, consultant, and executive trainer, Dr. Maes' areas of specialization include communication skills, conflict management, partnering, team-building, and leadership. Her articles have appeared in numerous national and international publications, and she has made presentations to such groups as the American Bar Association Section on ADR, the Society of Professionals in Dispute Resolution, the Alabama Governor's Task Force on State Agency ADR, and the Florida Dispute Resolution Center, and others. Additionally, she has served as a volunteer district court mediator and is an arbitrator.

Jeanne D. Maes, PhD, Professor
Department of Management, Mitchell College of Business,
University of South Alabama, Mobile, AL 36688
Phone: (251) 460-6737 · Email: jmaes@usouthal.edu

Colonel Andrew W. Backus assumed Command of the Norfolk District, US Army Corps of Engineers on June 12, 2009. As District Commander, he manages the Corps' water resources development and navigable waterways operations for five river basins in the Commonwealth of Virginia. These include the Rappahannock, York, James and Chowan rivers and the Chesapeake Bay coastal basin. He is also responsible for the Corps' military design and construction projects for Army, Army Reserve and Air Force military installations throughout Virginia. He manages the Corps' regulatory, environmental restoration, flood damage reduction (including

BIOGRAPHY

hurricane and storm damage reduction) and disaster response activities, and also provides engineering support to our nation's Overseas Contingency Operations.

Colonel Backus recently completed his Senior Service College year as the Army's Leadership and Management National Security Fellow at Harvard University. Prior to attending Harvard, he served as a Human Resources Manager in the Senior Leader Development Office on the Army Staff at the Pentagon.

Colonel Andrew W. Backus, PE, PMP
District Commander, Norfolk District, US Army Corps of Engineers
(O) 757-201-7601, (Fax) 757-201-7115
andrew.w.backus.col@usace.army.mil

William A. Sorrentino, Jr. has served the Government for 25 years beginning his service with the U.S. Army Corps of Engineers in 1977. He has served in various positions in the Corps, which includes structural design, project management, construction management and operations management, both in line and staff positions. Mr. Sorrentino is currently serving as the Chief, Technical Services Division at the Army Corps of Engineers, Norfolk District. In this position, he has responsibility to manage and lead the district's largest division which includes Planning, Engineering, Construction, Operations, Regulatory, Real Estate and Emergency Readiness. He serves as a principle advisor and consultant to the Commander on technical and key matters.

Willam A. Sorrentino Jr., PE, PMP, DBIA
Norfolk District, US Army Corps of Engineers
William.A.Sorrentino@usace.army.mil

BIOGRAPHY

Jim Moore is a consultant offering technical, management, and facilitator services. He has over 28 years of experience in managing large organizations and public works projects. Since 1976, he has designed, constructed, and managed real property for various Government Agencies. In 1999, Jim served as the Chief Engineer for the Base Camp Coordinating Agency in Kosovo. In 2001, he consulted with the Polish Government on the design, construction, and repair of levee systems. He is a subject matter expert in Hazardous, Toxic, and Radioactive Waste, and taught a number of courses in this field. He facilitates partnering services for a variety of clients in Israel, Qatar, and Egypt, served on an AGC Task Force to reinvigorate the Partnering Process, and authored several articles on the process. Jim resides in Mt. Pocono, Pennsylvania. He is a registered professional engineer in Pennsylvania and a CMCI Certified Construction Manager. His education includes a BS in Civil Engineering from the Penn State (1976), and an MS in Management of Technology from Lehigh (1999). He is a member of ASCE and Chi Epsilon. Among his awards are the deFleury and Army Achievement Medals.

James P.Moore, CCM, PE
US Army Corps of Engineers
Jim.Moore@usace.army.mil

BIOGRAPHY

Robert A. Shearer has served as Vice President for Planning and Assessment at Brevard Community College, and Assistant to the President for Academic Affairs and Professor of Management at the University of South Alabama in Mobile. A member of the Florida and Virginia bars, he is a certified state and federal court mediator and arbitrator. He has presented numerous programs at conferences sponsored by organizations such as the American Bar Association Dispute Resolution Section, the Florida Dispute Resolution Center, the Florida Academy of Professional Mediators, the Alabama Governor's Task Force on State Agency ADR, and the Society of Professionals in Dispute Resolution in the areas of mediation, arbitration, conflict management, interest-based negotiation, team-building, and workplace legal issues. In addition, he conducts executive training sessions on these topics and has chaired public employee grievance hearing panels. As a partnering consultant and facilitator, he has worked with private contractors and government agencies on complex, multi-party projects.

Robert A. Shearer, J.D., Professor
Mitchell College of Business, University of South Alabama
Mobile, AL 36688 · Email: rshearer@usouthal.edu

CHAPTER TWO

6

Exploring The World Of Pseudo Change

Thomas C. Head
Peter F. Sorensen, Jr.

Major Focus Of The Case

Pseudo change, while no doubt an ancient practice, has only recently come under investigation by organization development scholar practitioners. There are many different types of pseudo change, as well as many different causes, but in general they consist of activities that give the appearance of planned organizational change but actually involve no real alterations, or real changes unconnected to any motivating force. One can easily imagine many negative consequences of pseudo change ranging from wasted resources to disillusioned employees. While it has been speculated that often pseudo change is not deliberate, and may actually be a subconscious decision, it is important that managers learn to recognize pseudo change as it is happening (or ideally prior to its implementation) in order to avoid the significant repercussions. This case presents one illustration of pseudo change that not only illustrates what it involves, but also the dynamics of how it occurred. While presented as a single plant's experience the case actually is a conglomeration of three different location's events. This was done in order to protect the anonymity of the organization.

Introduction

Pseudo change is a common, but often ignored, problem constantly seen in a wide variety of organizations. Pseudo change can be defined as "the purposeful or unintentional implementation of a change effort in an organization that does not address the problem it is purposed to, and/or does not address an actual organizational problem or need, and/or involves engaging in activities that only give the appearance of change." (Head and Sorensen, 2011, p.1).

There are many reasons why pseudo change might occur. One possibility is that many managers suffer from the belief that action, any action, is better than analysis. Management simply perceives there isn't time to plan out a legitimate course of action, so they quickly develop and implement change initiatives (sometimes actually prior to establishing that a problem actually exists. Another possible cause lies in the compartmentalization present in many organizations, particularly those steeped in traditional bureaucratic thinking. This practice forces managers to adopt a very narrow functional focus in their thinking. In essence to the accountant everything is an accounting problem that requires an accounting solution, that marketer always advocates marketing solutions, and so forth. The blame for pseudo change doesn't just lay with management. "One pill" consultants, those who are only skilled in one intervention, will naturally view all issues revolving around their expertise. Every organization requires their expertise, whether there is a real issue or not. Often times powerful stakeholders, such as boards, unions, and investors, may also exert pressures on management to irrational acts. "A company that isn't changing is stagnant" is a philosophy inherently present in the short term thinking of many boards and investors. Certain practices may be identified as "untouchable" even though everyone sees they are dysfunctional. Given these, and the many other possible influences, it is interesting that pseudo change isn't actually more prevalent in organizations.

Even when pseudo change occurs with the best of intentions there will be negative consequences. After all, recall that by definition "Pseudo change is irrational. It is dysfunctional. By definition Pseudo change is undesirable." (Head and Sorensen, 2011, p. 5) Possibly the most obvious negative outcome of pseudo change is that actual organizational problems never truly get addressed. If the change actually does work it is entirely an accident akin to pushing a button that stops an out-of-control machine when one was simply looking for the light switch. Another possible consequence is that the employees could develop an apathy towards future changes. People will only take so many "this is the thing that will propel us to the next level" that fizzle before they lose interest in what is at "the next level". Obviously pseudo change will also lead to an extreme waste of time, effort, and other valuable (and scarce) organizational resources. While it is conceivable that pseudo change could show some occasional positive outcomes, the negative results will almost certainly outweigh any temporary gains.

Background of Focus Plant

The plant in question was one of many the large Fortune 500 company had scattered around the United States (and globally). This particular plant consisted of around 3,000 employees. Approximately 80 percent of the employees were line production workers and supervisors. There were 300 managers and professional support staff employees. The remaining 300 were various engineers working in product research and development. It is these engineers who are of interest. The engineers were divided among five departments. Mostly they consisted of electrical engineers as well computer software specialists, although there were a few mechanical engineers as well as a "smattering" of physicists. All these research and development individuals had been hired directly from respected universities, mostly through summer internship programs. Virtually 100 percent possessed a relevant undergraduate degree, and about half held a masters degree (about half of these were MBA's). Regardless of the department, the engineers all worked towards two general purposes: 1) to develop, and evaluate, improvements for current products, and 2) develop and test potential new products.

The Issue

Corporate policy mandated that all managers and professional staff (including engineers) be evaluated each year using a traditional, participatively set, management-by-objectives program. After several years the corporate headquarters staff came to the conclusion that very few, if indeed anyone, throughout the entire company actually took the management-by-objectives initiative seriously. Everyone created goals, and their performances were evaluated against them, but no one seemed to really care about the goals. Headquarters believed its employees all simply went "through the motions" and no one was particularly motivated by the system.

Corporate went to 16 of their plant managers and asked for their opinions. The results were inconclusive. Some managers didn't quite understand the issue. Others felt the management-by-objectives system was working fine. The remainder agreed with headquarters that the current system was flawed.

Headquarters staff knew they needed to act to correct this situation. While the organization hadn't reached the "problem level" yet, they felt it was only a matter of time, and an "ounce of prevention is worth a pound of cure." The only real question was "what should we do about this?" The answer came quickly as one of the corporate human resources executives was enrolled in an organization development class and had just learned about appreciative inquiry (Cooperrider & Srivastva, 1987). Could appreciative inquiry be incorporated into the management-by-objectives process so that the participants created more goals, more "stretch goals", took the goals more seriously, and accomplished more of their objectives? Headquarters selected three plants to serve as test subjects, one plant being the one of interest here.

The Intervention

The plant's intervention began with the corporate human resources executive, who first came up with the idea (and who was now doing this as a class requirement) coached the engineering managers in the appreciative inquiry process. This was done through a three hour on-site training program. Appropriately trained, the managers were instructed to call all of their direct reports together for an afternoon long meeting. These meetings were to consist of the combined appreciative inquiry management-by-objectives goal setting initiative.

The initial meeting with the engineers first involved explaining the agenda. The engineers would be taken through an appreciative inquiry process as a group. After that the engineers would be asked to create their personal work objectives for the year, and finally each engineer would meet one-on-one with her/his supervisor to review the goals.

The appreciative inquiry process began with each individual being asked to think of their "peak experience" time at the company, the time they enjoyed their job the most. Next the employees were asked to think about what was unique about these experiences that made them so enjoyable. The participants were then asked to share their own responses with the rest of the group, and the best of the unique traits were recorded on newsprint for all to view. It was at this point that each engineer was asked, referring to the newly generated list of characteristics, to write their own job objectives for the year. Before the one-on-one meetings the corporate human resources person was pleased to find that almost universally the engineers reported "liking" the process and thought it was truly helpful.

Knowing that the goal setting process was truly a year-long commitment, and based upon the overwhelming favorable response from the engineers, the corporate human resources executive decided to hold two more appreciative inquiry sessions throughout the year, one at four months and the second at eight months. These sessions were considered "boosters", taking the engineers through the process of identifying and sharing peak experiences and causal factors. The purpose was to reenergize and recommit to the goals. Each time the engineers were highly enthusiastic after the sessions, one individual (often quoted by the human recourses executive) shouting out "I'm pumped!, I'm really pumped!"

At the end of the year, wanting to collect further evaluative data on the new system, each engineer was asked for his/her opinion on the process. Over 90 percent of the engineers were reported to be "supportive" or "very supportive" of the new system. Armed with this statistic the corporate human resources executive (program creator and champion) received permission to begin diffusing the program throughout the remaining plants. The CEO could easily see what a great success this program was.

Fortunately, or possibly unfortunately, a few weeks later top management decided to slow the diffusion down. They believed the idea still possessed merit, but would need more effort. This slight change of heart was caused by a more detailed examination of other management-by-objectives factors. The engineering managers reported that there were no additional goals generated by the new system, nor were the goals that were established any more difficult than their pre-change counterparts. Perhaps the most significant finding was that the engineers' actual goal attainment percentages dropped five percent.

Change Post Script

The appreciative inquiry/management-by-objectives program was considered a true success by management. Plant managers were given the option, not a dictate, to adopt the program. Several plants did adopt the program over the next two years. No further evaluation had been performed, so the extent of the program's true benefits remain unknown.

Discussion

1. Discuss the concept of pseudo change, what it means, and how leaders tend to make pseudo changes.
2. Was this a case of pseudo change? Why or why not?
3. Assess the change process. What was done right? Wrong?
4. What were the clear outcomes of the change? What didn't change? Were the actual outcomes significant enough to warrant diffusion throughout the company?
5. Evaluate the corporate leadership's actions. What do you think of how they approached the entire process?
6. What are some ways the potential for pseudo change can be avoided?

Key Lessons In Leading Change

1. True change requires diagnosis and thought. First one must determine if a problem actually exists before launching an entire change process. Next the intervention selected to bring about the change needs to be carefully chosen based upon its ability to bring about the necessary change (problem solution), and not simply because it "sounds like a great idea."

2. Don't confuse a positive employee reaction with actual results. It is always heart-warming to hear that employees truly like a change. If nothing else it is easier to keep them from "back sliding" to their old ways when they enjoy the innovation. However is this enough for success? A child might like cake more than a vegetable, but a diet of all cake will not succeed in the long run. What is needed is a balance between what they like and what they need. If the two conflict than there is no question one must do what is needed (after making sure there is no way to combine the two).

3. Appreciative inquiry is a proven valid change technique. However, in and of itself, appreciative inquiry is not really an intervention. It is a methodology to lead one to identify interventions and action plans. Unfortunately, all too frequently, the appreciative inquiry process is used more as a feel-good group therapy activity and less as a path to meaningful change. When this occurs the process can actually "mask" the fact that no real change is being implemented. The key to successful appreciative inquiry is the action step, taking the "peak experiences characteristics" and identifying paths to make them the norm, rather than the exception.

References

Cooperrider, David, L. and Srivastva, Suresh (1987) Appreciative inquiry in organizational life. In Richard Woodman and William Pasmore, Eds. Research in organizational change and development, volume 1. Greenwich, Connecticut: JAI Press, Inc.

Head, Thomas C. and Sorensen, Peter F. (2011) Exploring the world of pseudo change. Academy of Management National Conference, San Antonio, Texas.

BIOGRAPHY

Thomas C. Head, Ph.D., is a Professor of Management and the Director Of Accreditation for Roosevelt University's W. E. Heller College of Business. He is a prolific author with 17 books and over 75 journal articles to his credit on a wide variety of topics. His current interests lie primarily with global organization development and related practices. He has served on the boards of the Academy of Management's Management Consulting Division, The Midwest Academy of Management and Pro-Change International. He has served as the editor for both The Journal of Pro-Change International and The Organization Development Journal. He earned his Ph.D. in Business Administration from Texas A&M University.

Dr. Head can be contacted at thead@roosevelt.edu.

Dr. Peter Sorensen is Professor and Director of PhD and Masters programs in OD at Benedictine University. He has authored over 200 books and articles, in the Academy of Management Journal, Group and Organization Studies, Leadership and Organization Development Journal, Journal of Management Studies, and Organization and Administrative Sciences. He is Past Chair of the OD&C Division of the National Academy of Management. His doctoral degree is from Illinois Institute of Technology.

Dr. Sorensen can be contacted at psoren@ben.edu.

7

Brandeis University: Selling Art or the Art of Selling Change?

Todd Jick

Acknowledgement: Nate Nickerson provided research and writing support for this case.

This case was originally published by Columbia CaseWorks of Columbia University as case number 100405 and is used with permission.

Major Focus Of The Case

Like many universities, Brandeis faced a serious budget crisis and its President faced a variety of difficult options. One of his recommendations, however, created a huge uproar – to sell valuable pieces of art from its esteemed Rose Art Museum. This threatened action was perceived by many constituents as unacceptable and led to considerable resistance. In addition, students at the University felt left out of the process of consultation and decision making. The President was confronted with negative reactions about both the actual proposed action as well as the process. Could it have been handled better? If so, how? After all, when organizations face budget crises, decisions and action taken are rarely popular, but perhaps it can be buffered by the way it is handled!

Introduction

On January 26, 2009, the *Boston Globe* reported that Brandeis University, located in Waltham, Massachusetts, had decided to close the Rose Art Museum and sell its more than 6,000 works by such celebrated modern artists as Andy Warhol, Willem de Kooning, Jasper Johns, and Roy Lichtenstein. The museum's director, Michael Rush, gave the *Boston Globe* a "No comment" – but did let the newspaper know that he had just been informed of the decision.[8]

The global financial crisis had hurt Brandeis particularly badly. Like virtually all universities, Brandeis saw its endowment substantially

---

8 Edgers, G. and Schworm, P. (2009, January 26). Brandeis to sell school's art collection. Boston Globe. Retrieved from http://www.boston.com

weakened by the recession. For Brandeis, a young school (founded in 1948) with a relatively small pool of alumni donors, this drop was significant. As a private liberal arts college, Brandeis was entirely dependent on its donors, many of whom had suffered serious financial losses due to Bernard Madoff's firm's fraudulent investment scheme.[9] The university faced a budget deficit of about $10 million, and in addition to closing the Rose it considered such measures as reducing faculty by 10%, increasing enrollment by 12%, and streamlining the way it organized majors. The Rose's collection was, according to Rush, assessed at $350 million in 2007.[10]

Brandeis's president, Jehuda Reinharz, said:

> *The Rose is a jewel. But for the most part it's a hidden jewel. It does not have great foot traffic and most of the great works we have, we are just not able to exhibit. We felt that, at this point given the recession and the financial crisis, we had no choice.*[11]

A former member of the board of trustees told CBS news:

> *Well, it's all about priorities isn't it? It's what do you value most? We've frozen salaries, we have a hiring freeze, we've cut expenses. If one of the compromises you're prepared to make is we may have to sell select works of art, I think most of the community...they'll understand that.*[12]

The decision of Reinharz and the Brandeis board of trustees (which, according to Brandeis's website, was "the final authority on all aspects of the university's operations" [13]) set off strong responses.

Museum Board of Overseers

On January 27, the day after the *Boston Globe* broke the story, the New York Times wrote a follow-on piece. The article quoted Rush, who said, "I was shocked. I'm still shocked," as well as Jonathan Lee, the chairman of the museum's board of overseers, who stated, "nobody at the museum – neither the director nor myself nor anyone else – was informed of this or had any idea what was going on."[14] The *New York Times* article also raised the question, not about the wisdom or morality of the decision, but of whether it was legal to sell the Rose's collection, since many of the museum's works of art had been given to the university as gifts.

9 Wee, G. and Lorin, J. F. (2009, January 27). Brandeis to close Rose Art Museum as endowment slips (update 1). Bloomberg. Retrieved from http://www.bloomberg.com
10 Wee and Lorin. Brandeis to close Rose Art Museum.
11 Edgers and Schworm. Brandeis to sell school's art collection.
12 Teicher, M. (2009, March 15). The art of survival: can a struggling cultural institution sell its artwork to balance its books? Some say no. Sunday Morning. CBS News. Retrieved from http://www.cbsnews.com
13 Board of trustees. Brandeis University. Retrieved from http://www.brandeis.edu/trustees/
14 Kennedy, R. and Vogel, C. (2009, January 27). Outcry over a plan to sell museum's holdings. New York Times. Retrieved from http://www.nytimes.com

A spokesperson for Massachusetts Attorney General Martha Coakley told the *New York Times* that her office was informed of Brandeis's decision on the same day that the story appeared in the *Boston Globe*. The spokesperson went on to say that Coakley's office would conduct a review of donors' wills and their agreements with Brandeis to determine whether any sales of art violated any contracts. "We do expect this to be a lengthy process,"[15] she said. A Brandeis spokesperson declined comment on the legality of the art sales.

The Art World

In both the *Boston Globe* and *New York Times* articles, art experts voiced withering criticism. They condemned, on principal, the general idea of hawking art in tough financial times, and also raised one particular concern: whether it was wise to attempt to sell art in what was, given the recession, an abysmal art market. "It couldn't be a worse time to sell expensive art," prominent curator and art historian Robert Storr told the *New York Times*. "It is not only unprincipled, but bad economics."[16]

On January 26 the *Los Angeles Times* carried an article about the Rose that included a statement from the Association of Art Museum Directors: "AAMD is shocked and dismayed to learn of Brandeis University's plans to close the Rose Art Museum and sell its collection. This is a sad day for the students of Brandeis, the University, and its community. ... AAMD's mid-winter meeting begins tomorrow and its members will discuss the ramifications of Brandeis' decision and any actions the Association may take in response to these regrettable plans." [17]

The *New York Times* also quoted a flabbergasted Jasper Johns, who said, "I find it astonishing. I've never heard anything like it." [18]

Faculty

Faculty also did not respond well to the announcement. In interviews with Inside Higher Ed, Brandeis professors complained that they had not, either as a group or through their committees, been asked their opinion of the sale. In addition, the article noted that art and museum associations specifically bar the sale of art for anything other than the purchase of other art.[19]

---

15 Kennedy and Vogel. Outcry over a plan.
16 Kennedy and Vogel. Outcry over a plan.
17 Boehm, M. (2009, January 26). Updated: Brandeis University to close art museum, sell connection. *Los Angeles Times*. Retrieved from http://latimesblogs.latimes.com
18 Kennedy and Vogel. Outcry over a plan.
19 Jaschik, S. (2009, January 27). Brandeis to sell all of its art. Inside Higher Ed. Retrieved from http://www.insidehighered.com

Students

Students spoke out loudly and clearly. In an op-ed in Brandeis's student newspaper, the Justice, a student lamented not only the decision itself, but also the way in which it was made. The closing, the student wrote, "reached the student body as a fait accompli, with no room for discussion. This decision from on high came as a particular blow to students who have been fighting for greater transparency in the budget cut decisions."[20] Another student, Jaclyn Saffir, wrote an op-ed for the *Boston Globe*, "A Lesson for Brandeis: Include Your Students," which was very critical of the process:

> *Although this week's decision …to sell the Rose Art Museum collection was an indicator of a bad financial trend for American Universities, equally troubling was that the trustees did not involve students in the decision…*
>
> *…the biggest unnecessary jab was at students, many of whom felt as if this was just another brick in the wall preventing student input in the university's financial challenges that would ultimately force students to sacrifice. This not only created a student backlash, with protests on campus, but also created headlines that would likely harm the reputation of the institution. While financial shortfalls may not deter some prospective students, a frustrated and ignored student body certainly will.*
>
> *In the end, the administration officials alienated a group that ultimately could have been on their side. While few would be happy to give up the Rose, most students and faculty understand that sacrifices have to be made and that academics cannot be jeopardized. Yet the announcement did not discuss alternatives or lay out why the decision was necessary.*
>
> *President Reinharz had a question-and-answer session Wednesday and explained the need for the decision, yet this presentation could have been given before the trustees voted. This would have allowed students to provide input into this process, and in the end, many, perhaps most, would have supported the decision.*[21]

---

20 Leifer, E. (2009, January 27). Op-ed: Rose shutdown risks our image. Justice. Retrieved from http://media.www.thejustice.org

21 Saffir, J. (2009, January 31). A lesson for Brandeis: include your students. *Boston Globe*. Retrieved from http://www.boston.com

A Parent Perspective

A mother of three students who attended Brandeis responded:

We're here to testify that Brandeis has never scrimped on its kids. So when they found they must cut, the administrators made darn sure it didn't crack the core of the university's top rated student centered programs and services. ...The Rose has been a wonderful resource for the community and a proud tribute to its generous and visionary donors. But Reinharz was right when he delicately described the museum as "for the most part...a hidden jewel." ... most Rose visitors find they are alone in its galleries.[22]

The President Responds

Shortly after the announcement and its backlash, Reinharz publicly backpedaled. In a letter to the Brandeis community dated February 5, he said it was never the intention of Brandeis's board of trustees to close the museum, nor to sell all of its artwork. "The Museum will remain open," he wrote, "but in accordance with the Board's vote, it will be more fully integrated into the University's central educational mission. We will meet with all affected University constituencies to explore together how this can best be done."[23] He apologized for the confusion over the information about the board's intentions and also for the fact that, as he said, "I did not find a more inclusive and open way to engage the Brandeis community in the deliberations that led to the Board's decision. I take full responsibility for causing pain and embarrassment in both of these matters. To quote President Obama, 'I screwed up.'"[24] Nevertheless, the reality was that the Rose, if the board had its way, would cease to be a public museum, and Brandeis would still reserve the option of selling some of its works of art.

22 Raub, D. F. (2009, February 6). A Brandeis mom's view of the Rose. Jewish Advocate.
23 Reinharz, J. (2009, February 5). Letter: Brandeis president apologizes for handling of museum issue. *Boston Globe*. Retrieved from http://www.boston.com
24 Reinharz. Letter: Brandeis president apologizes.

Reactions

In an article published on February 6, Bloomberg seized on the notion that Reinharz's words did little to change the state of play. Bloomberg reported:

> The chairman of the museum's board of overseers, Jonathan Lee, said Reinharz's statement is window dressing. *'This apology is a nice thing, but it doesn't change anything,' Lee said in an interview today. 'We're not going to be a real art museum any more. They're killing the museum. The museum director is going. We're not going to have big-time shows.'* [25]

On February 11 the *Boston Globe* reported that Rush had held a 90-minute town meeting at the museum. In attendance were students, faculty, and members of the broader community – all of whom got a surprise visit from Jeanette McCarthy, the mayor of Waltham. The mayor said that the Rose was very important to the city, adding that "art is a priority" and that "it would be terrible for it to go." The *Boston Globe* also quoted Brandeis English professor Ramie Targoff saying, "Everyone in this room will see that it is a sacred spot for many people in our community."[26]

The fight heated up on April 23, when the Rose's board of overseers issued a press release charging the Brandeis administration and board of trustees with usurping the overseers' authority. "Despite the existence of the current Board of Overseers for the museum," the release stated, "Brandeis has named a new committee to 'explore future options for the Rose.'" [27]

The release discredited the newly formed committee:

> *Two months after first announcing and then restating its intentions to close the Rose and sell off the artwork, the University released the mandate for its 'Committee for the Future of the Rose.'... According to Brandeis, the committee is designed to 'explore options' for the future of the Rose, but is specifically prohibited from determining the fate of the works of art that are the heart of the institution, leaving that to the administration and Brandeis Board of Trustees. Although the committee includes representatives from various constituencies, including the Rose Art Museum Board of Overseers, members were hand-picked by the administration and the Rose was not allowed to choose its own representative.[28]*

25 Lorin, J. F. (2009, February 6). Brandeis 'screwed up' in handling art museum's fate (update 2). Bloomberg. Retrieved from http://www.bloomberg.com
26 Terris, B. (2009, February 11). Hundreds seek ways to keep public access to Brandeis museum. *Boston Globe.* Retrieved from http://www.boston.com
27 Rose Art Museum board of overseers: systematic dismantling of the Rose Art Museum well underway even as Brandeis claims otherwise. (2009, April 23). The Rose Museum press release. Retrieved from http://www.businesswire.com
28 Rose Art Museum board of overseers: systematic dismantling.

The release included this statement from Meryl Rose, an overseer and a member of the family that founded the museum:

> *By forming the committee, Brandeis has turned a blind eye to the fact that the Rose already had an active board, in the Rose Art Museum Board of Overseers, to map out its future.*

She continued:

> *What is also terribly saddening to us ... is the role the Brandeis Board of Trustees played in this matter. We know that the trustees have only the best interests of the University at heart. ... Unfortunately, they have been led astray by a disingenuous administration motivated to push an agenda that involves looting the school's culture to simply balance the books.[29]*

On July 27 the *New York Times* reported that three overseers of the Rose had filed suit against Brandeis in Massachusetts state court in an effort to halt the sale of the Rose's art and the closing of the museum:

> *Jonathan O. Lee, Lois Foster and Meryl Rose, a member of the family whose donations created the museum in 1961 – contend that Brandeis's plans to close the museum 'contradict the charitable intentions' of the museum's founders, 'abrogate Brandeis's promises that the Rose would be maintained in perpetuity' as a modern and contemporary art museum, and violate its commitments to those who donated art to the museum.[30]*

The *New York Times* further noted that a statement issued by lawyers representing Brandeis called the suit frivolous and without merit.

---

29 Rose Art Museum board of overseers: systematic dismantling.
30 Kennedy, R. (2009, July 27). Lawsuit seeks to save art museum at Brandeis. *New York Times*. Retrieved from http://www.nytimes.com

Epilogue

In October 2009 Reinharz unexpectedly announced to the university community his intention to step down, ending his 15 years as president of Brandeis. Under his leadership, Brandeis's endowment had risen from $194M to $559M, applications for freshman admissions had increased from 4,321 to 7,758, and the university had become much more selective: the acceptance rate had gone from 68% to 32%. The chairman of the board dismissed speculation that Reinharz was "pushed out because of a band of disgruntled faculty, still smarting from last winter's controversy over the Rose Art Museum." [31]

Reflecting on the furor, Reinharz said:

> *The mission of the university is delivering the best education we can. Most of the controversy came from the Art world and I understand their passion, but I would dare say that many of them do not particularly care about Brandeis. Their care is for the Arts, but we are a university, first and foremost.*[32]

Finally, in his Brandeis University Magazine "exit interview," Reinharz reflected on the Rose:

> *First, it would probably have been a better course of action to have wider consultation with faculty and staff. Second, it was not necessary to issue a press release... [But] the Rose needs to be understood in the context of many other cuts we made ...including 76 staff positions.*[33]

On October 15 it was announced that:

> *A Massachusetts judge has denied a motion by Brandeis University to dismiss a lawsuit brought by three overseers of the school's Rose Art Museum who were seeking to stop the university from closing the museum and selling its works...the university pledged not to sell any artwork that had been donated by the overseers ... and said it would give the Massachusetts attorney general an opportunity for review if it decided to sell works donated by others.*[34]

On December 31 in an insert, "Bloom Was Off the Rose," the *Boston Globe* summed up the year's events at Brandeis after the announcement of the closing of the Rose Museum. The piece concluded, "After a public outcry spread from the campus to the art world, the university backed down and decided to keep the museum open, but let the director's contract expire and reserved the option to sell some works."

31 Hogan, C. (2009, October 2). Brandeis abuzz about Reinharz: the university takes stock of the man who transformed it. *Boston Globe.*
32 Hogan. Brandeis abuzz.
33 Gornstein, K. (Fall 2009). All good things. Brandeis University Magazine. p. 13.
34 Kennedy, R. (2009, October 15). Brandeis won't sell art donated by overseers. *New York Times.* Retrieved from http://www.nytimes.com

Discussion

1. In leading change, how you do things is as important as what you do. What can be learned from this case about what not to do and what should be done in making major changes?

2. Even the most effective leaders are often not well informed about how to lead change. How effective was President Reinharz in his 15 years at Brandeis and what could he have done different in handling the Rose Art Museum situation?

3. Who were the key constituencies in this case and what should their appropriate level of involvement have been and when should they have been involved?

4. If you could turn back the clock and had the opportunity to approach this situation differently, what would you have recommended step by step to the board?

5. Given the realities of what happened, what would you recommend that the board could do to address and possibly repair the damage that has been done.

Key Lessons In Leading Change

1. Some change decisions are not going to be popular, but perhaps are necessary, so how the process is managed will be critical

2. When and who to involve in change is a critical management choice. In general, the earlier the better. And in general, it is important to identify and include ALL the key constituencies

3. Public sector organizations have more constituencies to be considered than most organizations, especially when what is at stake is not just about "numbers" but also mission and values.

4. If leaders mismanage the change process, it will likely lead to more resistance than what was likely to arise on its own. Conversely, if the change process is managed well, it can allow difficult choices and decisions to be made.

BIOGRAPHY

Todd Jick is on the faculty of Columbia Business School. Previously, he was a Professor at Harvard Business School, London Business School, and Insead. He is the co-author (with Maury Peiperl) of the leading textbook in change management, called Managing Change, McGraw Hill, 2011, 3rd Edition. He has published numerous articles and more than 50 cases in the area of Change and Leadership. He has sat on a number of corporate boards and received Columbia's top teaching award.

Email: tdj2105@columbis.edu

8

Implementation Of Electronic Medical Records: Challenges And Lessons To Leaders

Tracy H. Porter

Major Focus

EMR's or electronic medical records are being adopted by numerous medical institutions with mixed receptions on the part of the medical staff. Though there is evidence regarding the benefits of EMR's, this dramatic change is also costly to install and challenging to train staff on and some doctors and staff are resigning rather than use the new system.

Change is the biggest constant in today's business world. All organizations at one time or another are finding that they need to innovate in order to stay viable. The management literature is full of stores of organizations that have experienced tremendous problems trying to implement major changes. It is imperative that organizational leaders develop skills in effectively managing the change and that they learn to involve and engage key stakeholders in the change process. This case illustrates the problems which can ensue when change is not well planned and implemented.

Introduction

Megan Kelly is the COO of a large metropolitan hospital system, Shaker Hospital Systems, in the Cleveland Ohio area. This hospital system is comprised of three main hospitals, 10 satellite buildings and five physician practice buildings. For over 120 years Shaker Hospital has been a solid member of the Cleveland area and has maintained a reputation for quality and excellence.

Kelly has been the COO of the organization for the past 3 years now and has been an employee in some capacity for over 20 years. During this time she has developed a reputation for quality and excellence. Staying current with industry trends is primary to the COO and the other top members of the organization. As part of this trend the COO has been activity striving to improve processes and systems in order to make the organization more efficient. This included many updates to the computer systems, communications systems and ultimately the records management system. Kelly therefore feels it is important to bring electronic medical records (EMR) into the hospital to improve efficiency and ultimately to cut costs.

EMR's are a way for medical personnel to organize patient medical records. They are medical records that are based within the hospital's computer system. EMRs are integrated within the hospital system and allow for physicians and nurses alike to access and input all information through their computer.

Past Methods and Relationships prior to Change

Since its inception the hospital has done all of its record keeping through traditional pen and paper charting methods. Many of the physicians have been with the hospital all of their professional careers and have no experience with computers of any sort. Kelly, in her tenure as the COO, has enjoyed a cordial relationship with the physicians and has envisioned her position as one of support to the clinical staff needs. She has maintained a good relationship with the clinical staff primarily because she has always understood her position within the hospital and has understood the importance of not getting involved in clinical issues. The COO is in charge of the efficient running of the hospital.

Investigating EMRs

Kelly proceeded to research EMRs extensively in preparation for this tremendous organizational change. Before making a decision to move forward, she spent several months assessing the benefits and challenges of EMRs and talking to executives in hospitals using EMRs. She was thrilled to discover that across the board she only heard positive results about the cost savings to their organizations. Kelly was so impressed with what she was being told that she did not spend any time asking about the downside to EMRs, the challenges in implementing EMRs, or ways the executives might have implemented EMRs differently.

Making a Decision to Implement EMRs

Since Kelly felt that there were no individuals who were unhappy with EMRs she didn't see a need to involve others in researching EMRs and also didn't see a need to form a committee to evaluate the pros and cons of EMR and plan the change process. Believing the clinical staff would be thrilled with this "time saving" tool at their disposal, Kelly ordered the EMR equipment and had it installed throughout the hospital system. She assumed that this change would be immediately embraced by all the medical staff members.

The Reaction of the Medical Staff

When the medical staff arrived at the hospital on Monday morning they were greeted with a memo announcing the installation of EMG and a comprehensive "how to" manual which demonstrated how the equipment was to be used. Certainly the medical staff had noticed a bit of construction going on in recent weeks. However, they assumed this was simple maintenance. Part of the "how to" manual given to each staff member listed optional training sessions which were offered during the first weeks after installation. The real challenge though was the clinical staff was expected to begin working on the EMR system immediately. Kelly felt the system was very intuitive and the medical staff could easily "figure out the system". This is what Kelly had been told by the executives at other hospitals.

The first morning after installation the physicians had varied responses at first. Some ignored the EMR equipment, some became very angry with Kelly, and several actually left the hospital in angry protest. One of the more vocal protestors was heard to state, "I have never used a computer in the past and I see no reason to begin now. Computers are too confusing and will actually cause more mistakes". This sentiment was echoed by numerous other physicians. The following conversation took place in the Doctor's Lounge that afternoon:

Dr. Young, "Who does she think she (Kelly) is to decide this without consulting us?"

Dr. Hopkins, "I think she has lost her mind with this EMR idea and how much do you think all that equipment cost the hospital?"

Dr. Young, "Millions!"

Kelly, overhearing this conversation from directly outside the door, entered the Doctor's Lounge to angry glares. Before she could even begin to explain how this transpired the physicians had her surrounded and were talking all at once. Kelly could not get a word into the conversation and eventually just stopped trying, sat down and listened. Later that day Kelly began to rethink her decision after she had a similar response from the nursing staff. She began to seriously question the way in which she handled this change.

Discussion

1. Kelly is a skilled leader with an excellent record. However, she has not been trained in leading change. What mistakes did she make in making the EMR change?

2. Why was the medical staff so upset with Kelly and how did this affect their motivation to implement the new EMR system and make it a success?

3. What are some alternatives a skilled change leader could have taken to approach this change project in a way that it would have a high probability of success?

4. Given the present situation what could Kelly do to correct the situation?

Key Lessons In Leading Change

1. Organizations should make training in leading change a high priority for leaders at all levels of an organization.

2. While not all major change decisions can be made by involving key people in investigating, planning, and implementing changes, this should be the norm rather than the exception.

3. Mistakes will be made in implementing changes so it is important for leaders to have small egos and an open leadership style so mistakes or alternatives can be freely discussed and corrections made.

BIOGRAPHY

Tracy H. Porter is a College Lecturer with the Department of Management and Labor Relations of Cleveland State University. She has extensive experience in the higher education field and as a management consultant. She received her Ph.D. in Organizational Leadership from Regent university with a concentration in human resource development. Her current research interests are in leadership development, impression management and spirituality in the workplace.

Email: t.h.porter@csuohio.edu

9

Leading Change The Wrong Way And The Right Way: The Importance Of Executive Sponsorship

David A. O'Brien

Major Focus Of The Case

Few leaders have been trained how to lead and implement change. This case is about a CEO who learned how to lead change the hard way. His first effort at making a major change in his company failed. When the persistence of the Human Resources Senior Vice President finally got his attention, he took a totally different approach to organizational change and saw much better results. The case provides many valuable lessons on leading organizational change.

Dan's First Approach to Much Needed Change

Noble Insurance (NI) like many US based life insurance providers was beginning to feel the effects of the economic downturn in Q1 2005. For the first time in its proud 42 year history, NI failed to meet revenue goals for the previous year. Despite the fact that earnings had been off for the two previous quarters, Dan Arnold, NI's Chairman and CEO did little to act on this until early 2005. With concern growing among his executive team, Dan decided that it was time to act. With minimal input from his Board or senior team, Dan announced that all departments in the company were to reduce operating expenses by 20% effective immediately. In addition to cost cutting measures, department heads were expected to eliminate any open positions and were told to be prepared for staff reductions in the future.

Within the first three months following Dan's cost cutting mandate, employee morale had sunk to an all time low. Not surprisingly, a decline in productivity followed. Even the most well intentioned and motivated employees were beginning to feel the stress that resulted from the cost savings initiative. People were being asked to do considerably more with less and despite the efforts of some leaders; most people were completely unaware of what was behind this new and painful direction. Ambiguity led to fear which in turn led to a very distorted rumor mill at the company.

By the time Kim Jeng, NI's SVP of HR got involved, several of the top employees had left to join competitors. Citing input and concern from her staff around the country, Kim informed Dan that the pace of change and resulting ambiguity had become a major barrier to organizational success. She went on to say that if NI didn't act soon, the long term viability of the company might be in jeopardy. As a long time, trusted member of Dan's team, her feedback got Dan's attention.

Despite Kim's good work in developing an organizational response strategy, Dan refused to be part of the process. He went on to say that this was a people issue and that people issues were best handled by HR. He was also quick to say that due to the demands placed on other executives, that this new change management initiative should be driven by mid level managers under the direction of HR.

The HR Executive's Efforts to Influence Needed Changes

In early Q3 2005 Kim and her team had selected an external resource for helping to implement and manage the change management project. It was determined that all managers would go through a full day of change management training and that all employees would attend a similar ½ day workshop. Following all of the training which took three months to deliver, the change management vendor met with Kim and her team to review progress and to make recommendations for the future. At first glance, the project appeared to be a success. Nearly 75% of all leaders and 82% of employees had attended the training. Dan was pleased with seeing this project come to a close. It was one more initiative to check-off his list. *Things were sure to be better now* he thought.

While the change management training did produce some benefits, it was widely perceived as a *band-aide* approach. Many of the leaders who did attend the training commented in private that they felt isolated from the big picture issues that were driving change in the first place. They also expressed a sense of resentment for Dan and his executive team for their lack of participation and support. Some managers actually went as far as to sabotage employee attendance by not allowing employees to attend the ½ day sessions under the guise that scheduling was too cumbersome and complicated.

As the beginning of 2006 rolled around employee morale at NI had declined to a point where nearly all employees began to have serious doubts about the future of the organization. Despite some communication clarity and consistency from field office middle managers, the rumor mill was in high gear across the organization. Most of the rumor mill exchange focused on *how good* things used to be and *how terrible* things had become at NI. Not surprisingly, Kim and her team of dedicated HR professionals began to notice a huge spike in Employee Relations cases. The daily average of employee sick days per department also spiked to an all time high.

A Proactive and Persistent HR Executive Finally Reaches the CEO

Frustrated and deeply concerned about the future of NI, Kim decided that it was time to get Dan involved in more than an ancillary role. She and her team began to research *best practice* approaches to organizational change and workplace resilience. After nearly two months of research, she was convinced that Dan had to lead the change charge.

In her meeting with Dan, Kim explained that she was still proud to be part of NI but that she felt very strongly that Dan needed to play a much more active role in helping the organization to move forward. She went on to say that all of her research pointed to the critical need for the CEO to not only drive the change initiative but also to embrace it as a long term process.

Kim's dedication and impressive record of accomplishments over the previous 18 years at NI helped in getting Dan to consider her recommendations. He admitted to Kim that he also sensed that NI was not the great company that it had been in years past. Almost sheepishly, he went on to say that he felt responsible for allowing NI to get to this point. He too wanted to believe in the future of NI and was now prepared to do his part in getting the organization back on track.

The CEO's New Approach to Leading Change

The first action that Dan took was to assemble his executive team for a long overdue conversation about NI's current state. He was surprised to learn from Kavi Jete, NI's General Counsel that most of the executive team shared in Kim's frustration and concern. Like most organizations their size, they all had been more than a little bit busy and distracted by the day to day demands of their functional areas. After listening to Kavi Jete and other members of his executive team for nearly two hours, Dan acknowledged that he was ready to lead the charge.

Recognizing that the current level of employee morale and reduced productivity were major barriers to success, Dan decided to seek input from employees across the organization. He wanted to know what was on their minds and what they needed from him and other leaders to help return NI to greatness. Unlike the first failed attempt at workplace resilience, Dan decided that he would lead this initiative. Within only three weeks, Dan personally visited all six of NI's locations. Through the help of Kim and her HR team, Dan was able to speak with nearly 80% of all employees through informal breakfast and lunch group meetings. At first, many of the employees were skeptical. After all, Dan had not been to most of these locations in over 2 years and many remembered his lack of involvement in the last change management initiative. Even more than this, they remembered his almost random cost cutting mandate that had produced such ill will across the organization. Sensing this wide spread skepticism, Dan admitted to the employees that he had not done a very good job last time around and that he had decided to take full responsibility for allowing NI to get to this point. He also informed them that they would be seeing a lot more of him and his executive team because now, they were all going to be responsible for helping NI to get back on track. Dan went on to say that they needed everyone's help and that this would be no small undertaking but that together, they would make NI a great place to work at once again.

Dan and Kim were both a bit surprised by the consistency of the feedback from employees across the organization. Sure there were those who were still very negative, but the vast majority of employees wanted to believe in a brighter future based in no small part on their proud past. With very little exception, the top three things that employees wanted answers to included, *what is happening? - why is it happening?* and *what do you expect from us?*

Realizing the importance of a consistent leadership response to these three critical questions, Dan and Kim decided to start with the executive team. Dan personally contacted each member of his executive team to discuss the employee feedback and instructed them to consider the three key questions. Within two weeks, Dan and his team met to discuss their communication strategy relative to the three key questions. The group quickly agreed that the sequence of questions made sense and that it was in everyone's best interest to keep things simple and clear. Like some executive teams, Dan and his team had been known to allow hubris to distort and dilute some executive communications in the past.

With the help of Kim Jeng as the facilitator, the executive team was able to agree to a real and meaningful response to each of the three key questions. They agreed that what was happening was that NI, like most insurance providers was being impacted by many external forces of change like; competition, demographics, regulations, technology and the overall state of the economy. After considering each of these external change factors, the group was able to see that these factors not only represented what was happening but also why it was happening. Finally, the group agreed that what was expected of each employee was no different from what the executive team expected of each other, to act with integrity and purpose, to stay positive and hopeful and to remember that we're all in this together and that when one of us succeeds, we all succeed.

While Dan was very pleased with the outcome of the executive team meeting, Kim expressed some caution. She went on to say that while this was a very powerful message, it might not reflect the thinking of the broader leadership across NI. After all, the many front line mangers that would need to carry the message across NI should have some input on what was being communicated relative to the three key questions. Dan agreed with Kim's assessment and instructed her to set up a series of meetings with leaders across the organization. Over the next four weeks, Dan and Kim held eight communication strategy meetings with all leaders across NI.

The reaction from most leaders including many other employees was very positive. This was the second time that Dan had visited their location in under a year and once again, he was looking for their input. In each of the leadership communication strategy meetings, Dan shared what came out of the executive team communication strategy session. He indicated that he thought that it was a good start but that he was sure it could be improved upon by leadership groups across NI.

While there were some varying opinions on the overall content of what was being communicated relative to change at NI, Dan and Kim were able to build clarity and consensus across the leadership ranks at NI. By using the three key questions as framework, the leadership team now had a clear and consistent story to tell about organizational change and transformation at NI.

Not content to leave leadership communication to chance, Dan asked all leaders to develop a proactive process for sharing the new leadership communication across the organization. As a beginning point, they agreed that Dan would do a company-wide communication once per month to update employees on NI's progress and also to seek input from employees about what leaders could be doing to help them succeed. It was agreed that Dan's first monthly communication would include the leadership team's answers to the three critical questions as well as lessons learned to-date.

One of the many important lessons that Dan and his executive team learned through the process was that some employees need more help than others to navigate organizational change. To this end, Dan enlisted the help of Kim and her HR team to offer change specific training across NI. He also initiated a monthly leadership conference call to update leaders on financial performance and to allow all leaders to share lessons and successes relative to the organizational transformation. Not surprisingly, this monthly exchange of leadership thinking went a long way in building further clarity and consistency around leadership communications.

Dan and his executive team worked diligently over the next two years to be role models for change by being more visible and engaged in the change process. The monthly conference calls and employee updates from Dan served to create many important outcomes including improved morale, collaboration, clarity and purpose.

The Results Of Effectively Leading Needed Change

Today, nearly six years after Dan's ill fated cost cutting mandate, NI is enjoying double digit growth and employees have a renewed sense of hope in the future. Dan continues to do his monthly conference call for leaders and is now doing a quarterly employee communication that includes performance data, leadership strategy and updates on the three critical questions related to organizational change and transformation.

Discussion

1. Evaluate the CEO's initial approach to change in 2004 – 2005 and the consequences of this approach.

2. As a leader leading change, how could the CEO have approached the need for change differently? What would be some alternatives to require an across the board 20% cut in operating expenses?

3. As a potential change champion yourself, what can be learned from the way the HR SVP finally got the attention of the CEO?

4. Discuss why it is important for leaders to have a leadership style that welcomes open communication and feedback and the correlation between leadership communication and employee morale.

5. What did the CEO do to lead change the right way the second time and what different outcomes were achieved?

6. Are there other things the CEO could have done to more effectively lead the change process the second time and could more have been accomplished and how?

7. What value does leadership transparency play in reducing the rumor mill?

8. Why is executive sponsorship critical?

Key Lessons In Leading Change

1. Organizational change and transformation is a continuous process not an event.

2. Announcing decisions without the dialog and agreement of key stakeholders on what is to be changed and how is an approach to change that is almost sure to fail.

3. As the pace of change accelerates, employees want and need more information.

4. Absent clarity and consistency from the leadership team, employees feed the rumor mill.

5. Most employees want to believe in the organization and its future.

6. Executive sponsorship of organizational change and transformation is critical.

7. Every leader is a role model for the organization.

BIOGRAPHY

David O'Brien is the President of WorkChoice Solutions, LLC, a trusted provider of Human Resource and Leadership Development consulting services that was founded in 2000. His consulting career spans twenty five years and includes key leadership positions such as Senior Vice President and General Manager of Lee Hecht Harrison, a global consulting company, Managing Director of Oak Technologies, a regional provider of Human Resource consulting, and his current role as President and founder of WorkChoice Solutions. His clients include such market leaders as Aetna, Avery Dennison, ESPN, KPMG, Mass Mutual, MetLife, Otis Elevator, PeoplesBank, St. Mary's Healthcare, The Hartford, Travelers, United Technologies and U.S. Airways. He also works with a variety of nonprofit and public sector clients. His strong commitment to community service has resulted in numerous awards including Employer of the Year and Business leader of the Year for his volunteer work. His first book, The Navigator's Handbook, 101 Leadership Lessons for Work & Life is available on-line and in bookstores nationwide. His second book, Tapping Your Leadership Wisdom is expected in bookstores in the fall of 2012. His leadership articles have appeared in a wide range of local, regional and national publications. To learn more, please visit www.workchoicesolutions.com.

David A. O'Brien
President
WorkChoice Solutions, LLC
P.O. Box 467
Bloomfield, CT 06002
860-242-1070
dobrien@workchoicesolutions.com

10

Mistakes In Managing Strategic Change

Sharon E. Norris & Tracy H. Porter

Major Focus Of The Case

The strategy of a firm needs to support the mission of the organization, or its reason for being, and the execution of the strategy provides the method for gaining competitive advantage. As the competitive environment changes, both the strategy and the execution methods, in tandem, must be reevaluated. Some firms make the mistake of creating strategic plans without conducting the due diligence necessary for executing the new plan. The existing structure, infrastructure, processes, and procedures may not be capable of converting new philosophical commitments at the executive level into appropriate actionable processes and initiatives. Kaplan and Norton (2008) have argued that it is for this very reason that it is important to connect strategy and execution in order to gain competitive advantage. This case focuses on the approach that a CEO of an equipment manufacturer in the medical instruments industry followed and the learning process that she and the members of the organization experienced as they struggled to link strategy and execution within a rapidly changing and competitive environment.

Introduction

Strategy is a military term that comes from the Greek word strategos that refers to the general of an army, and over time the word strategy was used to describe the way a general utilized armed forces to either protect the vital interests of a city-state or defeat an enemy. In business management, the word strategy was extended to describe the compilation of ideas or grand design regarding how a particular firm will operate and compete within a specific marketplace. In modern businesses, revenue, earnings, market share, cash flow, and return on investments are performance measures that have typically been associated with evaluating the effectiveness of a corporate strategy. Yet, corporate strategy does not refer to day-to-day plans but rather the way by which future, long-terms goals are attained. From an economic standpoint, corporate strategy is developed based on the values of the organization, future state of the environment, recognition of environmental threats, responding capacity to those threats, feasible avenues for development, and the resources necessary for moving in the intended new directions (Sutton, 1980).

In order to execute a corporate strategy, strategic management is required. Strategic management refers to a process of managing strategic change, linking developmental initiatives, and helping the organization gain competitive advantage through economic development. The most important aspects of strategic management include the capacity of organizational leaders to legitimize the need for change, translate philosophical commitment to change into action, and help the organization emerge from the strategic change process with a significant competitive advantage. In other words, strategic management involves effective change leadership and coaching. Kotter (1996), in his popular book, *Leading Change,* identified eight stages in the change process that included 1) establishing a sense of urgency; 2) creating a guiding coalition; 3) developing a vision and strategy; 4) communicating the change vision; 5) empowering employees for broad-based action; 6) generating short-term wins; 7) consolidating gains and producing more change; and, 8) anchoring new approaches in the culture.

Background on Central Services

Central Services (not the real name of the company) is an equipment manufacturer in the medical instruments industry that employs 200 employees. Kathleen Watson has been the President of Central Services for the past six years. During those years, she witnessed rapid technological advances in the industry. Watson was well aware that industry experts were predicting that medical instrument revenues would reach over $20 billion within the next five years. Unfortunately, she was also aware that foreign competitors, such as those in China, were quickly gaining market share. During Watson's presidency, Central Services had gained only small revenue increases each year.

Watson sat around a mahogany table in the top floor conference room at the corporate headquarters with the firm's board of directors. The board members raised questions about why Central Services had failed to keep pace with industry growth rates. In fact, over the past three years, Central Services actually lost market share. Watson had been pondering the same issues herself. Because Watson believed that her job was on the line, she had started searching for a solution to turn things around. The previous week, Watson attended a strategic planning conference after which she was determined that creating a strategic plan would solve the firm's problems with decreasing revenues, earnings, and losses in market share.

When the Chairman of the Board turned the table over to Watson, she introduced her new idea for creating a strategic plan for the company. In the previous week, she had even constructed a new budget of which she presented to the board. The board members were impressed with her strategic plan and were pleased to see a proposed budget with increased earnings as well as projected financial gains in earnings, return on investment, and improved cash flows. To her relief, the board approved her plan, and Watson left the meeting elated over the approved budget and plan for change. Now she just needed to sell the idea to her executive staff and the employees of the firm.

The following week, Watson called a meeting with the Central Services leadership team and announced her strategic plan and presented the approved budget. In essence, she told the leadership team that the new strategic plan called for a ten percent increase in revenues each year for the next three years with a gross profit margin of forty percent each year for the next three years. She also told the leadership team that she had created the strategic plan after attending an industry conference, and she informed them that the board already approved the plan and budget.

Included in this plan was a requirement for the company to develop and launch four new products each year over the next three years, and existing products would be actively marketed in new territories. The members of the leadership team left the meeting in public agreement with Watson's plan. They were told to begin holding meetings with all of their department supervisors to share the strategic plan. Each department was required to provide a detailed report within three weeks detailing out how they would meet these growth objectives for their departments.

The Change Management Process Begins in Chaos

One by one, the members of the leadership team met with their department supervisors to share Watson's strategic plan. The department supervisors, accustomed to the top-down initiatives from Watson over the past six years, voiced strong concerns with the plan. Employees had started calling Watson's ideas for change the "flavor of month," and the strategic plan announcement by far had the most unappealing flavor to date.

When the department supervisors learned that they were required to provide the details to back up Watson's plan, there were expressions of anger, frustration, dismay, and discouragement. They had grown tired of being responsible for carrying out Watson's half-baked ideas and getting blamed for the inability of the organization to support her initiatives. The department supervisors then met collectively the next day, and there were widespread complaints. Some stated that the changes came from on high, and there was no choice. Others were convinced that the strategic changes would fail.

The leadership team was fearful over the situation because they also knew that Watson had planned pay reductions, benefit cuts, and a reduction in force within the year. Some of the leaders were concerned that the attitudes expressed by the department supervisors would be considered insubordination. Other leaders indicated that their department supervisors were right in their assessment of Watson's approach. Soon the news was being discussed in hushed tones in small groups throughout the organization. Subsequently, the managers began to notice the productivity levels were declining even further, rework was on the rise, and customer claims for defects were rising. Employees at all levels of the organization were complaining to the human resource department, and rumors were spreading that the company was going out of business. There were even rumors within the community that the company was going out of business.

How Not to Manage Change

Too many leaders regard change as a short-term event. Many strategic planning consultants convince executive clients that strategic change can be managed effectively by simply creating and announcing strategic plans and then requiring employees to implement the changes and submit progress reports toward change. Financial consultants on the other hand convince their clients that the best way to create sustainability is by cutting expenditures and reducing headcount. In combination, these traditional business models can ultimately damage organizations.

Another problem with many strategic change initiatives is that they are too top-down. The need for change is not legitimized, and employees view the initiatives as disruptive rather than helpful. As a result, the focus during implementation turns toward an effort to break down the resistance to change of stubborn employees. When the need for change is not legitimized, employees see no need to fix what is not broken. Additionally, leaders often miss the point that it is the people within the organization who come up with the creative ideas of what needs changed and how to make improvements. Leaving the employees out of the process can produce disastrous results.

Effective Change Management

Key components to any effective change process are organizational diagnosis, employee involvement, and effective communication. By limiting a diagnosis of the problem to financial and/or marketing data, key aspects of organizational functioning are left unexamined. Without an appropriate understanding of the problem, changes can produce unintended results, diminish productivity, and weaken quality of work life. In addition to a comprehensive organizational diagnosis, employees need to be involved in the process. Employees at all levels hold knowledge that may be instrumental in making breakthroughs that can strengthen the business.

Keeping people informed at each step of the project is also necessary but not sufficient on its own. Leaders sometimes mistakenly believe that delivering an announcement message or brief updates are enough for employees. However, what is really needed is a much more comprehensive system of communication and social networking. The most effective change leaders use facilitation skills to draw valuable information from employees, customers, suppliers, and other constituents and also encourage social networking among professional and expert groups of employees to keep one another informed.

Managing not only the formal communication but also the informal communication such as social networks and the grapevine can be vital to communication efforts during strategic change. Top down, social, formal, and informal networking messages are vital in effective organizational communication.

Helping employees begin talking about change and sharing ideas could involve leaders forming cross-functional committees and focus groups to ask questions such as: "What would you see as the benefits of doing X?" or, "How would you implement this in your area?" Then, other key employees can be drawn into the process of asking questions about how to go about addressing issues associated with change. By involving employees all levels of the organization in the change process, the odds of resistance to the change are greatly reduced.

References

Kaplan, R. S., & Norton, D. P. (2008). *The execution premium: Linking strategy to operations for competitive advantage.* Boston, MA: Harvard Business School Publishers.

Sutton, C. J. (1980). *Economics and corporate strategy.* New York, NY: Cambridge University Press.

Kotter, J. P. (1996), *Leading change.* Boston, MA: Harvard Business School Press.

Discussion

1. Discuss the process the CEO used for developing and implementing a strategic plan and the response and why people responded the way they did. Do you think this is a typical or atypical process used in organizations to make important changes?

2. If you were an executive coach retained to work with the CEO, what would you coach the CEO to do differently in developing and implementing a strategic plan, and what would you coach the CEO to do knowing that the approach used has failed?

3. What are some things that can be done to make the strategic planning and implementation process more valuable, meaningful, engaging, motivating, and successful, and what could you include in the strategic goals that would help build the organization into an effective organization?

4. What are some of the key reasons employees resist change, and what can be done to overcome resistance to change?

5. How important is open communications to successful change, and what are the payoffs when you have open communications and costs when you don't?

Key Lessons In Leading Change

1. It is important that leaders realize that any strategic plan needs to be developed from an organizational diagnosis and with input from all levels of the organization. By doing so, valuable information will be gathered from all levels which can then be used to develop a plan which will be viable.

2. To simply develop a strategic plan at the top and prescribe change to the other organizational levels is like inviting the lower levels to resist the change. Change is not easy for anyone to readily accept and organizations are no different than individuals. The change needs to be legitimized before employees will buy into it.

3. It is important for leaders to spend a significant amount of time developing a strategic plan. Very often the strategic plan is quickly developed, quickly deployed, and then a great deal of time is spent dealing with the numerous constraints and barriers that arise. Often these issues could have been avoided if more time had been spent on the initial plan.

4. Managing both formal and informal communication during change initiatives is vitally important. In the absence of formal communication, people will rely on information gained through the grapevine. Such water cooler talk can quickly become rumors that spread both within the organization and into the external environment.

5. Strategic management involves coordinating multiple initiatives. If each department supervisor develops an initiative without collaboration, difficulties will likely follow. For that reason, strategic management requires the identification of strategic themes and objectives that will guide the process during the execution.

6. Leaders need to be trained in strategic planning and execution methods to ensure change initiatives are value-added with time to implement projects. The costs and risks of initiatives need to be appropriately assessed costs, and the organization needs to provide funding for new projects. Otherwise, conflicts will arise between the strategic initiatives and the operational needs of the organization.

BIOGRAPHY

Sharon Norris is an Assistant Professor of Business and Director of Graduate Studies, MBA Programs with the Gainey School of Business at Spring Arbor University. She holds a Ph.D. from Regent University in Organizational Leadership with a major in Human Resource Development.

Sharon E. Norris, Ph.D.
Assistant Professor of Business
Director of Graduate Studies, MBA Programs
Spring Arbor University
Gainey School of Business
106 E. Main Street, Station #35
Spring Arbor, Michigan 49283
snorris@arbor.edu

Tracy Porter is a Lecturer with the Management at Cleveland State University. She has extensive experience teaching at both the graduate and undergraduate levels and as a management consultant.

Tracy H. Porter, Ph.D.
Lecturer
Cleveland State University
Department of Management
1860 E. 18th Street, BU 428
Cleveland, Ohio 44115
T.H.Porter@csuohio.edu

11

DA Consulting: A Failed Change Initiative

Johanna S. Hunsaker
Dan Amaro

Major Focus Of The Case

Leading change often meets with failure. "Change" in its broadest sense, is a planned or unplanned response to forces. A good metaphor for change might be the pinball machine or permanent whitewater (Vaill, 1996). Change today is simultaneous, unpredictable and turbulent. "Permanent whitewater" describes the complex environment in which we all try to navigate. Effective change leaders know how to create a sense of urgency, recruit powerful change leaders, build a vision and effectively communicate it. If you do these things you have a better chance of making the change a part of your organizational culture. (Kotter, 1995). This case focuses on the failed change efforts of DA Consulting, a start up technical consulting company that contracted an Organizational Development consultant to help them. The case is told from the perspective of the manager of the consulting practice, Don.

Introduction

Under the best of circumstances nearly 70% of change efforts fail (Miller, 2002). One of the primary reasons why many change efforts fail is because leaders do not consider change from a recipients' perspective. In any change effort, leaders need to address the concerns that people have when they are asked to change. Most change efforts fail for predictable reasons: the fact that the change leaders do not involve or address the concerns of the people involved in the change. People will give buy-in to an organizational change if they believe that they have a voice in the process. (Lencioni, 2002)

The Concerns Model of addressing organizational change was originally developed by a team of researchers at the University of Texas who were studying the failure of educational objectives that initially tested well, but failed to achieve the targeted results. The concerns model identifies six predictable reactions to change initiatives: information concerns, personal concerns, implementation concerns, impact concerns, collaboration concerns and refinement concerns. When change leaders pay particular attention to the first three, the rest of the change will most likely take care of itself. (Hall and Hord, 2011, Hall and Loucks, 1978)

Table 1: **CONCERNS MODEL**

Stage of Concern	Expression of Concern
Information	I would like to know more about... Why is the change needed? What is wrong with the way we do things now?
Personal	How will this affect me? What's in this for me? Will I be able to adapt to this?
Implementation	How will I manage all of the work I have now and learn the new system? How long will it take? What should I do first?
Impact	Is the change worth it? Will the change really make a difference? How will this affect our work product?
Collaboration	Who else should be involved? How can I relate what I am doing to what others are doing?
Refinement	How can we make this change even better?

Don's Experience at DA Consulting

I thrived in fast-paced, high energy environments, and was a perfect fit for DA Consulting. Work was fun; we were learning and growing together. We all struggled with this new organization and were thrilled to be involved at a company that was in its infancy. We were building a technical consulting organization and there was an inherent sense of cohesiveness. The future was bright and the opportunities seemed endless.

After years of struggling to find our rhythm, the owners of DA Consulting finally realized what the rest of the employees had already come to realize: that this operation was not sustainable. We had been operating in the red since the company's inception. We had been hurriedly heading down a path of mediocrity and ultimately failure and there was no readily apparent answer. We had to change the organization drastically and very soon if we were serious about our survival.

As a consulting organization our survival depended on billing clients. Very simply put, we had to provide enough value to clients to be able to send them an invoice that they would happily pay. We could do this well enough to have respectable revenues. The issue was with overhead. The company expanded into office space that was unnecessary, hired (and fired) high-profile executives and invested in projects for new product lines without proper due diligence. We were a startup company that focused on status and appearance. Finally, the leadership contracted an Organizational Development consultant to help us address needed changes.

I had the honor of being involved in the executive vision/strategy sessions. They were held on Saturdays so as not to disrupt the regular work week. The players in the room consisted of the owners, two Principals, Chief Financial officer, Legal counsel, Directors of Operations and Sales and finally, me. My job was the management of the consultants and clients on a daily basis. I was the most connected to the line employees and understood the pulse of the organization: the go-between for the executives and the worker-bees.

The executives were surprised to hear that the employees did not share their same perspective on clients, work and the organization. I shared with the strategy/vision team that the employees did not believe in the mission, vision or values of the organization as they had not been included in the development of them in the first place. It was decided, almost on the spot that this would have to change. We were going to re-invent the company from the ground up and from red to black! A few of the high level goals were: establish a new company culture; break down the walls between functional groups to increase communication; have a profitable year. In order to accomplish the goals, it would take a herculean effort as well as buy-in from all levels of the organization. We had a long and difficult road ahead and, frankly, success was not guaranteed.

The Organization as Culture

Our company culture had definitely changed over the years. We started as a hungry, tenacious young group that was determined to win. As time passed we became complacent. Our culture had become accustomed to repeated and seemingly meaningless change and with that, we stopped caring. I personally had four bosses in a period of eighteen months. All of my bosses had been hired with the intent of guiding the company to the "Promised Land." And when they could not achieve the impossible within the overly-ambitious timeframe established by the owners, they were swiftly removed. Everyone wondered about the hiring practices utilized by the owners. More often than not, the leaders that were hired were in fact not qualified for the job, but would gain employment through a perceived pedigree. This often led to an attitude of arrogance and the overly used phrase "this is how we did it at..." Due to the constant turmoil our focus turned from one of client focused excellence to internal-focused mediocrity.

The employees had become skeptical of any organizational change and were immediately resistant to any sign of it. When the executive team would meet in the conference room and rumors would start flying around the office of change, the employees would desperately seek shelter from the impending hurricane that would surely ensue. The impulsive changes made by the organization had given rise to a closed culture. The individuals within the company were solely concerned with self-preservation. They had become alienated and resentful of the power that had been wielded over them. The environment and culture had become toxic.

Change was necessary, and so the strategy/vision team started with the fundamentals. Each employee was encouraged to anonymously submit their ideas for new, improved and meaningful Core Values for the company. We wanted to include all employees in the process and begin to create a culture of collaboration. Some employees responded well, whereas most responded with reluctance and skepticism. I remember specifically coaching a few employees and ensuring them that this time the change was different. And even though this may have been true, I had trouble believing it myself.

We established Fridays as "Pizza Friday." The idea was to have an all-hands lunch meeting and as the name implies, we would serve pizza. Attendance was not mandatory, but truancy was noted. The intent was to encourage open and honest communication while highlighting the major achievements of the week. The sales department was always eager to share the action in the sales pipeline whereas most other departments were content with eating cold pizza. The Organizational Development consultants loved the idea of "Pizza Friday." In theory, it should have contributed to the intended open and collaborative culture.

As a final capstone to our journey of cultural change, we held another all-hands meeting to unveil the newly established Core Values as well as the new Mission and Vision statements. At the suggestion of our Organizational Development consultant, we broke into sub-groups and discussed what the Core Values meant to each of us. It was a way to personalize the Core Values and own them as individuals. We then shared our findings with the whole company. The entire process lasted a total of thirty five minutes.

I was instructed by the strategy/vision group to speak and rally the troops. The idea was that if I had bought into the organizational change, so would the others. Again, I was not completely convinced myself. However, I knew, from the bright looks on the owners faces that I was especially convincing. I was a line-employee at heart and could never get past the feeling of being manipulated. I did not believe that my real concerns, or those of others, were being taken in to account.

While the culture of the entire organization was suffering, sub-cultures at the department level were also being established. The Consulting team was inherently collaborative. The Sales team was competitive and driven by numbers. One major issue within the organization was the interaction between these two sub-cultures. They were highly dependent on each other, but had entirely different performance metrics and values. Without Sales the Consultants would not have work and without Consultants, Sales would have nothing to sell. We were caught up in a kind of sub cultural warfare, as the blame of the failure of the company was quickly passed like a potato with an obscenely high temperature.

The attempted organizational change failed. We did not establish a new company culture, the walls between departments still existed and we were not profitable. There were many reasons why the change had failed. We were operating in such a dysfunctional organization from many perspectives. In order to effectively change, we would have had to take a much longer and more difficult path. We only considered company culture while ignoring other salient areas necessary for a successful change.

References

Hall, G. & Hord, S. (2011) *Implementing Change: Patterns, principles and potholes.* (Boston, Massachusetts: Pearson)

Hall, G. & Loucks, S. (1978) Teacher Concerns as a Basis for Facilitating and Personalizing Staff Development. Liebermann and Miller, eds. *Staff Development: New Demands, New Realities: New Perspectives* (New York, NY: Teachers College Press)

Kotter, John. (1996) *Leading Change,* (Boston, MA: Harvard Business School Press.)

Lencioni, Patrick. (2002) *The Five Dysfunctions of a Team*, (San Francisco,CA: Jossey-Bass)

Miller, D (2002). Successful change leaders: what makes them? What do they do that is different? *Journal of Change Management*, 2 (4) 359-368.

Vaill, Peter B. (1996) *Learning as a Way of Being*, (San Francisco, CA: Jossey-Bass)

Discussion Questions

1. Based on what you know about best run organizations discuss the major strengths and opportunities for improvement of DA Consulting prior to the culture change effort.

2. Well designed change efforts are usually based on an assessment of present realities and future ideals so change efforts can be based in reality and not assumptions about reality and those involved will have a common understanding of reality and the need for change. What was done to assess the organization and what was the change plan based on?

3. Leaders are the primary shapers of organization culture. Evaluate the involvement of the leaders in leading the change process to change the organization culture. Also, discuss the pros and cons of the approach used to change the culture. Do you believe that Pizza Fridays will change culture or is something more needed?

4. What are some ways an organization can deal with opposing cultures such as the Consultant versus Sales Cultures?

5. What aspects of leadership were lacking in the leaders at DA Consulting? What could be done to help the leaders and the leadership team become more effective?

6. Evaluate the approach that was used to reinvent the company. Using the Concerns Model, which of the six concerns were addressed in the change process? What would you have done differently to reinvent DA Consulting and achieve the high level goals that were established?

Key Lessons In Leading Change

1. For organizations to perform at their best leaders need to be skilled in building healthy, high performance organizations and effectively leading change.

2. The creation of a particular corporate culture is not just about inventing new slogans or acquiring a new leader. It is about what amounts to a new way of life. Successful change has to create a sense of urgency, recruit powerful change leaders, build a vision and effectively communicate it.

3. The reality is that people are not so much resistant to change as they are resistant to poorly managed change and being controlled. When an organization tries to sell change to people affected by the change instead of involving them and addressing their concerns, the change initiative is likely to fail.

4. Successful change would have started with the employees. Employees need to be included in an open discussion about where the company should go. Employees should contribute their outline vision for success as a company, and then jointly design a path to achieve the vision. After creating a vision and a path, they could have split up responsibilities and identified leads throughout all levels and disciplines of the organization to drive that change. It would have spread out responsibility and taken down the walls between departments, leadership and employees.

5. Powerful leaders symbolize many aspects of their organization and the leaders were only interested in becoming profitable, not particularly in the change necessary to get there. When leaders reduce the concept of corporate change to a set of discrete variables that they could control and manipulate like creating an equation that would magically lead to a profitable situation, the change effort will fail.

BIOGRAPHY

Professor Johanna Hunsaker has been a faculty member at the University of San Diego since 1981. Currently she serves as Department Chair for the Management, Law and Ethics group. International teaching is a passion, and she has taught at universities in France, Germany, China , Italy, Turkey, Spain and the U.S. Mariannas. Concentrating in effective teaching and curriculum design, she has designed numerous new courses and is consistently ranked in the top 10% of instructors. She has served as a consultant to numerous companies and has been an expert witness in over seventy five court cases involving sexual harassment and workplace discrimination.

Johanna S. Hunsaker
Professor of Management
University of San Diego, School of Business Administration
5998 Alcala Park, San Diego, CA 92110
619-260-4858 · Email: hunsaker@sandiego.edu

CHAPTER THREE

12

The Importance of Self-Awareness in Leading Change

Jacqueline M. Stavros & Jane G. Seiling

Major Focus Of The Case

A leader of change must first look at self from the standpoint of needed individual change and development in order to most effectively lead and manage self and others during a change process. Based on the organizational reality of leaders being involved in fast paced and chaotic global and virtual environments, the practitioner and manager must see themselves as at all times being leaders of change. Based on this reality, we seek to emphasize three points:

1. The change leader must stay mindful of the ongoing need for personal learning and development in order to effectively utilize lead and support change initiatives;

2. Learning starts with assessing one's leadership capacity and capabilities, and

3. The effective leader of change recognizes the presence of the use of self-as-instrument of change.

This case portrays the journey of a faculty member who has been asked to lead a major transformational change and the self-evaluation the faculty member goes through in preparing to lead the change. This writing begins with recognizing the importance of self-as-instrument in leadership development and change. Then, we present a leadership self-assessment process to discover how one can, by being mindful and knowing thyself, aspire to effectively make proactive improvements to one's ability to lead change.

Introduction

The question asked in this writing is: How does a leader, wherever they are in an organization, grow personally to become a mature and effective leader of change? We see the element of "maturity" in this area as dependent on the experience, learning, and growth of the leader. Maturity of leadership makes it possible to become an effective instrument-for-change.

For this case study, a "leader of change" includes those who are faced with being change agents and aspire to gain competence and confidence in effectively leading change at any organizational level. Today's leaders lead in fast-paced and uncertain environments; therefore, they must see themselves as prepared to be an effective change leader change. Based on this reality, we seek to emphasize three points: 1) the change leader must stay mindful of the ongoing need for personal learning and development in the area of change, 2) learning starts with assessing one's leadership capacity and capabilities, and 3) the effective leader of change recognizes the presence of the use of self-as an instrument of change – mindfully seeking alignment with the organization's values, vision, and mission (Stavros & Seiling, 2010).

This writing begins with agreement with Eisen (2010) that, for effective organizational change to occur, leaders must view themselves as being an instrument for change. The starting point for becoming an instrument for change is the need to *know thyself* – the leader must first investigate the need for personal change. Then, a change leadership self-assessment process is highlighted to discover how one can aspire to effectively make proactive improvements to one's ability to lead change. Unless noted, the terms "leader" and "practitioner" are interchangeable.

Self-as-Instrument for Leading Change

Eisen (2010) suggests that the "personhood of the practitioner" is under emphasized as a key variable in achieving effectiveness in leading change. He adds that "there are three elements that must interact appropriately in your leading change process: *awareness, perception and behavior*" (p. 526, italics in text). These elements are emphasized as relating to knowledge and feelings that are basic to effective performance as a self-as-instrument and change leader in *Figure 1*.

Figure 1: **A MODEL OF SELF-AS-INSTRUMENT**

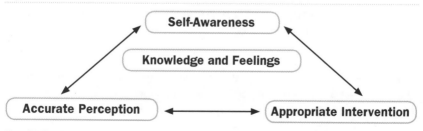

Eisen (2010) in 'Practicing Organization Development', Third Edition, p. 529. Used with permission.

Performance as a good, technical leader, that is, *knowing* and *doing* the role of leader of change, cannot occur without balancing personal *cognitive strategies* (knowledge) with *feelings* (emotions) that provide the capacity to perceive accurately and fully what is going on around the leader. Eisen (2010) suggests the central role of feelings, stating, "Having feelings is a basic aspect of being alive: feelings give color and dimension to our thoughts and actions" (p. 529).

Change is inevitable in organizations, causing concern and loss, making it necessary for the leader to intervene (or design and utilize appropriate interventions) empathically but with an eye on the achievement of positive change. Leader perceptions must be as accurate as possible and reached through the eyes and minds of self and others. This suggests the benefits of having "trusted advisors" (coaches) who are willing to be straight-forward with advice and evaluation during the self-awareness process. Elements unknown to your self can strongly influence your view of data, decisions taken, the nature of your motivations, your actions (behaviors), and more.

Know Thyself

The most basic competence of the change leader is located in identifying his or her ability to "know thyself" before leading others. Knowledge of change processes is located in the *head*. Self-awareness of one's role and capabilities in addressing the emotions involved with loss, concern for the member, and authentic caring for the people involved in the change is located in the *heart*.

In order to legitimately and authentically lead, the leader should consider three questions:

1. How well did I lead today? What did I do that was meaningful?
2. How might I lead better tomorrow that is useful to the vision and mission of this organization?
3. Why would anyone want me to lead him or her?

Taking these questions seriously requires awareness, reflection, and input from self and others. This requires leaders to do the genuine self-assessment and reflective thinking essential to make necessary personal changes. Then, they must *step back* and examine their basic understandings regarding their own values, vision (direction), and mission (purpose), and how these important elements impact their ability to lead others.

Then, leaders of change must also understand their leadership style, personal strengths, opportunities, and aspirations, and be willing to make *intentional* changes to further develop their model for leadership (Boyatzis & Akrivou, 2006; Stavros & Hinrichs, 2009). To take steps to continually improve one's personal leadership style shows others that being mindful of personal development is ongoing – especially as it pertains to leading others. While emphasizing personal development and change, every leader can build trust, confidence, and rapport with those he or she works *within* the organization.

Kotter's (1996) research and his book with Cohen (2002) emphasize that highly successful change efforts reflect a central challenge of transforming behaviors (of leaders and others) in the direction needed to move the system to a most preferred future (vision). Achievement of transformational personal change, as mentioned earlier, involves deep thinking and reflection, interviews, and writing. This case study will focus on the first three transformational factors: values, vision, and mission alignment within one's self and with the organization. The remaining part of this case study introduces a self-assessment process that helps the change leader assess oneself as an instrument of change. In this case, the change leader is a faculty member at a private university. Remember, leaders of change exist at all levels of an organization.

The Change Leadership Self-Assessment Process

Change requires time, dedication, input from others, and a willingness to learn about you from others. Advisors must be identified who can and are willing to participate openly in the process as trusted advisors. A self-assessment is a futile effort unless there is a willingness of the advisors to talk authentically and a willingness of the leader to believe what has been heard. Finally, there must be a desire to act on the assessment by taking intentional steps toward change. The following are key factors for assessing self: values, vision, mission, leadership competencies, and writing the authentic self report.

Values: While Meglino and Ravlin (1998, p. 354) characterized values as "oughtness" and how one ought to behave, Feather (2003, p. 34) conceived of values as "general beliefs about desirable ways of behaving or about desirable general goals." Identifying one's values provides the foundation for writing one's vision and mission statements. Values identification helps to answer the following questions:

- What do I want to live and work by each and every day?
- How do I want to treat others?
- What do I stand for?
- What do I care about?
- How do I show I care about others?

Values are only "good intentions" unless you take time to consciously reflect on their impact on your actions each day – especially when making key decisions. (Satisfaction with decisions comes with making decisions while being mindful of your core values.) In identifying your values, you should be able to locate your *five core values* without much thought or hesitation. It is in reflection on why you have selected these values that supports identification of what will be important to you and where to focus in the future.

Table 1 offers an example of a leader's value set (in this case, the faculty member). She understands that her living values are based on her history and experiences so the listing is also provided. Her values are bolded. The additional information is her descriptions/meanings of her values.

Table 1: **VALUES LISTING**

History:	I grew up in a family of six in Detroit. We lived a simple life. There was plenty of love, a lot of sibling rivalry, and lessons learned while growing up. We lived in a flat above Grandma near a large automotive plant and next to a 76 gas station until my parents had enough money to move to the suburbs where we could attend public schools. Now my family and extended family provide unconditional love and support.
Family:	In my family value, "family" includes close friends. For family to be real, it includes connection and belonging, feelings of acceptance, and feeling like my presence matters to those I care about. Family comes first.
Integrity:	It provides the basis for living. Each of us has purpose in life. And, we need to model our purpose through being genuine and honest in our relations with self and others to gain trust and respect. Living with integrity makes it easy for me to sleep at night!
Respectful-Kindness:	I strive to see a "sense of worth" in people and situations. In doing so, I strive to use consideration and kindness no matter how tough or frustrating the situation may get. This allows me to be honest with people and help them grow.
Energy:	I value the energy that I awaken with each morning and the opportunity to renew it when I go to sleep at night. In order to live my values and take care of my family and career, I need a balance of physical, emotional, mental, and spiritual energy. If you find your passion and define your vision and know your mission based on what you are passionate about, energy is fueled. You need energy to go after your dreams! I live my life trying to make sure that I have a full energy source.
Humor, Health and Humility:	Mental health (along with the field that I work in) requires that I live with humbleness and the presence of ambiguity and uncertainty. My life never fails to give ample opportunities to encounter ambiguity. Laughter is healthy and I use it to diffuse situations. I try to bring humor and laughter into my life every day.

This change leader's organization's values are: teamwork, integrity, excellence, respect, and sustainability. There is a connection between her core value of "integrity" and her organizations value of "respect," plus, although not an exact word match, the values of "teamwork" for her organization and her "family" value connect. The leader sees an alignment of her values with her organization's values. This enables her to make good decisions that impact her ability to effectively lead change.

Vision

One's vision is an extension of one's personal values. Leading scholars and practitioners have stated that vision is a key differentiating factor when comparing leaders to managers (Bennis & Nanus, 1985; Buckingham, 2005; Kotter, 1996). Having a vision is about providing the power to take action toward reaching that future. Leaders use their vision as a mental image to provide the power (energy) to fulfill their leadership roles and responsibilities and to inspire self and others. According to Kotter (1990):

> The direction setting aspect of leadership does not produce plans;
> it creates a vision and strategies ... it is ... simply a description
> of something (an organization, a corporate culture, a business, a
> technology, or an activity) in the future, often the distant future, in
> terms of the essence of what it should become. (p. 36)

Thus, the impact of a powerful vision is that it provides a clear direction that *motivates movement forward.* This view is also supported by Tichy and Devanna (1986):

> The vision is the ideal to strive for. It releases the energy needed
> to motivate the organization to action. It provides an overarching
> framework to guide day-to-day decision and priorities and provides
> the parameters for playful opportunism. (p. 123)

These statements are no less true about the need for a personal vision statement. In an organization, visioning is a process of creating and communicating the direction of the organization as it impacts every stakeholder, especially the organization members and customers. An ongoing process of education, training, questioning, communicating, and inspiring must be used to bring the vision to life for each organizational member. The vision statement found in the strategic plan, a website, or on the wall must find a way into the behaviors, attitudes, purpose, and hearts of the people. For the self, visioning provides internal direction setting that, without question, impacts the actions of the leader and, potentially, those around the leader.

Returning to our example, the mindful leader's organization's vision is "to take a leadership role in preparing our students to be global leaders while creating a sustainable society." The president's vision is "to create a more humane and sustainable world community by global thinkers and leaders." There is alignment of the president's vision with the organization's shared vision. And, the change leader's vision is "to strive for authentic simplicity and engage in energizing relationships with a meaningful and sustainable purpose." Her vision aligns with the president's and the organization's vision. There is a shared direction for everyone to serve the mission through daily actions. She used the following questions in preparation for writing her vision:

- Think of a future you feel strongly about. What do you want your "ideal self" to be experiencing in this future? How does vision relate to your ideal future?
- What is your organization's vision? Is there alignment?
- How can your vision act as an instrument of alignment for others?
- How does your vision reflect your values?
- How could you communicate this vision to others?
- How could your vision be an instrument-for-change in your organization?

A mindful person often has visions for different parts of his or her life, but a person's dominant vision can change/adjust other visions at any given time. Be aware of the alignment between them. Not to do so can create damaging disconnections between the multiple visions, creating a dilemma of contrast that can be difficult to work through. Again, having a meaningful personal vision provides "the ideal to strive for" and a basis for action in other domains of life. Being mindful of one's personal vision is critical to it having an impact on one's work and life.

Identification and communication of a set of core values and a vision (both personally and organizationally) are a strong first step. Yet, a vision is only effective if actions taken reflect the meaning of that vision. The next step in this assessment is to identify one's mission that stimulates ongoing action.

Mission

Mission is purpose. It focuses and stimulates what you do each and every day to live by your values and strive for your vision. A mission statement helps you to focus on what should be done. It can energize the highest and most creative energies to execute a strategy and attain set goals. This suggests the benefits of writing a good *personal* and *professional* mission statement. Mission statements, like vision statements, take time to write and require deep reflection to achieve alignment across one's values, vision, and mission. Consider the following as a place to start in writing a personal mission statement.

My **mission (statement of purpose)** is _____
(use action verbs) for what: _____ (principal or cause)
to/with or for (whom) _____

The university president's mission is "develop and deliver distinctive and innovative management programs that maximize student human potential." This change leader wrote a mission that is simple yet parallel to the organization's and president's mission. Because she is a faculty member that serves the students, her mission is "learn and serve with others to create a sustainable future for the students, myself, and my organization." There is alignment of the faculty member's mission to both her leader's and organization's mission. This allows her to be effective in dealing with others in getting the work done.

The questions she considered in creating the mission is "what is the guiding purpose that pulls me closer to realizing my vision?" Continuing with the above change leader illustration, the organization's mission is "developing leaders through innovative and agile programs that focus on the sustainability issues for organizations." *Sustainability* is defined as including the whole system in efforts to collectively consider social and environmental factors as it relates to profit that can result in a better world for self, this generation, and generations to come.

As noted above, effectively identifying your values, vision, and mission statements requires awareness, dedication, reflection, and concentration on the task. Next, we will briefly introduce the importance of identifying and strengthening leadership competencies because competencies influence and make possible the formation of personal values, vision, mission, and the ability to lead effectively.

Leadership Competencies

A leader's competencies will manifest themselves in demonstrated actions. The areas where a leader is strong will receive more attention (action) and show through – whether or not they are beneficial competencies. A study by Stavros (1998) shows that outstanding capabilities come to the surface as the mindful change leader functions with organizational members. Skills, like oral communications, networking, self-confidence, initiative, and attention to detail, may be the hallmark of a particular leader's activities.

In Stavros' studies of leaders, the ability to take the initiative in identifying one's values, creating a vision and mission, communicating the vision and mission to others, giving attention to detail, feedback, and having the confidence to move forward, demonstrates the essence of effective leadership skills and the ability to lead change in organizations. Many resources can be identified by searching the web to help you identify your competencies as a leader. Table 2 provides a list of leadership competencies developed by Richard Boyatzis (1998) that we have found the most helpful is located at the end of this case study.

The Self Report

Finally, the mindful leader gathers all of this information into a self-report that is useful as an authentic instrument for change. Sharing it with your coach(es) supports accountability for action. Reviewing this information regularly also supports efforts to perform as a self-as-instrument for change.

Table 2: **LEADERSHIP COMPETENCIES TO EFFECTIFELY LEAD CHANGE**

(*Note:* Adapted with permission from Boyatzis, 1998)

Efficiency Orientation:	The ability to perceive input/output relationships and the concern for increasing the efficiency of action.
Planning:	The ability to define goals/objectives, strategy, tactics, and resources to be used to meet the purpose (mission).
Initiative:	The ability to take action to accomplish something, and to do so before being asked, forced, or provoked into it.
Attention to Detail:	The ability to seek order and predictability by reducing uncertainty.
Flexibility:	The ability to adapt to changing circumstance, or alter one's behavior to better fit the situation.
Networking:	The ability to build relationships, whether they are one-to-one relations, a coalition, an alliance, or a complex set of relationships among a group of people.
Self-Confidence:	The ability to consistently display decisiveness or presence.
Group Management:	The ability to stimulate members of a group to work together effectively.
Developing Others:	The ability to stimulate someone to develop his abilities or improve his performance toward an objective.
Oral Communications:	The ability to explain, describe, or tell something to others through a personal presentation.
Pattern Recognition:	The ability to identify a pattern in an assortment of unorganized or seemingly random data or information.
Social Objectivity:	The ability to perceive another person's beliefs, emotions, and perspectives, particularly when they are different from the observer's own beliefs, emotions, and perspectives.

Summary

This case study highlights and discusses the importance of change leadership self-assessment, transformation, and becoming a 'self-as-instrument' to model and mindfully lead change. Tesser, Martin, and Cornell (1996) suggest people must attempt to change their own performance through self-evaluation in order to lead and orchestrate deep change, move in a positive direction, and/or to improve performance in an area of concern. Self-awareness through self-evaluation requires *self-motivation*. Thus, self-motivation must be present to expand or stabilize the desire to develop one's leadership practices and to stick with it when competing tendencies or forces interfere with the determination to change.

This is a journey within. The journey begins, first, with identifying personal values. Second, this core value set is used as a foundation for setting your vision (direction) and mission (purpose) statements. Third, an assessment of leadership competencies is completed to gain more information on effectiveness to lead change. Self-assessment involves reflection and sensemaking, interviews with trusted advisors, assessment of responses, and writing about thoughts regarding self and others. It is assumed that, as a leader, the presence of awareness at a *deep personal level* can be a tool to build capacity to lead change (Quinn, 1996).

In this case study, the faculty member's illustrations demonstrate her willingness and ability to effectively lead change being mindful of self and who she leads. We thank her for sharing her illustration with us and know that she continues to effectively lead change in various roles both internal and external to her organization.

Key Leadership Lessons

1. To have credibility in leading change, leaders must also be willing to learn, grown, and change.
2. The way you lead change can make or break the success of the change. It is important for change leaders to be self-aware and to welcome feedback and coaching.
3. It is important for change leaders to prepare for leading change and to assess the alignment of their own values, mission, and values with those of the organization they are leading change in.
4. Leadership can be a lonely job, It is important to find trusted advisors or mentors who are able to give you honest and helpful feedback and provide coaching and wisdom.

Discussion

1. Leaders play a critical role in the change process and the way they lead change can make or break the changes. Discuss the concept of self-as-instrument of change and what you believe to be a leader's role in leading change.

2. What are possible personal blind spots leaders have in leading change?

3. Discuss your understanding of each of the three items (values, mission, vision) mentioned in the Change Leadership Self-Assessment Process. Would you add anything to the list?

4. Have each person in the group prepare and share what they would include in their personal values, mission, and vision statements and who they might select as a trusted advisor(s).

5. Briefly discuss each of the leadership competencies shown in *Table 2*:

6. Have each person in the group share a few insights they gained from this case.

References

Bennis, W., & Nanus, B. (1985). *Leaders: The strategies for taking charge.* New York: Harper and Row.

Boyatzis, R.E. (1998). *Transforming qualitative information: Thematic analysis and code development.* Thousand Oaks, CA: Sage.

Boyatzis, R. E., & Akrivou, K. (2006). The ideal self as the driver of intentional change. *Journal of Management*, 25(4), 624-642.

Buckingham, M. (2005). *The one thing you need to know: ... about great managing, great leading, and sustained individual success.* New York: Free Press.

Eisen, S. (2010). The personhood of the OD practitioner. In W. J. Rothwell, J. Stavros, R. Sullivan, & A. Sullivan, *Practicing organization development: A guide for leading change (3rd Edition).*, San Francisco: Jossey-Bass.

Feather, N. T. (2003). Values and deservingness in the context of organizations. In S. W. Gilliland, D. D. Steiner, & D. P. Skarlicki (Eds.), *Emerging perspectives on values in organizations*, pp. 33-66. Greenwich, CN: Information Age Publishing.

Kotter, J. P. (1990). *A force for change: How leadership differs from management.* New York: The Free Press.

Kotter, J. P. (1996). *Leading change.* Boston: Harvard Business School Press.

Kotter, J. P., & Cohen, D. (2002). *The heart of change.* Boston: Harvard Business School Press.

Meglino, B. M., & Ravlin, E. C. (1998). Individual values in organizations: Concepts, controversies, and research. *Journal of Management*, 71, 492-499.

Quinn, R. E. (1996). *Deep change: Discovering the leader within.* San Francisco, CA: Jossey-Bass.

Stavros, J. M. (1998). *Capacity Building: A Relational Process of Building Your Organization's Future.* Dissertation, Case Western Reserve. Cleveland, OH.

Stavros, J.M., & Hinrichs, G. (2009). *The thin book of SOAR: Building strengths-based strategy.* Bend, OR: Thin Book Publishing.

Stavros, J., & Seiling, J. (2010). Mindful leadership development: Assessing self for leading change. In W. J. Rothwell, J. Stavros, R. Sullivan, & A. Sullivan, *Practicing organization development: A guide for leading change* (3rd Edition). San Francisco: Jossey-Bass.

Tesser, A., Martin, L. L., & Cornell, D. P. (1996). On the substitutability of self-protective mechanisms. In P.M. Gollwitzer & J.A. Bargh (Eds.), *The psychology of action: Linking cognition and motivation to behavior* (pp. 48-68). New York: Guilford.

Tichy, N. M., & Devanna, M. A. (1986). *The transformational leader.* New York: Wiley.

BIOGRAPHY

Jacqueline M. Stavros, DM. possesses twenty years of strategic planning, marketing, international, and organization development and change experience. Stavros is an associate professor and DBA program chair for the College of Management, Lawrence Technological University, where she teaches and integrates strengths-based practices such as Appreciative Inquiry and sustainable development concepts in leading organizational change, strategic management, organization development, and leadership. She has worked and traveled to over a dozen countries in Australia, Asia, Europe, and North America. Clients have included ACCI Business System, BAE Systems, Fasteners, Inc., General Motors of Mexico, Jefferson Wells, NASA, Tendercare, United Way, Girl Scouts USA, gedas International, Orbseal Technologies, and several Tier 1 and Tier 2 automotive suppliers, nonprofit organizations, and higher education institutions. She has co-authored and edited many books, book chapters, and articles. Books include: *Thin Book of SOAR: Building Strengths-Based Strategy, Practicing Organization Development: A Guide for Leading Change, Dynamic Relationships: Unleashing the Power of Appreciative Inquiry in Daily Living,* and the first *Appreciative Inquiry Handbook: For Leaders of Change.*

Dr. Jacqueline M. Stavros
Associate Professor, DBA Program Chair
Lawrence Technological University, 8657 N. Christine Drive, Brighton, MI 48114
810-229-6776 (home phone number),
248-204-3063 (university phone number)
Email: jstavros@comcast.net

BIOGRAPHY

Jane Galloway Seiling, Ph.D. is a professor, consultant, and writer on leading change and capacity building in nonprofits, accountability in organizations and sensemaking, and sensemanaging in organizations. Her activities include six years as a senior editor of a book series with the Taos Institute, author, and adjunct professor. Jane brings to her interests twenty years of working inside organizations and ten years as an organization development consultant.

Her work has appeared in various academic and practitioner journals and chapters in edited books. Her books include *The Membership Organization: Achieving Top Performance Through the New Workplace Community,* 1998 winner of the Society for Human Resource Management Book of the Year award; *The Meaning and Role of Organizational Advocacy: Responsibility and Accountability in the Workplace* and co-editor of *Appreciative Inquiry and Organizational Transformation: Reports from the Field.*

Dr. Jane Galloway-Seiling
The Taos Institute, Cleveland Ohio
1501 Riverview Drive, Lima, OH 45805
419-991-0959 (home phone number), 419-236-8455 (cell phone)
Email: janeseiling@aol.com

13

Leading Change: One Leadership Team's Experience

Janet McCollum & Ken Murrell

Major Focus Of The Case

Leaders live in an environment that demands constant change of themselves, their team, and their organization. On the one hand, leaders are well aware of the risks and detrimental effects that an unsuccessful change effort has on their organization. On the other hand, leaders appreciate that change is required for their organization's continued success. The challenge that leaders face is how to develop the organization's capacity to change and become adept at changing while maintaining a high level of performance. This case study examines how one leader and his team developed the capacity to become change-adept while maintaining, and in fact improving, the organization's level of performance.

Introduction

Today's organizations are experiencing accelerated rates of change that are increasingly unpredictable (Cameron & Quinn, 2006; Lawler & Worley, 2006). Organizations are struggling to handle the multitude of change demands – some competing, some complementary. Approximately two-thirds of change efforts undertaken either do not meet expectations or fail completely (Beer & Nohria, 2000; Cameron & Quinn, 2006). If a change effort is unsuccessful employees become frustrated, cynical, and untrusting and low morale prevails which in turn leads to low organizational performance. The high failure rate of changes and the resulting consequences create an urgency for leaders to develop skills in leading change. However, the learning process is not an easy one. Leaders face the dilemma of knowing that change can be risky and potentially detrimental to the business of the organization and yet change is required for organizations to succeed. The challenge for leaders becomes one of learning how to lead successful change and developing the capacity of organizations to change while maintaining a high level of performance.

Change

Change as it is used in this context is not just about coping with new demands. Rather change is about developing the capability of the organization to move forward and take advantage of new demands and opportunities. Given the environment of change that leaders face, understanding the implications and ramifications of various change approaches is critical. A comparison of two different approaches to change, planned and emergent, follows.

Planned change. The traditional Organizational Development way of viewing change is based on planned change, where the change process is planned, implemented, evaluated, and aligned and organized to be sustained. In this approach an agreed upon strategy is developed by some combination of leaders, change agents, a change team, and other stakeholders. Successful completion of the steps should lead to the specified change outcomes. Most frequently used change approaches are based on this model of planned change. It should be pointed out that even though the emphasis is on a planned approach the process is a dynamic one that requires adapting to changing situations and conditions.

Emergent change. Responsive and organic change that leads to unexpected results is a key element of emergent change. Emergent change may include intentional change that includes anticipated outcomes, but does not include a programmatic approach. Change is continuous with no beginning or end. Emergent change evolves over time and is dynamic, ongoing, complex, and nonlinear in nature. Emergent change requires change-adept organizations that have the capacity to understand the nature of the overarching change context in which they live and to continuously move a step ahead of the need for change.

Change-adeptness. According to Lawler and Worley (2006), "If organizations are to be successful in the future, they must build their capacity to change and become adept at the process of changing while maintaining a high level of performance" (p. 19). Cameron and Quinn (2006) state that "through the process of building a change-adept culture, changing becomes an integral part of organizational life and organizational performance" (p. 11). Kanter (1997) describes a change-adept organizational culture as one that "anticipates, creates, and responds effectively to change" (p. 3) is "open to new possibilities, challenge, learning, and change" (p. 25), and where "productive change becomes a natural way of life" (Kanter, p. 3). The challenge for leaders is how to develop a change-adept organizational culture, where changing and high performance are the norm.

Background of the Acme Waste Case Study

Acme Waste (a pseudonym, the company prefers to remain anonymous) provides waste and environmental services in North America (U.S., Canada, and Puerto Rico), including waste hauling, landfill, and recycling operations. The Acme culture is action biased, hard working, results focused, and metric driven. A common description of the culture offered by Acme employees is "we are a ready-fire-aim culture." The subtext would read "and proud of it." This approach leads to what managers self-describe as a "hair on fire" approach (reactive).

Note: The quotes in the case study are taken from interviews the researcher conducted with the members of the leadership team.

Initiating Conditions – A Precursor to Change

The President/COO view. The President/COO (P/COO) discovered that an area in the southern U.S. was more profitable, with higher EBIT and margins, than other areas. However when the P/COO looked at the area's metrics, he found high turnover, high maintenance costs, safety issues, and low productivity and he began to wonder how much more profitable the area could be if the metrics improved. The P/COO considered that perhaps the metrics indicated that the people and equipment were being worked too hard. He surmised that the area would achieve better metrics if people enjoyed their work and were proud of the place where they worked. The P/COO decided to experiment and address conditions that caused people to leave.

The core team. To address the conditions, the P/COO brought together a cross-functional group of mid-level managers (core team) to analyze area data, identify key focus areas for change, and pilot recommended changes. The core team included five District Managers (DMs) and five functional managers, led by the Area Vice President (upper level manager). Two internal consultants provided ongoing support, coaching, and process facilitation to the core team. After analyzing the data from the area and discussing their experiences, the core team identified five key focus areas for the pilot – compensation, organization and standardization, recruiting/ retention, training, and culture.

The pilot district supporting mechanisms. A pilot district was chosen to experiment and test the core team's recommendations. Because the DM of the pilot location was an active member of the core team, the core team provided peer group support to the DM. One of the internal consultants was assigned to coach the DM on leadership and team facilitation.

Top management demonstrated interest throughout the pilot by requesting ongoing progress reports, attending some core team meetings, and periodically visiting the pilot district.

Pilot measurement. The core team identified measurements to determine the success of the pilot. Over the 18 month pilot, metrics and financial data were tracked quarterly. Employee survey results, employee listening session results, and manager culture survey results were compared year over year. In addition, the internal consultant took notes on manager conversations, interviews, and observations. The manager quotes, paraphrases, and observations that follow are taken from the internal consultant's notes (the lead author of this case).

Action research as a foundation. An action research approach (Coghlan & Brannick, 2005) was used as the foundation for the core team process, the district leadership team process, and the DM coaching process. Action research is based on an iterative, participative, collaborative process that incorporates continuous learning through diagnosing, planning action, taking action, and evaluating results. Key to action research is reflecting on lessons learned to determine what worked well and what might be done differently.

The District Pilot

All 200 district employees participated in the pilot. The DM created a cross functional team to serve as the pilot district leadership team. This team, which consisted of ten people, including the District Manager (DM), District Operations Manager, Maintenance Manager, Dispatch Manager, Route Managers (RM), Customer Service Manager, Billing Manager, and Sales Manager, had not previously worked together as a team.

The DM's initial reaction was, "Corporate is always coming up with ideas for the field to implement without asking the field what might work. We already do these things, we know our business, and we are profitable. We don't need to change." As the core team created a vision and defined what that vision meant for the field, the pilot DM became committed to the idea and process for becoming the "best place to work."

Inquiry process – developing a district leadership team committed to changing. When introducing the new compensation system to the district leadership team, the DM posed a series of questions and presented some facts/ideas to consider. Most importantly, the new pay system significantly increased the pay of certain drivers and rewarded drivers for safety, attendance, and productivity. The district leadership team responded,

"We can't do that, it costs too much money." Because of previous core team discussions around the same monetary concerns and one-on-one coaching sessions with the internal consultant, the DM was able to use a questioning and consideration dialogue process to encourage the leadership team to develop a broader systems perspective, embrace multiple perspectives, develop complex thinking skills, and consider possibilities. Some questions and considerations used to facilitate the dialogue process follow.

Questions: What is the impact of reducing absenteeism? What if drivers are more productive and safe? Considerations: If absenteeism is reduced, fewer temporary employees are needed, thereby reducing costs. The more productive the driver, the less time a driver is on the road, the less exposure the driver has to accidents. Fewer accidents results in lower insurance rates. Savings on insurance rates increases the bottom line profitability. In addition, if drivers return earlier to the yard in the evening, both drivers and supervisors can get home earlier, resulting in happier employees and happier families. Happier employees tell others, making recruiting employees easier and enhancing the view of the company as a good place to work.

As the DM became more adept at using the questioning and consideration dialogue process, the team became more adept at participating and adding their own questions and considerations. As the DM effectively modeled the new process and invited participation, over time the capability of the entire leadership team increased.

Month 1. Managers focused on what was NOT happening. The comments were generally negative, and blamed others or the environment ("managers can't coach because we have to constantly put out fires"). Managers saw little relationship between their issues and other departments' issues. However, managers were aware of salient employee issues – lack of trust, lack of training, conflicting rules, and no employee recognition. Managers' listed complaints that "someone" should fix. No solutions were offered. During month one, the DM introduced the pilot and discussed making the district "a better place to work." Four out of the ten managers stated, "We could do a better job if everyone worked together."

Month 2. Employee surveys were administered to all employees. To foster an open environment, the results of the survey were posted for all employees to see. Although managers had articulated key employee issues, they were shocked when the survey results substantiated their comments. Faced with employee confirmation that issues really existed, the managers realized they needed to address the issues but were unsure how to proceed.

The managers stated that they had done their best for their employees; that the managers were also trapped in the system. By taking this stance, the managers tried to justify continuing with business as usual. The DM framed the survey results as a positive opportunity to create a "best place to work."

To better understand the employee survey results, the internal consultant held employee listening sessions for each department. Each employee group was asked to agree on the three most positive survey items and why they were important and agree on the three least positive survey items and provide suggestions on changes to make the district a "better place to work." The listening session results were posted.

The employees identified positive areas (i.e., the future of the company is important to me; customer satisfaction is one of our priorities; my job allows me the freedom I need to use my own judgment; and overall this is a good place to work) and discussed specific reasons why these areas were positive. The employees identified areas for change (e.g., trust between employees and management; recognition for a job well done; management is fair and honest and cares about employees; there is cooperation and teamwork among the people; training to do the job; and communicate and keep employees informed) and provided specific suggestions for changes.

At this point, managers' comments became more hopeful and their attitudes toward the employees and making changes became more positive. Managers began to think about what could be done differently based on the employee listening session feedback. Managers indicated a willingness to shift their perspective (e.g., "the need to develop people" or "perhaps the maintenance budget is just a guide"), thus fostering the development of emergent change that occurs as part of an organic responsive process. Managers discussed the "need to work together to solve problems" and "the need to understand what each other does" to move the team toward a more interdependent approach. The leadership team spent time talking, but no action was taken.

Months 3 through 5. The DM provided leadership to the team by modeling the desired changes of interdependent team work, developing a "best place to work", experimenting with new or different alternatives, and listening to and acting on employees' suggestions. The leadership team moved from thinking of ways to do things differently to actually experimenting with ideas by putting them into practice. The managers began to recognize that the pilot was "not a formulaic or packaged solution, but rather an experiment" and that "change is a process, not an event" indicating further embracing of emergent change. The managers incorporated an action research approach, viewing change as an ongoing process where learning occurs through experience and participation and collaboration with others.

Through leadership team discussions, employee survey and listening session feedback, and talking with employees, managers became more aware of their changing role with their employees. RMs talked about the need to "grow drivers internally from the helper ranks by sending the helpers to driver's school and then promoting those who did well. "The managers began to understand the importance of working together. In a team meeting, a manager reported that "dispatch received compliments from sales and customer service and RMs praised maintenance." The managers began to think more broadly and systemically as they practiced the questioning and consideration dialogue process and experienced success as they experimented.

During month three, the managers participated in a "managers' culture dialogue." In this meeting, the managers discussed the employee survey results, the listening session data, and each manager's Organizational Culture Assessment Inventory (OCAI) (Cameron and Quinn, 2006) results. Based on these three data sources, the leadership team considered the current culture and preferred culture for the organization. To move the district in the direction of the preferred culture, the team identified the following three key focus areas and actions to take during the year. To address communication with employees, the leadership team agreed to communicate department and staffing changes to employees, work on better communication within the leadership team, and agree on and implement standardized policy changes to create consistency across departments. To develop a more interdependent collaborative leadership team, managers agreed to spend time in other departments to get to know the people and use a cross functional systems approach for addressing issues. To foster employee involvement and participation, managers agreed to form cross functional employee teams to address ways to recognize employees and create teamwork/cooperation. A list of action items, due dates, and responsible managers was published and reviewed at the leadership team meetings.

Months 6 through 10. DM coaching sessions with the internal consultant continued. The sessions focused on how to encourage the development of individual members of the leadership team and continue to foster the development of the identity of the leadership team.

The DM actively fostered the development of the managers in team meetings and individual conversations. The DM and managers demonstrated complex thinking, self awareness, and use of reflection. The leadership team became more integrated and self directed as they developed confidence in their ability to work together, their comfort and success with experimentation and the action research approach, their ability to change direction if something didn't work, and greater respect and trust in their employees' abilities. They followed through on the commitments made during action planning. RMs noted positive changes in the language and attitude of the drivers. Employees began talking about "raising the bar and drivers talked about being 'A' players." The DM and District Operations Manager actively coached RMs and reported progress stating that "now some managers are willing to listen to employees about what employees need to be more efficient and productive and also to commend those employees who are doing a good job." Managers actively pursued getting to know other departments. As part of new hire orientation, new drivers sat with customer service and dispatch, new customer service representatives sat with dispatch and billing and went on a route with a driver. District-wide appreciation of each others' departments grew. Managers reported that "everyone was excited that maintenance and operations were working together on a new truck check-in process" – a first in a long history of animosity. The DM noted that as "managers started to communicate with each other, the effect trickled down to employees and everyone started talking to each other." The managers became role models for employees.

Months 11 and 12. Managers continued to demonstrate more optimistic complex thinking. The leadership team exhibited even greater collaboration and willingness for joint action. A manager reported that "even quiet people are speaking up in the meetings." In the words of one manager, "the buzz is on and it is spreading." Managers noted continued positive behavior changes in employees and themselves. The leadership team responded to employee concerns about the facilities by paving the employee parking lot, fixing an upstairs bathroom, and installing new coffee machines. These actions resulted in employees commenting to each other and to their managers on how much the work environment had improved. The employee committee planning the district holiday party sought input from other employees – a first. This inclusion demonstrated a visible sign of communication moving throughout the organization.

In the midst of all the positive changes, Maintenance unexpectedly retreated into their silo and for first time the leadership team voiced a concern over retreating to the past. The district maintenance manager reported to both the DM and the area maintenance manager (AMM). The AMM controlled the maintenance budget. He was not part of the pilot or core team and had no knowledge of the district changes. Therefore, the AMM was operating under the old rules and beliefs – the maintenance budget was sacred, trucks did not need to be repaired "like new", they just needed to work, and drivers caused the maintenance problems because they did not take care of their trucks. The focus was on short term cost and blaming. The AMM pressured the district maintenance manager to revert to old behaviors.

Months 13-14. As maintenance withdrew into their silo, the district maintenance manager attended leadership team meetings less frequently, eventually dropping out completely. The other managers became discouraged by this development. Based on their experience with maintenance, the managers noted that "the organization was fragmented. Everyone had their own agenda and different goals." The gains in cooperation and momentum of the previous period seemed to be lost or subdued. Most of the managers' comments were negative, similar to the beginning of the pilot, focusing on what was wrong without offering solutions. The leadership team felt they must make a choice – to retreat to the known or to continue to evolve and change. The team questioned whether they wanted to put forth the effort to continue; whether they would be successful if they put forth the effort; and whether the other team members were really committed to making the effort required.

To help the team move forward, the DM refocused the leadership team's attention on the employees and becoming a "best place to work." To remind the leadership team of what they achieved over the past year, the DM and internal consultant conducted a reflective session to review the accomplishments of the team and each department. At the end of the session, one manager stated, "I had forgotten how much we accomplished. We have come a long way." In month 14, the second employee survey was administered and the results were posted.

Months 15 and 16. The review of the leadership team accomplishments and the positive survey results helped managers return to a more positive view. A year over year comparison of the employee survey results and employee listening session comments showed improvement in all key areas – although managers agreed that trust, recognizing employees, keeping all employees informed required continued focus. The leadership team expressed a readiness to move forward and once again squarely face their leadership responsibilities. One manager summed up the leadership team's attitude by stating, "It is time to move from good to excellent."

The managers' Organizational Culture Assessment Inventory reports and subsequent discussions showed movement toward the preferred culture described the previous year. Some changes to the preferred culture were recommended for the coming year, however these were not major shifts. The two greatest changes suggested for the coming year revolved around systems thinking and included the need for the district to become more entrepreneurial, something previously seen as unnecessary by the leadership team, and helping the employees understand the broader market, customers' value to the company, and the importance of their day-to-day job.

Month 17. Managers clearly articulated the importance of an overall system approach. Managers internalized and further developed self awareness/ self discovery as a foundation for leading. Managers reported using reflection to consider how their actions impacted the way others act. Collaboration was growing and the managers increasingly recognized the need for the differentiation of different departments while creating an integrated whole that successfully worked together. One manager noted "A systems approach for addressing issues helps you know what to expect from other managers." Experimentation became more deeply embedded into the culture. RMs viewed drivers as professionals with responsibilities and accountability for "taking care of their equipment, being safe and productive, and taking care of the customer" while also learning to be more self managing. The leadership team reported that they now "volunteer to try different corporate pilot programs if we think the district can benefit." Over the life of the pilot, profitability measures indicated considerable positive gains and all key metrics showed positive trends.

References

Beer, M., & Nohria, N. (2000). Introduction: Resolving the tension between Theories E and O of change. In M. Beer & N. Nohria (Eds.), *Breaking the code of change* (pp.1-33). Boston, MA: Harvard Business School Press.

Cameron, K. S., & Quinn, R. E. (2006). *Diagnosing and changing organizational culture: Based on the competing values framework* (Rev. ed.). San Francisco, CA: Jossey-Bass.

Coghlan, D., & Brannick, T. (2005). *Doing action research in your own organization* (2nd ed.) Thousand Oaks , CA: Sage.

Kanter, R. M. (1997). *Rosabeth Moss Kanter on the frontiers of management.* Cambridge, MA: Harvard Business Review.

Lawler III, E. E., & Worley, C. G. (2006). *Built to change: How to achieve sustained organizational effectiveness.* San Francisco, CA: Jossey-Bass

Mntzberg, H. (2009). *Managing.* San Francisco, CA: Barrett-Kohler.

Discussion

1. This case describes 17 months of changes in an organization that resulted in a change adept culture, a high performing and collaborative leadership team, improved teamwork throughout the organization, improved performance and morale, lower turnover, and greater attention to safety issues. Discuss the key changes that occurred that made this possible with the goal of learning as much as possible about leading successful change.

2. Some changes such as the ones described in this case need outside expertise to help guide and coach the process. Discuss a few guidelines on when expertise from outside the group is needed.

3. Assessments were used early on in the process to discover present realities and later to evaluate progress and plan for the future. Why are various types of assessments during the change process important in achieving successful change?

4. Discuss the skills leaders need to develop to effectively foster and lead a change-adept culture.

5. Discuss the changes in the leader/managers' perspectives and behavior during the change process and the impact this had on how employees perceived the district, their work, and their relationship with each other and their manager, and how they performed.

6. Significant changes will invariably run into difficulties and challenges. Discuss what happened in months 13-14, how it was dealt with, and anything you would do different in handling this situation.

Key Lessons In Leading Change

(Quotes are taken from interviews with the leadership team.)

1. DM comments about the process. "When we developed the process it seemed unorganized and a bit stressful. We didn't know what the end result would be. We didn't know what we were really trying to accomplish. It was not comfortable. It was a good process to go through. Now we have structure, but flexibility is important."

Lesson: Leaders should be flexible and adept at emergent change processes.

2. DMs comments on the business impact. "Finances are still improving. The organization is now built to change, or we are moving in that direction. We strive to achieve, be adaptable, and agile. We have a vision and when we get people together we can make it happen."

Lesson: As change occurs in an organization, leaders must also pay attention to business needs. Leaders create the vision and get people together to achieve the vision.

3. A manager's comments on the positive approach to change. "The initiative reminded us of how things should be. We need to build on strengths. If you focus on the positive, you look at things from a different perspective."

Lesson: For change to happen, leaders should build on the strengths of the organization and its people.

4. A manager's comments on local adaptation of change. "We tried, tested, and benchmarked, but still had the flexibility in developing and adapting solutions to fit our district."

Lesson: Leaders should not be afraid to experiment, develop, and adapt solutions to local conditions.

5. The DOM's comments on culture. "How to change a culture? Before I thought you needed a volcano to erupt or something to pull everyone together. Now I realize it's how you treat employees and what you expect of them. You can't do one thing to make a culture change; you have to do a lot of different things everyday to make a culture change. Now I believe you can make a culture change by how you are."

Lesson: Leading change is about how you treat others, what you expect of others, and knowing who you are.

6. DM on sustainability of changing. "To sustain the initiative it needs to be worked into the normal routine. Now we are getting pretty good at changing."

Lesson: Change is a way of life for a successful organization. Leaders need to be good at developing the capability of an organization to become change-adept.

BIOGRAPHY

Dr. Janet McCollum is currently an Assistant Professor at Pennsylvania College of Technology in the business department. Janet has twenty plus years experience leading Organizational Development and Training departments in a variety of industries including waste, oil and gas, computer manufacturing, electronics, and real estate development. She also has international consulting experience and has worked in the international non-profit sector. Her doctoral degree is from Pepperdine University in Organizational Change. She has a Masters degree in Telecommunication Management from Southern Methodist University and a Masters degree in Educational Research from the University of Houston. Janet has presented numerous papers and workshops at the Academy of Management, OD Network, OBTC, and ASTD. Janet lived in Moscow, Russia for 5 years and loves to travel and experience new places and cultures.

Janet McCollum
Assistant Professor
Pennsylvania College of Technology
One College Avenue
Williamsport, PA 17701
Email: jkm2@pct.edu

BIOGRAPHY

Dr. Ken Murrell has been in the field of Organization Development for over 30 years and has had the privilege of working with many wonderful colleagues all over the world. His doctoral degree is from George Washington University and his MBA in international business was granted by the American University in Washington D.C. Whenever possible he also teaches in Europe, Asia and Latin America. Ken held corporate positions with G.D. Searle in Chicago and on his second sabbatical spent a year working with Bell South in developing their interrnal OD staff. He has had decades of experience consulting to several leading international organizations, three different Baldridge Award winning companies, and the United Nations Development Program.Ken's publications and research papers number over 100 and his interests range from Organization Devlopment globally to looking more deeply into the nature of human development and the ethical considerations that tend to align themselves with one's own development level.His passion in his work is in international development and Ken has lived, worked and traveled in somewhere from 60-70 countries on six continents but has yet to visit Antartica but wants too before he leaves this world.

Ken Murrell
Professor of Management and MIS
University of West Florida
11000 University Parkway
Pensacola, FL
Email: kmurrell@uwf.edu

14

The Internationalization Of A Deep-South University: A Study In Leadership Vision And Execution

Jack Hawkins Jr. & John A. Kline

Major Focus Of The Case

Leaders who desire to be agents of change must begin with vision. A strong, well-articulated vision separates leaders from mere managers, but the execution of a vision separates dreamers from leaders. Proverbs says that without vision the people will perish. Likewise, without vision the purported leader will flounder.

Implementing organizational change is a difficult and critical task, even for the most seasoned leader. It has always been that way and is getting more so with the accelerated rate of change in most organizations. Thus, the danger of "change fatigue," is real, and those up and down the organizational chain of command may wonder if the latest idea is a product of sincere vision or simply a whim of the moment. The implementation of vision – the execution of the plan – can be summarized in three words – communicate, communicate, communicate. This case focuses on how implementation of vision transformed a public university in the rural American South. The lead author is also the change agent and a subject of this case, so in many ways this is a personal story of applying leadership lessons learned.

Introduction: The Seed of Vision

Troy (Alabama) University was founded in 1887 as a teacher-training institution. By 1989, the year Jack Hawkins, Jr., became Chancellor, the University had grown from a single small campus in Troy, a town of some 13,000 in southeast Alabama, to a comprehensive University with four campuses in Alabama. Beginning in the early 1970s then-Troy State University began to assume a global dimension by receiving a Department of Defense contract to provide degree programs on military bases in Europe. The end result was a University with two distinct personalities, one a campus in Troy serving traditional-age college students 18 to 23; the other a network of campuses and teaching sites focusing on the adult learner. The traditional campus is the primary focus of the case.

It is axiomatic that a leader's vision is influenced by current events. The world events that occurred during the first few years of the Hawkins Administration at Troy University were monumental: the fall of the Berlin Wall and the end of the Cold War, U.S. troops in the Middle East, economic downturn, and the creation of the first web page. The post-Cold War world was about to give way to the age of globalization. As Thomas Friedman wrote in The Lexus and the Olive Tree, (Farrar, Straus & Giroux, 1999), ". . . the globalization system, unlike the Cold War system, is not static, but a dynamic ongoing process: globalization involves the inexorable integration of markets, nation-states, and technologies to a degree never witnessed before – in a way that is enabling individuals, corporations, and nation-states to reach around the world farther, faster, deeper, and cheaper than ever before . . ."

In his inaugural address at Troy University on October 12, 1990, Chancellor Hawkins set forth the vision to match this dynamic new reality: "Troy State University 2000 will not be classified simply as a research regional university. We are worldwide in our outreach and we are becoming international in our perspective... The measuring stick of educational progress no longer is our Southern neighbors because we now compete in a global village."

The Chancellor's vision placed new requirements on Troy University. In order to transform the institution from a regional university to a global one, it would take more than operating satellite branches on military bases overseas. Troy University owed its students the opportunity to be globally competitive. That meant implementing a "three-legged stool" of recruiting international students, growing a study-abroad program, and developing faculty through international exchanges and teaching opportunities at Troy University's international sites.

Overcoming Challenges to the Vision/Execution of the Vision

Troy University faced several potential hurdles on the road to internationalization, most relating to the recruiting of international students to the main campus in Troy, which in the early 1990s enrolled about 5,000 students. One barrier was on-campus resistance to change and the notion that internationalization was too grand a vision for what once was a teacher's college. The other was the possibility that students of other nations, cultures, and religions would not be accepted in a college town located in the heart of the Southern Bible Belt.

Many organizations struggle to change because people fail to grasp the vision and understand the implications. Change expert William Bridges outlines four "P" steps necessary to implement vision and launch change. They are purpose, picture, plan, and part. At the time, the University leadership did not consciously consult the Bridges methodology in implementing a program of internationalization at Troy University. In looking back, however, Bridges' formula explains well the process of implementing change at Troy University.

Purpose: From the outset, University administrators told both internal and external audiences the reason for internationalization was to prepare all Troy University students to succeed in the global marketplace that awaited them after graduation. While some people could not grasp why we were investing in a program of international recruitment and study abroad, they could grasp the importance of student preparation. Most important, University leaders were ready to answer the question: What will happen to Troy University if we don't change?

Picture: Purposes can be abstract; people need a picture of how things will be after the change occurs. It was necessary to paint a picture of the Troy Campus that included hundreds of students from other lands contributing to the environment on campus. To provide a concrete picture of our vision, the University transformed one of its largest and most prominent traditional residence halls into an international living and learning center where U.S. students would voluntarily room with students from other countries. This important move enabled the campus and the community to see a physical manifestation of an abstract idea.

Plan: Many people in senior leadership positions do not need a plan; they find a way to the destination once they have the picture in mind. Most people, however, need to know how the organization will get from here to there. Elements of this plan included appointing an international programs staff to establish responsibility for student recruitment from the outset, establishing a fund to assist faculty members who wanted an overseas academic experience, and charging the deans of each academic college to begin devising formal study-abroad programs.

Part: Even the best purpose, picture, and plan leave doubt in the minds of people if they do not know the role they are to play. First, they need to know how they fit into the changed organization; second, they need to know how they will interact with others; and third they need to know the role they will play in implementing the change.

Leadership Styles and the Internationalization of a University

Until the faculty commits to the concept of university globalization, it will not occur. The commitment cannot be limited to the office of the president or chancellor. The CEO must be a strong advocate, but he or she cannot be the sole champion. It follows then that the role of the CEO in this case was to first champion the cause and then look for others to assume the role of champions of internationalization. Chancellor Hawkins, who served as an officer in United States Marine Corps, was comfortable with a "lead from the front" attitude that promoted the vision while at the same time seeking input from those who might have reservations about the initiative.

Leadership case studies abound contrasting autocratic styles of leadership with more inclusive styles. This particular situation required a measure of autocracy only to the point of setting the goal of internationalization and even that crucial first step was taken only after including senior administrators and the University Board of Trustees in the discussion. The execution of the goal required a more inclusive style of leadership embracing clear communication with all constituents. On-campus communication of the vision included a prominent discussion of internationalization in the chancellor's annual address to faculty, the announcement of the special fund to aid faculty through academic channels, and regular briefings with the Faculty Advisory Council.

This process of communication produced a cadre within the academy dedicated to globalizing the University. It also made it easier to implement the second phase of the communication plan – celebrating incremental success. In his award-winning book, Leading Change, John P. Kotter advocates generating short-term wins because change often takes a lot of time and short-term wins encourage others to stay the course. Kotter points out that a good short-term win has three characteristics: It is visible, unambiguous, and clearly related to the change effort.

Celebrating incremental victories has remained a key component of our communications plan. For example, each year in the Chancellor's annual address to faculty we include examples of those who are furthering the cause of internationalization throughout Troy University. We encourage our publications staff to include stories about internationalization in our faculty newsletter and alumni magazine. Most important, we encourage administrators at all levels to give positive feedback to those who champion globalization.

Results

The internationalization effort at Troy University began in earnest in the 1994-95 academic year. Progress has been made in several key areas:

1. **Recruitment of international students** – Troy University enrolled 55 international students in the fall term of 1995. By fall term of 1999, that number had increased to 205; to 402 in the fall terms of 2004 and to more than 850 in 2011. Approximately 60 nations are represented in Troy University's international student enrollment.

2. **Study-abroad programs** – In 1995, Troy University's study-abroad offerings consisted of an annual trip to Paris and an annual trip to Latin America by students taking foreign languages. Today, our students travel abroad to nations such as England, Sweden, Belgium, China, Costa Rica, France, Germany, Kenya, Mexico and Ecuador, among others.

3. **Faculty development** – Over the last four years, our Chancellor's International Initiative fund has helped fund international study for an average of 10 faculty members a year.

4. **Confucius Institute** – Partnerships with universities in China led Troy University officials to the Office of the Chinese Language Council International in Beijing and ultimately to the development of a Confucius Institute at Troy University in 2007. Troy University's Confucius Institute is part of a global network dedicated to the promotion and development of Chinese language education, and cultural and business exchange with the People's Republic of China.

5. **Overseas campuses** – In 2004, Troy University established degree programs in Vietnam in partnership with three universities in Hanoi and Saigon. As a result, in 2008 Troy University became the first U.S. university to award the baccalaureate degree in a nation once viewed as an adversary of the United States. Today, Troy University enrollment in Vietnam exceeds 1,000 students and many have matriculated from campuses in Hanoi and Saigon to complete their studies in Troy.

6. **Stronger brand identity** – Today Troy University is recognized as "Alabama's International University."

7. **Overall University growth** – Troy University has grown from 14,000 students enrolled worldwide in 1989 to approximately 30,000 today. Internationalization played a key role in the overall growth of the University as more U.S. students sought an international experience, as the University increased its distance-learning offerings, and as the University opened more teaching sites outside of Alabama as part of the overall program of globalization.

References

Friedman, Thomas (1999). *The Lexus and the Olive Tree*, Ney York: Farrar, Straus & Giroux

Bridges, William (1991) *Managing Transitions: Making the Most of Change*, Reading Massachusetts: Addison-Wesley

Kotter, John P. (1996) *Leading Change*, Boston: Harvard Business School Press

1. Briefly discuss Troy University at the beginning of the case and what was accomplished by the end of the case so you will understand what is possible when leaders understand change leadership and realize what you can accomplish through effective change leadership.

2. Discuss and list the lessons you learned in this case about change leadership. Are there other lessons you would add to your list?

3. Discuss your understanding of the Four P model developed by change expert William Bridges and how it was applied to transforming and changing the culture of Troy University.

4. Leadership style plays a key role in leading change. Discuss the leadership style of the university President Chancellor and then list leadership style characteristics that help facilitate change.

5. Communicating regularly, keeping communications open, and planning and celebrating incremental progress (quick wins) are all important to successful change. Discuss how these three important change principles were accomplished in the case and other ideas you might have in accomplishing each.

Key Lessons In Leading Change

1. Effective leaders begin with a clear vision, and then they communicate and continually affirm that vision. Nowhere is the saying, "If you can't communicate, don't try to lead" more true than in communicating the vision.

2. Many would-be-leaders grasp the notion of being "idea people" but they fail in the execution stage. True leaders begin forming the implementation plan almost simultaneously when creating the vision and then they involve others, giving them parts to play in implementing the change.

3. Change and transition are not the same. Change is the event and transition is the process of getting there. Good leaders know the difference and they focus on the human side of change – the transition groups and individuals must go through for the change to occur.

4. Leaders incentivize change by removing obstacles, allocating resources, empowering individuals, and giving positive feedback to those making substantial contributions to implementation of the change.

5. Leaders persevere and inspire perseverance in team members by publicizing and celebrating incremental or short-term accomplishments and success on the way to fulfilling the vision. Nothing breeds success like success.

BIOGRAPHY

Dr. Jack Hawkins, Jr., a native of Mobile, Alabama, was named Chancellor of Troy University Sept. 1, 1989. He earned his bachelor's and master's degrees from the University of Montevallo and his doctorate from the University of Alabama. Upon completion of his bachelor's degree in 1967, Hawkins was commissioned a lieutenant in the U.S. Marine Corps and served as a platoon leader during the Vietnam War. For his combat duty, he received the Bronze Star, the Purple Heart and a citation from the Korean Marine Corps. Dr. Hawkins has overseen an era of change and growth at TROY, as worldwide enrollment has more than doubled from 14,000 in 1989 to approximately 30,000 today. He led the merger of the worldwide Troy State University System into the unified Troy University, an initiative called "One Great University." More than $200 million has been invested in capital improvements by the Hawkins Administration, including new academic buildings on all four of TROY's Alabama campuses. Chancellor Hawkins served as the catalyst for the University's evolution to an international institution, as TROY has attracted record numbers of students from other nations and established more than 60 teaching sites around the world. During his tenure, academic standards for admission have been increased, new degree programs were established in all academic colleges, and intercollegiate athletics joined the highest level of NCAA competition.

Jack Hawkins, Jr., Ph.D.
Chancellor of Troy University
216 Adams Administration, Troy University, AL 36082
334-670-3200 · Email: jhawkins@troy.edu

BIOGRAPHY

Dr. John Kline was born and grew up in Iowa, lives in Montgomery, Alabama, and is the Distinguished Professor of Leadership and Director of the Troy University Institute for Leadership Development. He is a graduate of Iowa State University where he completed his bachelor's degree in English and speech. Next he earned both Master's and Ph.D. degrees in Human Communication from the University of Iowa. After serving as professor at both the University of New Mexico and the University of Missouri-Columbia, Dr. Kline accepted a teaching position in 1975 as a civilian professor at the USAF Air University located at Maxwell Air Force Base, Alabama. From 1991 until 2000, he was the Air University Provost with responsibility for faculty, academic programs, libraries, technology, budget, and support of 50,000 resident and 150,000 distance-learning students annually. In early 2000, Dr. Kline joined Troy University (Alabama) as a Professor of Education. In 2003 he assumed his present position. Dr. Kline speaks and writes on leadership and communication and conducts training on writing, speaking and listening. His most recent books – both published by Pearson Prentice Hall are: Listening Effectively: Achieving High Standards in Communication, and Speaking Effectively: Achieving Excellence in Presentations. He has many recent articles on Leadership and Communication and a book chapter on servant-leadership.

John A, Kline, Ph.D.
Distinguished Professor of Leadership and Director
of the Troy University Institute for Leadership Development
260 Smith Hall, Troy University, AL 36082
334-670-3389 · Email: jkline@troy.edu

15

Successfully Managing Major Changes: The Merging Of Two Companies

Edward H. Rockey

Major Focus Of The Case

BioBehemoth* is in the process of acquiring SoloMed. Depending upon what criteria are used to evaluate the success or failure of mergers and acquisitions, most studies report a failure rate of over fifty-percent. Though there are strategic and financial factors (e.g., paying too much for the acquired company) that can lead to the failure of mergers and acquisitions, the following seven leadership and behaviorally-oriented issues arise consistently:

1. Leadership styles that clash.
2. Mismatch of organizational cultures.
3. Colliding egos among upper management.
4. Difficulties in communicating between companies.
5. Departure of key talent from the acquired company.
6. Failure to lead change management effectively.
7. Failure to have a sound plan for integrating employees, processes, and systems, and values.

BioBehemoth was once very much like SoloMed – small and innovative, with a dynamic and loyal workforce who, as devoted and empowered members of a very special company, have felt proud and inspired. Though still a widely-admired and successful corporation, BioBehemoth has become more bureaucratic over the years, and it has lost a bit of its employees' sense of being special. Also, BioBehemoth's original company growth and fame have begun to swing away from its original highly-innovative roots and to veer towards growth through mergers and acquisitions and through developing and marketing less innovative products.

* Not the real name of the company

The focus of this case is to help the BioBehemoth/SoloMed acquisition succeed by reducing or preventing the six failure factors referred to above from ruining this acquisition effort.

The Case Background

SoloMed has recently developed an FDA approved highly successful medication, but the fledgling venture has limited resources to enable it to meet consumer demand. Physicians have begun to prescribe the product at a rate much higher than the company's capacity to deliver. The eight-year-old company has a staff of 344 people and is NASDAQ traded. Sales of its newest blockbuster product approach a billion dollars. Though the company has a sound basic financial position, it is unable to expand facilities and enlarge personnel in congruence with with marketplace success and future promise. SoloMed employees tend to be a tight-knit group who pride themselves on their achievements, who treasure the innovative reputation of their enterprise and share a culture similar to that of a select, distinctive coterie of very creative high-tech firms – playful, slightly irreverent companies that show disdain for bureaucracy and also treasure personal connectedness and a commitment to be collaborative.

BioBehemoth, on the other hand, has already demonstrated its ability to meet market demand for highly-successful products. It has vast revenues and over three billion dollars in cash. It has 3,780 employees and is widely recognized as a very sound company. Although its shareholder return over the past eight years has been very rewarding (36%), the shareholder return at SoloMed has been even higher (52%). Significantly, BioBehemoth slipped off of the top tier on the list of "Best Companies to Work For". It has lost some of the close family feeling experienced by employees in its early years.

When a proposed acquisition was announced, industry opinion and a few newspaper and magazine articles raised a red flag about the impending acquisition. Is this a wise move for BioBehemoth? How will the staff at SoloMed respond? Some anonymous quotes from SoloMed employees included, "We're not afraid of unemployment; we're afraid of disempowerment", "We really don't know how this came about. We've been kept in the dark" and "What'll happen to our scientific culture, our keen sense of being part of a special innovative culture?"

Discussion

1. Assume that a **Change Team** consisting of influential people from BioBehemoth and SoloMed has been appointed to successfully plan the acquisition of SoloMed by BioBehemoth. What should the Change Team do to get organized and prepared for their assignment?

2. Discuss and list five to ten steps the **Change Team** could recommend to the Top Leadership Team to achieve a successful integration of the two companies. One of the steps should be clarifying the roles of the top level leaders in the change process. List 3-5 roles you would recommend.

3. Assume that your **Change Team** has identified a number of goals they would like to achieve in the successful integration of the two companies. What goals would you recommend to the Top Leadership Team particularly keeping in mind goals that would help avoid the seven leadership failures that often occur in mergers and acquisitions mentioned at the beginning of the case.

4. What kind of working relationship should the **Change Team** try to arrange with the Top Leadership Team?

5. What kinds of feedback mechanisms could the **Change Team** build into the change process to make sure the change process is going well?

Key Lessons In Leading Change

1. Leaders need to assure that major changes are carefully planned.

2. Leaders need to play an active role in providing the leadership necessary for successful changes.

3. People support what they help create. Involvement of key stakeholders in the change process is important in planning and implementing changes.

4. Teams such as **Change Teams** can play a valuable leadership role in planning and implementing changes.

5. It is important to have knowledgeable internal or external professionals or both involved in planning and implementing major changes.

BIOGRAPHY

Professor Rockey is the author of and has presented at conferences in Sweden, Australia, Switzerland, Italy, New Zealand, Hong Kong, Canada, Mexico and the USA.

He is a member of the World Association of Case Research and Application and has published in their academic journal and proceedings. He has done training or consulting for Amgen, Prudential Insurance, Proctor & Gamble and other corporations and has presented at management clubs for Lockheed, Litton and several other firms. His Ph.D. is from New York University, and he taught previously at Brooklyn College (CUNY).

Edward H. Rockey, Ph.D.
Professor of Applied Behavioral Science
Graziadio School of Business and Management
Pepperdine University
Westlake Graduate Campus, 2829 Townsgate Road,
Westlake Village, CA 91361
805 496-8796 · erockey@pepperdine.edu

16

The Importance Of Storytelling
In Leading Fundamental Change

Robert B. Morris II & W. Warner Burke

Major Focus Of The Case

Every leader who has attempted to implement organization change knows what a difficult, messy process it can be. The reality of organizational life is that change will happen, whether leaders embrace it or not. As the continued high failure rates suggest, despite our abundant experience with it we are still woefully bad at bringing about long-term, sustainable change in organizations. Mergers and acquisitions are particularly challenging change efforts, and they fail at least 75% of the time (Burke & Biggart, 1997; "How Mergers Go Wrong", 2000). One reason we continue to struggle in this regard is there are few case studies illustrating success. As such, those leaders who do step up to the challenge have little to go on other than their personal experience and talent. The primary purpose of this case is to address this limitation by describing the approach of one CEO who led successfully a merger between two banks.

Introduction

The difference between leadership and management is well established, with the essence of leadership centering on transformational change. Until the 1970's, the terms leader and manager were used interchangeably to describe anyone who rose to a position of authority. In his seminal article, Zaleznik (1977) identified the key differences between leaders and managers. While others have expanded on these (Burns, 1978; Bennis & Nanus, 1985; Burke, 1986; Kotter, 1990), core to the argument is the notion that leadership is more about change (i.e., transformation) and management is more about maintaining the status quo.

Although organizations constantly change, fundamental organization change, like transformational leadership, is rare. Fundamental organization change is defined as "a major overhaul of the organization resulting in a modified or entirely new mission, a change in strategy, leadership and culture" (Burke, 2011, p.1). Such a change is considered to be revolutionary (as opposed to evolutionary), and it requires leaders who can create a vision that connects to the needs and goals of their followers, then communicate in a way that motivates people to implement the vision going forward.

For this reason, Gardner (1995) claims that storytelling is one of the most important things that leaders do. Leaders connect with the emotions of their followers by telling powerful stories that symbolize who they are and how they lead. He distinguishes between direct and indirect leadership. Put simply, indirect leadership involves influencing through symbolism, while direct leadership involves directly relating stories to followers. Appealing to followers' ideals and values in charismatic ways is the essence of Burns' (1978) definition of transformational leadership, and it is the key to our CEO's success in the case that follows.

Background

Our case begins in the mid 1800's with the founding of two savings banks in Brooklyn, New York. The first, Dime Savings Bank of Brooklyn, was founded on the principle that even the most humble of New Yorkers should save. To enable this, the minimum deposit was just one dime (10 cents). Dime showed early signs of growth through innovation by becoming the first to offer banking by mail during the Civil War, thereby permitting soldiers on the front line to deposit money for their families back home. The second bank, Anchor, was founded around the same time to serve Navy families in the local community. Like most savings banks of that era, both focused on the local community as their primary market. Over the next 100 years, Anchor and Dime grew separately by way of mergers and acquisitions that enabled regional expansion as well as growth in the types of services offered to customers.

Fast forward to 1995 when, following a rough period for both banks, the two decided to join forces. This merger occurred because the two CEOs and their boards of directors saw the potential for growth in a shrinking market. By merging into one bank focused more on the commercial aspects of banking and less on the savings, the banks could potentially increase cost savings by reducing overhead and sharing critical resources. Even more important, they could grow quicker together compared to the time it would take each of them individually. Like many companies before and after them, Dime and Anchor quickly learned why mergers rarely succeed. On first glance it would seem that the two banks would be very similar because of their histories, size, location, customer base, etc., but their likeness ended there. Instead, the bank cultures were highly dissimilar as each emphasized the values formed early in their history that were reinforced over time. For example, the culture of Anchor stressed attention to detail, while Dime's highlighted seeing the bigger picture. The competing values of the distinctive bank cultures presented a significant obstacle – and a great opportunity – for leadership.

Recognizing the difficult task ahead, the banks sought consultative help with the merger. In the early stages of the merger, the consultant worked with the bank to identify its new mission. From this, the values and norms that would form the new culture were determined. Following a series of organizational surveys that identified the priorities for change, the CEO worked closely with the consultant and the head of human resources to design and implement a 2 ½ day leadership program for the top 125 leaders in the company. The focus of this program was communicating and inculcating the values of the newly merged bank. A key objective of this workshop was the development of self-awareness, specifically regarding the six values and their associated behaviors.

Launching the Change Effort

The CEO was eager to participate in the workshops, so the consultant designed space for him to talk with the participants of each workshop and coached him to talk about personal values that underpinned his own leadership. Larry Toal, the CEO, went to each of the five 2 ½ day programs to talk about his values regarding leadership and change. The consultant further advised Toal not to talk about leadership per se, just to be a leader. He elected to demonstrate leadership by telling personal stories from his past about key lessons that helped form his leadership approach. What stood out in Toal's presentation was his value of anticipation and how important this strongly held belief is to effective leadership.

In each of the workshops, Toal relayed two stories to emphasize the importance of anticipation. The first story involved Toal's career history and his family. In brief, he and his wife raised two boys and changed homes many times throughout his career. With each move, he and his wife would determine right away the shortest route from their new home to the nearest hospital. He believed that with raising boys sooner or later he and/or his wife would be taking them to the emergency room with a broken arm, a deep cut, a severe abrasion, etc. His point? Anticipation that this trip would likely be necessary at some stage was highly important in the raising of their boys. Of course, his forward thinking paid off in spades the first time they actually made that trip...and they made a few over the years.

The second story concerned his leadership in the U.S. Navy. He rose through the ranks and became the executive officer (#2) of a battleship. He explained that when at sea as part of a large convoy, anything can happen. When steering the ship in a convoy, one must anticipate the possibility of a ship in front of you will for some reason veer either to the right or left, "starboard" or "port" in naval language. When such an event might occur the ship's commander must decide which maneuver to take in order to avoid a collision. Anticipating such a possibility was key to making sound, timely decisions. And the point of Toal's story was the fact that such an event occurred when he was at the helm. While at sea on a convoy, the ship ahead of his ran into trouble and had to initiate its own maneuvers. He subsequently made a decision and gave the command of "port" at so many degrees. The commander of the ship (#1 in charge) immediately overruled Toal's command by saying "No, Starboard!" As it turned out, this was the wrong decision and they began to get into trouble with maintaining their position in the convoy. Finally Toal was able to re-position the ship and continue safely on their journey. Later, in private, the ship's commander had a word with his executive officer, Toal, and said to him: "You were right to go to port; I was wrong in over-ruling the decision. And even though wrong, you were also right not to disobey my order. Your skill in the end corrected the mistake."

With this second story, Toal was not only illustrating again the importance of anticipation, he was also addressing the nature of followership by being careful not to contradict and embarrass his commander in front of the sailors on board the ship. The commander exercised leadership later by having his private chat with Toal. These two stories that Toal told his executives resonated with them. It is highly likely that today, many years later these executives could easily recall the two stories and the importance of anticipation.

1. Discuss some of the differences in management (planning, organizing, directing, controlling, executing etc.) and leadership (providing vision, direction, and inspiration, making changes etc.), the need for both, and why leadership is a key to successful change.

2. What is your dominant orientation (leadership, management, both, or neither) and what are the strengths and limitations of your present orientation and what could you do to change so you would be more effective and have a greater impact?

3. John Kotter is his book The Heart of Change points out that for change to be effective it must appeal to the emotions as much or more than the mind. Story telling is an example of engaging people by appealing to the emotions as well as the mind. What are other ways to reach the heart as well as the mind of people in leading change?

4. Leaders need to find ways to effectively communicate the values and culture they want to instill and the changes they desire to make. As a leader, what personal value would you most want to instill in people? Take out a sheet of paper and craft a logical argument as to why this value is important to you. With a partner, persuade him/her without using a story as to why it should be important for them as well. How did your partner feel after hearing your argument?

5. Using the value you identified above describe the experience that brought this to life for you or create a story to describe or illustrate the importance of the value. With a different partner, share your story. How did your story make your partner feel?

6. Evaluate the consultant's approach to coaching the CEO. What worked well and what were the risks of such an approach?

Key Lessons In Leading Change

1. There is an appropriate time and place for leadership and for management. Mergers and acquisitions are by their definition fundamental/revolutionary change efforts that demand leadership.

2. The CEO enables fundamental organization change by spearheading the charge to create a new mission and inspiring others, especially the top leadership team.

3. When leading change, aligning individual values and behavior with the organization's new culture is critical.

4. Leadership is emotional and personal. A common pitfall for leaders is underestimating the amount of emotion - and overestimating the impact of rationality and logic - when influencing others.

5. Knowing your own predisposition, i.e., being self aware, is a critical first step in determining your own leadership effectiveness. Know your story and share it with others at the appropriate time to gain buy-in and commitment to shared ideals.

6. Organization development (OD) professionals partner with and coach their clients to effect change. As illustrated in this case, OD consultants should influence change indirectly rather than attempting to be in the spotlight themselves.

References

Bennis, W. G., & Nanus, B. (1985). Leaders: *The strategies for taking charge*. New York: Harper & Row.

Burke, W. W. (1986). Leadership as empowering others. In S. Srivastva and Associates (Eds.), *Executive power: How executives influence people and organizations* (pp. 51-77). San Francisco: Jossey-Bass.

Burke, W. W., & Biggart, N. W. (1997). Interorganizational relations. In D. Druckman, J. E. Singer, & H. Van Cott (Eds.), *Enhancing organizational performance* (pp. 120-149). Washington, DC: National Academy Press.

Burke, W. W. (2011). *Organization change: Theory and practice* (3rd ed.). Thousand Oaks, CA: Sage.

Burns, J. M. (1978). *Leadership*. New York: Harper & Row.

Gardner, H. (1995). *Leading minds: An anatomy of leadership*. New York: Basic Books.

How mergers go wrong. (2000, July 22). *Economist*, p.19.

Kotter, J. P. (1990). *A force for change: How leadership differs from management*. New York: Free Press.

Zaleznik, A. (1977). Managers and leaders: Are they different? *Harvard Business Review*, 55(3), 67-78.

BIOGRAPHY

Rob Morris is a business psychology consultant and the Head of the New York Office for YSC, Americas. YSC is a global consultancy specializing in leadership and organization development. Rob graduated with a degree in leadership psychology from the United States Military Academy, West Point, and he served for twelve years as an Infantry Officer in the United States Army. A graduate of the US Army Airborne and Ranger schools, Rob led several teams and staffs from the platoon to the Division level, including two roles as a company commander in light infantry units. He spent four of those years designing leadership development programs and teaching leadership at West Point. In addition to leading YSC's Northeast team, Rob manages the executive coaching practice for YSC, Americas where he has consulted to several global companies in the financial services, FMCG, entertainment, and not-for-profit sectors. He holds an MS in counseling and leadership development from Long Island University and a PhD in Social-Organizational Psychology from Teachers College, Columbia University.

Robert B. Morris II
General Manager, Northeast US, YSC
295 Madison Ave, 19th Floor. New York, NY 10017
212-661-9888 · Email: rob.morris@ysc.com or rbm2123@gmail.com

BIOGRAPHY

Dr. Burke is professor of psychology and education and coordinator for the graduate programs in social-organizational psychology. He is also Associate Editor of the Journal of Applied Behavioral Science. Professor Burke earned his B.A. from Furman University and his M.A. and Ph.D. from the University of Texas, Austin. Prior to coming to TC in 1979, he served in senior positions at Clark University, the NTL Institute, and as executive director of the OD Network. Professor Burke's consulting experience has been with a variety of organizations in business-industry, education, government, religious, and medical systems. A Diplomate in I/O psychology through the American Board of Professional Psychology, he is also a fellow of the Academy of Management, the Association for Psychological Science, the Society of Industrial and Organizational Psychology, and past editor of both Organizational Dynamics and The Academy of Management Executive. He has authored over 150 articles and book chapters in organizational psychology and authored, co-authored, or edited 17 books. He has received numerous awards, including in 1989 the Public Service Medal from the National Aeronautics and Space Administration, in 1990 the Distinguished Contribution to Human Resource Development Award, in 1993 the Organization Development Professional Practice Area Award for Excellence-The Lippitt Memorial Award-from the American Society for Training Society and Development, and in 2003 both the Distinguished Scholar-Practitioner Award from the Academy of Management and the Lifetime Achievement Award from both the OD Network (2003) and Linkage (2010).

W. Warner Burke
Edward Lee Thorndike Professor of Psychology and Education Coordinator, Programs in Social-Organizational Psychology
Chair, Department of Organization and Leadership Teachers College, Columbia University
220 Zankel, 525 West 120th Street. New York, NY 10027
212-678-3831 · Email: wwb3@columbia.edu

CHAPTER FOUR

17

Leading Employees Past Difficult Organizational Transitions

Mitchell Lee Marks

Major Focus Of The Case

Transition management is very difficult – only about 25 percent of mergers and acquisitions attain their financial or strategic objectives and most downsizings provide one-time-only cuts in the cost of doing business but fail to return organizations to financial health or leave the organization with any true enhancements in how work is accomplished (Marks and Mirvis, 2010). Mismanaged – and even just undermanaged – transitions exact a heavy toll on employee well-being, work team performance, and organizational life (Marks, 2003). Thus, it is increasingly common for executives to encounter "transition-weary" workforces – employees who survive a merger, downsizing, restructuring or other major transition but have not realized any enhancements to their personal work situation or to overall organizational effectiveness. This case describes an organization which was created in a "merger of equals" but suffered from poor leadership, a lack of teamwork, and culture clash. In the course of five years, employees endured three waves of downsizing, two restructurings and the arrival of a new CEO from outside the company. It focuses on the role of the CEO in leading employees following a series of disruptive transitions.

Introduction

As they cope with and move through the global economic crisis, executives' spirits may be buoyed by new business opportunities – perhaps the adoption of a new strategy, the introduction of a new technology, product or service, or even the elimination of a competitor. They anticipate that after a difficult struggle, victory in a decisive battle is within reach. They see the goal and confidently rally their troops on the mission at hand. Then the cry will come to charge ahead and take the prize.

However, in many workplaces, the troops will be neither ready nor willing to move forward. They will be looking back, holding on to and unable to let go of the pain behind them. Their vision will be obscured by the emotional residue of anger, distrust, and depression built up over years of false promises and unmet expectations. Nor will the troops have the confidence that they can capture the prize – their self-esteem will be battered and their faith in their leadership broken. Most significantly, the troops will not see how any personal gain will result from organizational success. Instead, they will fixate on memories of their fallen comrades: the casualties of layoffs and downsizings, and the "walking wounded" whose careers were sidetracked by acquisitions and restructurings.

The EuroTel Story

EuroTel emerged from the rubble of a 2003 "merger of equals" between two staid European-based telecom companies.[36] According to company communications, the combined organization was envisioned to be a "dynamic worldwide force in telecommunications products and services." Both sides had been stable places to work, with clear career paths, ample fringe benefits and a value on long-term employment. The merger abruptly threw employees into the harsh realities of 21st century working life – in particular, a workplace characterized by continuous discontinuous change. They endured a diplomatic but conflict-aversive CEO who couldn't build teamwork at the top of the organization nor push integration through it and then attempted two languid restructurings before being ousted by the Board in 2004.

The new CEO, showing his Board he was a man of action, overhauled the company strategy and downsized the organization in each of the next three years. Then, in 2008, he announced the acquisition of a major U. S.-based competitor. Since the deal was founded on a sound strategy – EuroTel had never fared well in the North American market and this was an opportunity get a foothold in it – and most likely meant that EuroTel itself would not be taken over in an anticipated industry consolidation, the CEO fully expected it to be warmly received by his workforce as a bold and "game changing" move. Instead, EuroTel employees – who had survived three waves of downsizing, two restructurings and a new CEO within five years – reeled when they heard of their leader's intention to take over a major U. S. competitor and then eliminate redundant jobs.

---

36 While the details of the case are factual, the name of the organization has been changed at its request.

While prepared for some criticism of what was now the fourth downsizing in as many years, the CEO was overwhelmed by the persistence of employee upset. He eventually asked that focus group interviews be conducted to more fully understand employee viewpoints. The findings revealed a diverse set of barriers to a smooth combination. Some were forces within EuroTel itself, such as the "us versus them" dynamics still lingering from the "merger of equals" five years earlier, a sense of "burn out" from the serial downsizings, and high profile opinion leaders who kept talking about "the good old days" of longevity and loyalty. Other roadblocks pertained to the U.S. target; especially disconcerting to the Europeans was a perception that their new American partners were much more aggressive and would be highly political when competing for jobs in the combined organization.

Adding to their distress, EuroTel employees had received below industry-average compensation packages, along with promises from leadership that "better days were ahead" when people's hard work through the lean years would pay off. They were shocked upon hearing the announcement of the U. S. acquisition – asked one manager, "if the company had all this money sitting around, why didn't they pay us market salaries?" – and then stunned to learn that the head of Sales from the acquired firm was selected to be President of the Sales function in the combined company. "Who bought who here?" asked a EuroTel Sales director when the President announced his intention to downsize the lead company's Sales staff and integrate it into the acquired company's structure.

One of President's first actions was to tour the European partner's Sales offices. Staff had high hopes for the meetings, figuring this was their chance to share perspectives on the business and perhaps lobby for themselves with their new leader before he announced the new Sales organization. The highs turned to lows, however, as manager after manager reported that the American President completely dominated the meetings and "laid down the law that he was in charge, that what he said goes and, if anyone didn't like it, he would be happy to show them the door." Despite a consistent barrage of complaints about the President's style and intentions, the CEO stood by his selection and asked him to work with a consultant who could coach him on the post-merger integration and team building process. When the President refused the offer, the CEO reversed his course and showed him the door.

Shortly after, the CEO asked the chief executive of the acquired U. S. company – who was planning to retire – to stay on as acting President of the combined Sales organization for no more than twelve months.

Employees from both sides applauded the move. The acquired Americans felt they had a well placed executive looking out for them in the combined organization and people from the buyer were happy to have someone viewed as a consensus builder leading Sales. Still, a huge organization building task remained – the two companies had been bitter competitors, they had widely different cultures, and the false start of Sales President reinforced employee sentiments that their leadership was inept at managing major organizational transitions. Most critical, however, was the reality that EuroTel veterans were still licking their wounds from five years of transition turmoil.

References

Marks, Mitchell Lee and Mirvis, Philip H., *Joining Forces: Making One Plus One Equal Three in Mergers, Acquisitions, and Alliances* (2nd edition), San Francisco: Jossey-Bass Publishers, 2010.

Marks, Mitchell Lee, *Charging Back Up the Hill: Workplace Recovery after Mergers, Acquisitions, and Downsizings*, San Francisco: Jossey-Bass Publishers, 2003.

Discussion

1. The payoffs are considerable when leaders are skilled at leading change. However, the costs are also considerable when leaders do not understand how to lead change. Using this case as an example, what were the costs of ineffective change leadership?

2. After reading the case what lessons did you learn about how not to lead change?

3. What could the CEO do to re-build trust and get employees to feel more like "architects of change" rather than "victims of change"?

4. If you were a consultant retained by the CEO to coach the CEO on how to successfully deal with existing issues and build the two former competitors into one successful company, what kind of process would you recommend?

5. Ideally, what should the CEO and board look for in hiring a new President of the merged companies who would have a high probability of being able to build one healthy, high performance company and effectively lead the change process?

Key Lessons In Leading Change

1. Transitions – even when for the better – are difficult events for organizations and their members.

2. Employees need to let go of the old before they can accept the new.

3. The earliest days of the transition – when the organizations and people are relatively unfrozen – provide the best opportunities for leaders to begin the process of culture change.

4. Leaders pay now or pay later in transition management – they pay now by moving carefully and avoiding or minimizing missteps or they pay later by moving quickly and then dealing with the consequences of major mistakes.

5. It is difficult to run a business while managing a transition – executives need the full support of their leadership team.

BIOGRAPHY

Mitchell Lee Marks is an organizational psychologist, a member of the faculty in the College of Business at San Francisco State University, and president of the consulting firm JoiningForces. org. He is an internationally recognized expert on managing organizational transitions (including mergers, acquisitions, alliances, downsizings, and restructurings), corporate culture, and executive teambuilding. He is the author of six books, most recently the revised second edition of *Joining Forces: Making One Plus One Equal Three in Mergers, Acquisitions and Alliances* (co-authored with Philip. H. Mirvis). He is the author of several articles on leadership, organizational change, and organizational behavior in scholarly and practitioner journals including *MIT Sloan Management Review, Human Resource Management, Journal of Applied Psychology, Academy of Management Executive,* and *Journal of Organizational Change Management.* He is a frequent speaker to professional and scientific groups and is the recipient of the *Outstanding Scholarly Contribution to Organizational Behavior* award from the Academy of Management.

Mitchell Lee Marks, Ph.D.
College of Business
San Francisco State University, San Francisco, CA 94132 USA
(415) 436-9066
President, JoiningForces.org
Email: marks@sfsu.edu

.

18

Improving Customer Care Experience: A Case Study of a Large Private Hospital in Dhaka, Bangladesh

William J. Rothwell & Sohel M. Imroz

Major Focus Of The Case

This case study involves a large private hospital in Dhaka, Bangladesh, which used frequent, effective feedback and positive employee recognition to successfully change the way employees in its customer service department interacted with patients, doctors, nurses, and other hospital staff to improve the customer care experience.

Two important lessons may be learned in this case. First, one of the key responsibilities of a manager is to maximize employee performance so that they become conscious of their full potential. Managers need to play an active role in handling employee performance and development. One way to achieve this is through the delivery of frequent and effective feedback. Second, to paraphrase the best-selling authors of *The Leadership Challenge* – James Kouzes and Barry Posner – managers must tap into the hearts and minds of their employees, not merely their hands and wallets. Managers can achieve this by truly recognizing their employees. Positive employee recognition can be achieved via various means such as monetary awards, written communications, attention from senior management, etc.

This case study showed that the combined result of frequent, effective feedback and positive employee recognition was a team of motivated employees willing to do a better job to satisfy the needs of patients and hospital staff. Satisfied hospital staff provided better health care to patients, and patients in return chose the hospital for their health care needs. This cycle increased the hospital's profitability and success, making it one of the most prominent health care facilities in the country.

Introduction

The focus of this case study is how to improve the customer care experience by providing employees with effective feedback and by awarding and recognizing them for their performance. The case is organized into the following sections: (1) case background; (2) forecasting customer care needs; (3) effective feedback process; (4) employee recognition process; and (5) program results.

Case Background

The LPH Hospital – a fictitious name for a well-known private hospital in Dhaka, Bangladesh – faced several problems. A newspaper article published in early 2006 reported long wait times during patient check-in, unfriendly staff and professionals, and frequent altercations between patient parties and hospital staffs during patient check-out. The veracity of this report was further confirmed by an internal investigation that revealed inconsistent performances by customer care employees when answering patient inquiries about cost, procedures, policies, and available services. The internal investigation also found that these employees became agitated, defensive, and sometimes rude when confronted by patient parties about these discrepancies.

The LPH Hospital faced serious criticism from people at all social levels; its reputation took a heavy blow after the appearance of the newspaper report. While answering journalists' questions at a press conference, the hospital president personally assured the public that senior hospital executives would take immediate corrective actions to improve the situation. At first, however, there was a great deal of disagreement among senior executives about what needed to be done and who would be in charge.

One hospital executive suggested that the customer care department needed to be expanded from six full-time and two part-time employees to twelve full-time employees to accommodate a higher number of patients. He also suggested hiring a full-time customer care manager – a brand new position – to create new programs, policies, procedures, etc., and train and manage the newly revamped customer care department and its employees.

The hospital president took the proposal to the Board of Directors (BOD). The BOD approved it and identified improved customer care experience as a strategic goal. Two existing part-time employees were made full-time with increased salary and benefits, and four more full-time employees came on board. In addition, a new position titled "Customer Care Executive" (CCE) was created to serve as the manager of the customer service department and oversee, direct, and coordinate a full range of customer service-related programs and processes. It was also decided that the CCE would report directly to the hospital director. After three months of extensive recruiting efforts, Ms. Bizlee Khatun (also a fictitious name) was finally hired in May 2006 as the new customer care executive at the LPH Hospital.

Forecasting Customer Care Needs

The first step for Ms. Khatun was to clarify the existing needs of customer care department employees, particularly focusing on the patient check-in and discharge processes and identifying the root causes of less-than-supportive customer service levels. She met each employee one-on-one and listened to their stories, experiences, expectations, and concerns. After several weeks of meetings and personal observations, Ms. Khatun identified several problems. First, formal job descriptions did not clearly specify the roles and responsibilities of customer service employees. Second, employees seldom received any feedback from their managers about their job performance. Although employees had annual performance reviews, they were not very structured and often did not contain formative feedback identifying areas of improvement. Third, employees were unmotivated because they were rarely recognized or rewarded by senior hospital staff. "The upper management just doesn't care about us" was the typical comment offered by these employees.

Ms. Khatun immediately instituted two valuable yet rarely used processes in her department to improve customer service level. First, employees began to receive frequent and effective feedback from the manager, hospital director, and other senior hospital staff. Second, employees began to be recognized and rewarded for superior performance. Ms. Khatun formally enacted effective feedback and employee recognition processes. These are discussed in more detail in the following sections.

Effective Feedback Process

Effective feedback is an integral part of a healthy work environment. Feedback reinforces positive work performance and enables employees to improve when required. In Ms. Khatun's experience, most managers provided either praise or criticism to employees. But she believed that employees also needed feedback on both their successes and areas needing improvement. Therefore, her feedback process contained two types of feedback: motivational and formative.

Motivational and Formative Feedback

In motivational-type feedback, Ms. Khatun met with employees to discuss what they did well and encouraged them to repeat a good performance more often. She found this type of feedback to be confidence-boosting for the employees. In formative-type feedback, she told employees what could be done better the next time to improve their performance and productivity. This type of feedback was competence-boosting for employees.

Ms. Khatun believed that both types of feedback were equally important, and that the feedback needed to be provided with regularity and sincerity. The process of providing effective feedback to her employees included two major steps: (1) identification of the observed task, action, activity, or performance (a.k.a. incident) requiring feedback, and (2) delivery of the actual feedback.

Identification of Incident. The first step in the effective feedback process adopted by Ms. Khatun was to identify the incident that was problematic or praiseworthy. This step included identifying the details of the incident – such as nature, severity, and importance. The past work history of the employee was taken into account, and all relevant data and documentation were gathered.

Feedback Delivery. The second step consisted of providing the actual feedback to the employee. The most useful method was to meet the employee in person as soon as possible to discuss the incident. Ms. Khatun always ensured employee privacy when required, and allotted adequate time to discuss the incident. She found that effective listening skills were invaluable during these meetings and discussion sessions.

Depending on the type and severity of the incident, Ms. Khatun described its importance and clearly communicated her expectations to the employee. If the employee needed immediate performance improvement, Ms. Khatun not only stated this requirement but also supported the employee with the necessary tools, resources, and training opportunities. She made sure employees had an opportunity to tell their side of the story and encouraged them to provide suggestions and input for potential solutions.

Improvement plans and corrective actions were mutually agreed-to by Ms. Khatun and the employee. In addition, Ms. Khatun preferred to clearly specify the consequences of not rectifying a problematic incident within a specific period, summarize meeting notes in writing, give a copy of the summary to the employee, and keep a record in the employee's file for future reference. She found that employees really appreciated frequent feedback with balanced positive and constructive views from her and senior hospital staff.

Employee Recognition Process

Ms. Khatun firmly believed that effectively rewarding and recognizing customer care employees created a positive working environment that encouraged success. The employee recognition process is illustrated in *Figure 1.*

Figure 1: **EMPLOYEE RECOGNITION PROCESS**

Define Responsibilities, Goals and Objectives

Ms. Khatun's employee recognition process involved clearly defining the responsibilities, goals, and objectives of customer care employees and making sure that they were understood and agreed-to by team members and senior management. Primary responsibilities included correctly answering patient inquiries about cost, procedures, policies, and available services, courteously dealing with customer complaints, professionally maintaining a liaison relationship between patients and insurance companies, and effectively facilitating communication among patients, medical staff (doctors, consultants, nurses, etc.) and administrative staff (food, housekeeping, etc.). Secondary responsibilities included providing patient referrals, distributing paperwork, and making collection calls for due bills, and other administrative duties such as filing, data entry, etc.

By clearly defining responsibilities, Ms. Khatun communicated senior management's expectations of customer care employees, and provided a better understanding of the value of their services and where they fit within the big picture. Furthermore, clearly defined responsibilities, goals, and objectives enabled the customer care department to figure out what types of skills, experiences, and qualifications were going to be required of new employees or would be found on job postings available to internal applicants.

Ms. Khatun understood that to be successful, the recognition process needed to focus on employee accomplishments and behaviors that add value to the hospital. She believed that recognizing any behavior unrelated or detrimental to the hospital's mission could render the recognition process ineffective. The following factors were agreed-upon by the team members and senior hospital staff as being supportive to organizational mission and value: patient safety; long-term employment, positive attitudes, excellent customer service, dependability and punctuality, leadership and initiative, highly skilled employees, and team players. These factors were incorporated into the employee recognition process and were deemed recognition-worthy.

Develop a Budget

The next step was to develop a reliable budget plan, which needed to be approved by senior management before carrying out the employee recognition process. Ms. Khatun believed that a reliable budget plan helps an organization spend money wisely while minimizing debt. She found the following considerations useful in developing the budget: (1) time spent in designing and implementing the process; (2) time spent in presenting the award; (3) dollar value of the award and recognition items given; (4) time and cost of training employees; and (5) miscellaneous costs – such as promotional, administrative, food and beverage, etc.

Establish Guidelines

In order to reward customer care employees for outstanding performance and to improve the customer service level, Ms. Khatun initiated "Employee of the Month" – a formal award and recognition program. Recognition program guidelines were designed to ensure that the employee nomination and selection steps were performed in a fair and consistent manner. The guidelines included incentives, eligibility requirements, selection criteria, and selection process of the award recipients. Employees could be nominated for the award by their peers, managers, or senior hospital staff. With guidelines in place, customer care employees were more comfortable knowing that each nominee would be thoroughly reviewed by the customer care executive and the hospital director, and that the award would be given to the most-deserving candidate every month. Employee of the Month became the most coveted award at the hospital. The monthly award ceremony had hospital-wide visibility and was attended by most of the senior hospital executives.

In addition to the monthly awards, additional guidelines were also created to formally recognize employees during one-on-one meetings with their manager, or in front of the entire customer care department.

The key objective was to ensure that employees were recognized regularly and sincerely.

Select the Award

Ms. Khatun put a lot of thought into choosing the appropriate award for her employees. She knew that money was not the top motivator. Instead, employees valued personal thanks or a letter of praise from senior hospital staff as more motivating and encouraging. This observation led Ms. Khatun to the conclusion that awards should have value and meaning to the employee – otherwise, the entire recognition process would be fruitless. She realized that it would be easy to recognize employees and give awards, but much more difficult to reap the full benefits of the awards. Although employees can be awarded something as simple as verbal or written praise or as extensive as tangible gifts or money, the full benefits of awards can only be achieved when they are sincere, meaningful, relevant, and timely.

Present the Award

Ms. Khatun sought to ensure that the presentation of the award and recognition were laudable and worthy of the recognition being afforded to the employee. Awards and recognitions were presented in formal and informal ways. Formal ways included one-on-one meetings between employees and their managers, department-wide weekly meetings, and company-wide monthly Employee of the Month meetings. Awards presented formally typically included moderate- or high-cost recognition items such as company shirt or cup, books, gift certificates, cash, various household accessories, group lunch at nearby popular restaurants, office party, etc.

Informal recognition was spontaneous and as simple as walking by employees and personally saying "thank you", "good job", etc., and commenting on how much managers and senior hospital staff appreciated their hard work and dedication. Other informal methods of employee recognition included little- or no-cost activities such as presenting a certificate or plaque, flowers, movie tickets, letter of recommendation from the hospital director or even the president, posting the employee's name and photo on the hospital bulletin board, etc.

Program Results

After four years of dedicated efforts from customer care employees, managers, the hospital director, and other senior hospital executives, the employee feedback and recognition programs were hailed as successes by people inside and outside the hospital. The latest survey indicated the average patient satisfaction rating of "satisfied" compared to "very unsatisfied" four years ago, according to a five-point Likert scale (very unsatisfied, unsatisfied, neutral, satisfied, very satisfied). The employee retention rate increased by more than 80% during this time. The current LPH customer care department is now considered among the most elite and respected within the private hospital healthcare community in Dhaka; LPH customer care employees frequently receive job offers from other hospitals with higher salaries, perks, and benefits. Despite increased competition among private hospitals, the high rate of retention of customer care employees at the LPH Hospital has been promising. Beginning in 2011, new activities and programs were being developed to increase the patient satisfaction level to "very satisfied" within the next three years. If past experience is any indication of future success, LPH employees, managers, and senior staff are confident that they will achieve the goal slowly, but surely.

Discussion Questions

1. Behavior and performance in organizations can be significantly changed by providing positive leadership, a positive work environment, helpful feedback, and positive recognition. Describe the Customer Service Department before the new manager was brought in and after the new manager implemented changes in the work environment.

2. The first step in the change process was to gain the support of top level leadership and the board for change. Why is top level support important to the change process?

3. Ms. Khatun began the change process in the new Customer Service Department by assessing the present situation before making changes. Why is this an important step in the change process and what did she find out?

4. Describe what Ms. Khatun did to change the feedback and recognition processes and the impact this had on employees. What did you like and what would you change about the approach she took? Why do you think the changes were a success?

5. Change efforts can fail to achieve the desired results if employees are not properly valued and recognized for their efforts. What considerations should leaders make in using employee recognition, awards, and rewards in motivating change?

6. What are some insights you gained about leading and sustaining change efforts and what would you do to take customer service to the highest level?

Key Lessons In Leading Change

1. Providing positive leadership, a positive work environment, helpful feedback, and positive recognition are all essential to leading change and changing behavior and performance.

2. Change efforts are unlikely to be successful without the involvement of those who need to support the change and those who are most affected by the change.

3. It is important for change leaders to create opportunities for employees to offer candid suggestions and honest opinions and feedback for change to be successful and leaders to be in touch with the realities of what is working and not working.

4. Both motivational and formative feedback is necessary in leading change. Motivational feedback builds employee confidence and formative feedback builds employee competence.

5. Employee recognition is important in helping employees stay motivated and feel valued during the change process. It is also important to get wise counsel about how to recognize employees and to assure that recognition is sincere, meaningful, relevant, and timely.

6. Failure to understand what motivates employees and how they are experiencing changes can negatively affect change efforts. The incentive to change has to be greater than the incentive to stay the same for employees to stay motivated at a high level.

7. Leaders must have excellent listening skills to lead a change process. It can be helpful to work with coaches to develop listening and other change skills and these skills will become increasingly important in times of dynamic change.

BIOGRAPHY

William J. Rothwell, Ph.D., SPHR, is a Professor at Penn State University Park Campus. He leads the graduate emphasis in Training/Organization Development. Before arriving at Penn State in 1993, he was an HR professional for nearly 20 years and headed up HR efforts in a state government agency and then led a comprehensive Management Development program at a large insurance company. In addition to serving as a professor, he is also President of Rothwell & Associates, Inc., a consulting firm. He has authored, coauthored, edited, or co edited over 300 books, book chapters, and articles – including 68 books. His most recent books are *Invaluable Knowledge* (Amacom, 2011), *Effective Succession Planning*, 4th ed. (Amacom, 2010) and *Practicing Organization Development*, 3rd ed (Pfeiffer, 2010). In 1999, he published *Developing In-House Leadership and Management Development Programs: Their Creation, Management, and Continuous Improvement* (Greenwood Press).

William J. Rothwell, Ph.D., SPHR
Professor, Department of Learning & Performance Systems
310B Keller Building, University Park, PA 16802
Tel. 814-863-2581 · Fax: 814-863-7532 · Email: wjr9@psu.edu

BIOGRAPHY

Sohel M. Imroz is a Ph.D. candidate in the Workforce Education and Development (WF ED) program in the Department of Learning & Performance Systems (LPS) at Penn State University Park Campus. He holds a Master's degree in Management Information Systems, an MBA, and a Bachelor's degree in Computer Science. His research interests include leadership development, talent management, succession planning, organization development, and corporate culture. He is also a certified ITIL® (Information Technology Infrastructure Library) professional.

Sohel M. Imroz, Ph.D. Candidate
Department of Learning & Performance Systems
Pennsylvania State University, University Park, PA 16802
Tel. 402-547-7763 · Email: sxi5021@psu.edu

19

Managing Change In A High School

Neil Cranston

Jane Kelly was appointed to Happy Vale High School 6 months ago, a school with a history of success, but one that showed signs of decline. The teachers were of the view that the school had not received the kind of leadership and support it needed. The local community was also losing faith in the school.

Jane needed to re-engage the teachers and community in the school and in so doing, lead strategic change on what she perceived as many potentially unwilling participants. This case study describes how Jane embarked on a change journey for Happy Vale High School.

Happy Vale High School is located in a mid-size regional city, in an area which used to be predominantly professional middle-class in make-up. Recent changes in the area had seen a shift in socio-economic demographics, with a large influx of students from non English speaking backgrounds. Many of the staff were showing signs of being unable to cope with these "different" students and expressed a desire to return to the "good old days".

A decade or so ago, Happy Vale had been seen as relatively innovative, and very successful in achieving high outcomes for its students. Now, some staff blamed the administration for enrolling too many students with learning difficulties because of their backgrounds. Jane, as the new principal, also inherited a school leadership team that seems to lack ideas as to how to work with the teachers in the new and changing environment – they too, like many teachers, long for the good old days of certainty and stability.

The school physically was also in decline. While it has invested heavily in technology in recent years, in response to staff and parent demands for curriculum modernisation, the result was little investment in improving the buildings and grounds. The school finances were not healthy, with the school committed to a number of IT leases which tied school funds well into the future.

Understandably, there were low levels of community satisfaction with the school. Standards were dropping, and the school was in a state of limbo. Jane was young, energetic and a committed professional. She was not going to accept that what she inherited at Happy Vale was the way it had to be. She set out to make changes – and she saw these changes deeply embedded in the learning and well being of the students. The school had to change. The teachers had to change!

The Need for Major Cultural Change

Jane knew that this meant major cultural changes. Initially, she could not see how to achieve such a significant change within a realistic time frame. While she remained positive and forward-looking, even her optimism had its limits as she understood one could not impose the sorts of changes needed on the school too quickly. But there was not time to stagnate, as the students were suffering and unless something was done, the school may well close.

Preparing the Organization For Change

In preparing the school for change, Jane started to spend almost all her days wandering around the school trying to engage with staff and any parents who were visiting.. Several staff openly showed their scepticism when she had suggested a survey of student views about what they might like to see change in the school. Open forums with parents also were met with a lack of enthusiasm. One parent accused Jane of being 'anti-intellectual' when she talked about inclusive educational practices which valued all young people wanting to achieve an education.

Moving Forward

Not all change decisions can be made by consensus. Sometimes leaders simply have to lead and make unpopular decisions. Jane decided that despite a lack of enthusiasm by many, she would embark on what she called an "audit" of the school, both to see where it was at now, as well as identifying some strategic goals for the future. Not surprisingly, staff could not have been less interested in such a process. However, she identified a small group of teachers who had shown some enthusiasm for change – with this group, she explored different ideas about how to start a strategic planning process for the school. How could they get staff to look honestly at where the school was now? How could they overcome the cultural resistance to thinking seriously about the future? How could they engage people in planning, when they seemed so negative about the school?

Jane continued having informal chats with staff to get to know them, identify the roles they played in the school, and work out what the blockages to involvement might be. She also emphasised that she was in the school for the long haul and that she committed to change. She would not give up and it became clear to all that "this woman is for real" as one staff member commented.

Appointing a Steering Committee to Guide the Change Process

To help guide the change process, Jane set up a steering committee of volunteers to oversee the strategic planning process, ensuring that the committee included some of those who were positive about change. She chose to have a diverse group to reflect the range of stakeholders of the school, including staff and some parents and students. She wanted this group to be the core of the process, and to feel empowered. She began their involvement with a dinner and meeting, intending to help them establish strong, cooperative relationships and a strong sense of common purpose.

Engaging an External Consultant

The committee realised that staff and parents needed some objective data as to where the school was at. To establish this, an external reviewer with extensive and respected experience in education was engaged to collect and advise on currently available school data. The reviewer was also asked to conduct interviews with students from all year levels, teaching staff, support staff, administrators, the registrar, parents, community members. Jane insisted on this comprehensive first step for two reasons. Firstly, it would establish a robust information database for future decision-making, and should help resolve disagreements about the current situation in the school. Secondly, it would ensure that all key players had a chance to express their views, and so clearly demonstrate her commitment to universal engagement in the process.

Planning and Holding a Collaborative Forum to Engage Stakeholders

Jane planned to share the findings on the reviewer's findings at an open forum of teachers students and parents. She knew this was a high risk strategy, but believed open sharing of information was vital if teachers especially were to critically reflect on what was really happening (or not happening) in the school.

The forum was carefully planned such that participants were able to interact freely and to develop a respect and understanding of differing views. Jane believed the night provided an opportunity to model the behaviour that she wanted to instil within the school: an openness to discuss big ideas, an opportunity to challenge, and a commitment to working together.

Jane was delighted when the atmosphere on the evening was positive and challenging. People who had rarely spoken to each other engaged in vigorous debate, many for the first time. Some of the more reluctant staff participants could be seen in lively exchanges with parents. There was finally a process to get teachers, students and parents talking about positive aspects of education and what Happy Vale had to offer, rather than always focusing on the negatives.

Next Steps

Following the evening, a summary of outcomes was collated and then shared on the school website. A discussion blog was set up to encourage further debate. The steering committee considered the comments across the next week or so then developed: **(1) a working statement summarising achievements; and (2) goals for the future.**

Jane felt she was finally getting somewhere. While the statement was a tangible outcome of the process, she knew that what really counted were the new working relationships and enhanced respect in the school community: the first tentative steps towards a new culture in the school. Once momentum for change has been gained, change can be propelled forward or quickly lost depending on next steps. Now Jane was contemplating what needed to happen next to keep the momentum going and make needed changes.

Questions/Discussion Issues

1. Change leaders often find difficult and challenging situations to overcome in accomplishing what they think is possible. Discuss the challenges Jane faced and the forces she had working for her and the forces she had working against her.

2. It is important for change leaders to prepare organizations for change, build at least some support for change, and to identify and involve key stakeholders. What did Jane do to start building at least some interest and support for change and who are the key stakeholders she needed to involve and engage to make change possible?

3. In leading change it is often helpful for leaders to establish a change team (steering committee, guiding coalition etc.) made up of at least one senior leader and other respected and representative team members who will help plan and guide the change process. What should be the role of the steering committee that Jane organized and what should be the criteria for being on the committee?

4. It is often helpful to involve external expertise to help plan, guide, and facilitate the change process and work with a change team. What are the advantages and disadvantages of involving an outside consultant and what should you look for in retaining a consultant?

5. Now that Jane has built momentum for change and has a steering committee to guide the change process, what could she and the steering committee do in the next year to keep the momentum going and help build a successful school?

Key Lessons In Leading Change

1. Change leaders need to have a vision for what is possible and commitment to excellence and not settling for the status quo.

2. Change does not just happen. It needs to be well thought out and planned.

3. Change leaders need to understand the people and culture of the change context. Data driven decision-making can alleviate negative influences based on myth.

4. There are times when change leaders need to be bold and move forward even if there isn't a consensus to do so.

5. Change is not a singular activity and it cannot be done just by 'the leader'. Change needs to engage the staff so they own the change and become active participants in the change process.

6. Change is an on-going process the requires energy, vision and a lasting drive if it is to be sustainable in the longer term

BIOGRAPHY

Dr. Neil Cranston is Professor in Educational Leadership and Curriculum in the Faculty of Education, University of Tasmania. He researches, teachers and writes in the area of educational change and leadership and is the co-author of two books on leadership and many journal articles.

Dr. Cranston can be reached at: Neil.Cranston@utas.edu.au.

20

Despardi's Dilemma: Building Collaborative Relationships in the Extended Manufacturing Enterprise

David Coghlan & Paul Coughlan

Major Focus Of The Case

This case takes executive leadership beyond the boundary of an individual company into the extended manufacturing enterprise. It explores the dilemma of a purchasing manager of the system integrator who was confronted with a serious operational issue that lay within a supplier firm, i.e. outside of his own authority, and his desire to build a collaborative strategic relationship with that firm. The focus of the case, therefore, is where a leader does not have the direct authority over another company.

Introduction

Alfredo Despardi, the Chief Purchasing Manager with *ConTromo* parked his car and headed across the *PumpCo* car park. He was due to meet Marc Boudel, the owner-manager of *PumpCo*, one of his key suppliers. He wondered still what approach to take. A quality issue persisted with a plastic insert - a low cost, high volume component part. The defective component melted in service and the subsequent collapse of the control systems had severe knock-on effects for end-users. Despardi did not want to penalize *PumpCo* for poor performance. Instead, he could initiate a collaborative improvement initiative with *PumpCo* in order to tackle the issue and in doing so transform their relationship.

ConTromo specialized in manufacturing and assembling 'motion control' systems for different automotive and truck niche markets. *PumpCo*, a medium-sized firm with approximately 200 employees, delivered pump components to *ConTromo*. Within the automotive and truck industry the order winning criterion was price, whereas quality, delivery and technology were order qualifiers. Therefore, firms within these industries needed to monitor constantly the cost-structure throughout the supply chain in order to remain competitive.

The Critical Role of Collaborative Relationships and Teamwork

The competitive structure of the automotive and truck industry had some clear characteristics:

- Hierarchy in the market
- Strong distinction between part suppliers and system suppliers
- Economies of scale
- Focus on competitive pricing and quality products

Collaborative supply relationships were of strategic significance to firms competing in this industry. A system integrator, like *ConTromo*, needed suppliers that could apply strategic operations improvement with a strong focus on cost, quality and delivery. From this perspective, it would be essential for *ConTromo* to look for long term, involved, and dedicated partners that supported its business ambition. As such, in order to guarantee maximum use of supplier knowledge to increase efficiency, to improve quality and to reduce time to markets, closer collaboration with a limited number of suppliers would be needed. Yet, the quality problem with the insert needed to be solved immediately and might not tolerate the longer time to develop a more collaborative relationship.

The Challenge Despardi Faced

Despardi had a deep understanding of the contributors to quality-based competitiveness and was familiar with the practice of the classic Deming cycle: This well-established cycle of action and reflection in the area of quality management was central to many prior quality improvement projects. However, Despardi had become aware of the potential to deepen his understanding of that cycle in terms of the learning potential – beyond single-loop - and also the ways in which that potential might be realized in active and open collaboration between *ConTromo*, as system integrator, and its other suppliers.

As Chief Purchasing Manager, Despardi was well aware of the constraining and enabling potential of contractual relationships for supply and, in particular, how a contractual relationship both enabled and constrained the development of collaboration. An understanding of technologies and markets, shared between *ConTromo* and its suppliers, enabled a keen awareness of the critical nature of quality-related issues and their technical origins. He was aware also of how the shared, but unstated, understanding of the power balance in the contractual supply relationship constrained openness on critical intellectual property, the associated cost implications and the inter-organizational origins of quality issues.

ConTromo and *PumpCo* had collaborated intensively over a number of years. Despardi knew Boudel well. Both firms perceived their relationship as close, trustworthy and of strategic importance. For *ConTromo*, the importance of the relationship stemmed from its dependence on a specific component produced by *PumpCo*. For its part, *PumpCo* valued *ConTromo* as a customer. They had met frequently, shared improvement goals, and had clear plans for exchanging information. Over time, they had learned from each other with regard to operational and strategic issues. Recently, Despardi and Boudel had expressed a desire to develop a long-term dimension to the relationship between their firms. They expected strategic as well as operational benefits from engaging in further collaborative strategic improvement initiatives.

The Melting Insert

Over the preceding four years, a quality issue had persisted with a plastic insert - a low cost, high volume component part – manufactured and delivered by *PumpCo* to *ConTromo*. The issue originated during the injection molding process when vacuum bubbles occurred as a result of material shrinkage during the production process. In spite of many attempts acting alone, *PumpCo* had not been able to optimize its manufacturing process technically. Further, in spite of quality inspections and a high resulting internal scrap rate, a proportion of the inserts delivered to *ConTromo* for assembly into its control systems were still defective. The defective components melted in service and the subsequent collapse of the control systems had severe knock-on effects for end-users. In response, *PumpCo* initiated extra incoming quality checks which still did not address the issue. *PumpCo* faced the real possibility of claims for financial reimbursement from *ConTromo* in relation to these checks and the costs of failure.

Preparing for the Meeting with Boudel

As Despardi prepared for his meeting with Boudel, he was clear - he had to resolve the quality issue so as not to lose business. However, he faced a dilemma. On the one hand, he could penalize *PumpCo* for its poor performance and begin the process of finding an alternate supplier. On the other hand, he could try to build on the good relationship between the two firms and generate a collaborative approach to resolving the issue. At the core of this dilemma was that he could not guarantee that the collaborative relationship would resolve the quality issue in time.

Suggested Readings

Coghlan, D. and Rashford, N.S. (2006). *Organizational Change and Strategy: An Interlevel Dynamics Approach.* Abingdon, UK/New York: Routledge.

Coughlan, P and Coghlan, D. (2011). *Collaborative Strategic Improvement through Network Action Learning.* Cheltenham, UK/NewYork: Edward Elgar.

Slack, N. and Lewis, M. (2008). *Operations Strategy,* 2nd Edition, Harlow: Pearson Education.

Discussion

1. What is the dilemma that Despardi faces and what is at stake?
2. To what extent does his response to this dilemma impact on his survival as a leader?
3. How might he exercise his leadership in relation to *PumpCo*, an independent owner-managed firm on which he depends?
4. Effective leaders are skilled at collaborative leadership. What is your understanding of collaborative leadership, what are some of the payoffs, and how did Despardi use collaborative leadership in this case?
5. What are the implications of collaborative leadership for senior executives managing within a network of firms, where an executive does not have direct authority over what happens in another firm?

Key Lessons In Leading Change

1. Building collaborative relationships and teamwork is an important leadership skill in addressing issues and leading change.
2. Leaders face choices and trade-offs. They have to deal with both task and relational issues. Further, while they may focus on longer term and strategic issues, they are never far from the shorter term and operational issues. In dealing with these choices and tradeoffs, they need both to maintain control of the strategic and operational agenda and, in building and maintaining collaborative inter-organizational relationships, to be open to how these relationships generate new ideas and actions.
3. Peer interaction and influencing is a feature of relationships within and between firms. Leaders are not always in a position where they can decide and command action. They, therefore, need to be able to build collaborative relationships with leaders of other organizations and to be skilled at listening to their ideas, anticipating their concerns, and exerting influence as appropriate.
4. Firms may establish their network relationships as strategic, where the primary goals are economic, such as cost-reduction and supply chain efficiency. For longer term competitiveness, they may aspire to building a network relationship that extends beyond the strategic and which transitions to becoming a learning network.

BIOGRAPHY

David Coghlan is Professor of Organization Development at the School of Business, Trinity College Dublin, Ireland and is a Fellow of the College. He specializes in organization development and action research and is active in both communities internationally. Recent co-authored books include: Organization Change and Strategy (Routledge, 2006), *Doing Action Research in Your Own Organization* (3rd. edition, Sage, 2010) and co-editor of the four volume set, *The Fundamentals of Organization Development* (Sage, 2010).

David Coghlan
School of Business,
Trinity College, Dublin 2. Ireland
Ph. + + 353 1 8962323
Fax+ +3531 6799503
Email: dcoghlan@tcd.ie

BIOGRAPHY

Paul Coughlan is Professor of Operations Management at the School of Business, Trinity College Dublin, Ireland. His research interests include continuous improvement of manufacturing and product development practices, services innovation, action learning, action research, and commercialization of university research. He and David Coghlan have written *Collaborative Strategic Improvement through Network Action Learning*. (Edward Elgar, 2011).

Paul Coughlan
School of Business
Trinity College, Dublin 2. Ireland
Ph. + + 353 1 8962327
Fax + + 3531 6799503
Email: coughlnp@tcd.ie

CHAPTER FIVE

21

The Fundamentals Of Building High Performance Teams

D.D. Warrick

Major Focus Of The Case

The ability to build high performance teams and teamwork throughout an organization and the willingness to make the changes necessary to achieve a high level of team performance and teamwork may literally decide the fate of many organizations. Organizations that have teamwork at the top, within teams, and between teams have a significant competitive advantage. Unfortunately, though the need is great and the potential payoffs substantial, few organizations train leaders how to build high performance teams or do anything to build teamwork throughout the organization.

This case presents some fundamentals for building high performance teams and applies the fundamentals to helping change a dysfunctional top leadership team to a high performing team. The case is not intended to assume that there is a formula for building high performance teams so much as to present principles that can be adapted to the unique needs of teams. Actual names and places and specifics about the organization involved are not used so the focus can be on the fundamentals. The organization will simply be called Organization A and the team at the top that was involved will be called the Leadership Team.

Introduction

Virtually everyone believes in teamwork and leaders at all levels often preach teamwork. Effective teamwork has the potential to improve performance within and between teams, morale, cooperation, coordination, innovation, communications, the quality of decision making, the speed of getting things done, greater unity of purpose and commitment to carrying out plans, and even retention (McShane and Von Glinow, 2010). Many books and articles have been written about the many benefits of teamwork and the costs when teamwork is lacking (for example see Hellriegel and

Slocum, 2011, Katzenback and Smith, 1993, LaFasto and Larson, 2001, Levi, 2011). However, while it is obvious that teamwork plays a key role in the success of organizations, athletic teams, and symphonies, few organizations outside of athletic and military teams make teamwork a high priority that is systematically developed.

To put the level of teamwork that actually occurs in an organization into perspective, choose the organization you are presently working in or one you have worked in previously or are familiar with and answer the following questions:

1. Do you believe that teamwork is essential to the long term success of the organization?
2. Does the organization excel at teamwork at the top, within teams, and between teams?
3. Do you believe that the organization values and rewards teamwork?
4. What does your organization do to train leaders how to build high performance teams and teamwork?

Six Fundamentals For Building High Performance Teams

There are a number of models for building high performance teams. The most popular model was developed by B.W. Tuckman and M.A.C. Jensen (1977). The model includes five stages of team development: (1) Forming… getting to know the team members and the team; (2) Storming…team members struggle to establish roles, norms, and goals; (3) Norming…roles, norms, and goals are established; (4) Performing…team members have learned to efficiently coordinate activities, resolve conflicts, and work together with a high level of trust; (5) Adjourning…the team is about to disband and team members shift their focus from a task to a relationship focus. While this is an excellent model, the focus is primarily on forming new teams and showing the life cycle of teams. The model presented below includes six fundamentals that can be used for building existing teams into high performance teams, helping high performance teams continue to improve, and for forming new teams.

1. **A Team Leader Committed To Building A High Performance Team.** No amount of team building will replace the need to have a team leader who is committed to building a high performance team that performs above the norm. When leaders lead, great things are possible and when they don't it creates a leadership vacuum filled with a lack of purpose, focus, and unity and unwanted and often dysfunctional dynamics that handicap the team. Effective team

leaders are skilled at providing **vision** (a clear and compelling sense of purpose and picture of what the team needs to do to succeed; **direction** (clear goals, values, and priorities); and **inspiration** (leading by example, motivating people to meet the challenge and give their best, encouraging and developing people).

2. **Capable And Committed Team Members.** It is important to have or to be developing the right players for the team to build a high performance team. **You can't have an A team with C players.** An A player is a team member who has valuable skills that contribute to the success of the team and who is a committed team player. B players can also be valuable to a team. They are developing skills needed by the team and they are committed team players. A C player is a team member who either doesn't have the right skills needed by the team and appears unwilling or unable to develop the skills and/or is not a committed team player. One ineffective or disruptive team member can handicap the whole team.

3. **Knowing Present Realities.** It is important for a team leader to have a keen sense of reality about the strengths and opportunities for improvement of the team and team members. Leaders who are out of touch with the realities of the dynamics of their teams will make decisions that may be influenced by erroneous assumptions or incomplete information. However, it is also important for the team to do periodic reality checks. If you know reality you can almost always do something about it but without reality checks, teams can develop issues that accumulate and go unresolved. Reality checks can be accomplished in formal ways by surveying and/or interviewing team members or by getting the team together to evaluate what is working best and what could be improved or changed.

4. **Team Norms That Create A High Performance Culture.** Norms are standards of behavior that begin to shape the team culture, practices, and behaviors of team members. They can be positive or negative, helpful or harmful, and can have a significant influence on the performance and health of a team. Norms can happen by design or default so it is of course important to establish them by design by agreeing on the norms and what it takes to create them. It is also important for the team to agree on what to do if team members consistently operate outside the norms so there is a process for addressing issues.

5. Structuring The Team For Results. Another essential fundamental to building a high performance team is to structure the team for results. Some of the important structural issues that should be clear and designed to make the team successful are: (1) the mission of the team; (2) the responsibilities of the team, the team leader, and the team members; (3) a few high impact, clear, and motivating goals; and (4) how and when the team will meet, share information, and make decisions; and (5) simple but meaningful measures and controls.

6. An Organized Way To Improve Team Processes And Results. Curiously, it is not unusual for teams to **never** spend time focusing on how to improve the team and the team results. High performance teams don't become high performance teams by chance. It takes regular planned efforts to evaluate and improve how the team functions and the team results.

THE CASE: Efforts To Build A Dysfunctional Top Leadership Team Into A High Performance Team

Organization A was an organization of about 100 employees that had been in existence just under 40 years. It was an organization that attracted well educated employees that were willing to work at below industry wages because they believed in the purpose of the organization. The organization had been moderately successful but ran into difficult times because of the down turn in the economy. The President had resigned and the board brought in a new charismatic President with impressive credentials in hopes of turning the organization around.

The new President had a strong reputation for being a visionary, skilled, leader who was willing to make needed changes. He came to the organization with high hopes. However, after spending two months learning as much as possible about the board, his leadership team, the organization, and prospects for the future, he found that the organization was in far worse shape financially and organizationally than he anticipated. The board was a mixed assortment of well qualified and not so well qualified members. They showed little unity as a team and did not have a strategy for the future other than bringing in a new President. The Leadership Team consisting of the President and the top five leaders in the organization could at best be considered a dysfunctional team. They were dedicated professionals on a personal level but seldom operated as a team, had no vision or strategy for the future, and did not function well as a team though some did work well with other individuals on the team. Unresolved interpersonal conflicts, a lack of trust among some of the team members, and different levels of acceptance of a new president made the culture of the team somewhat toxic. The rest of the organization was in disarray with confusion and uncertainty over the future of the organization. Employees felt over worked and under paid and had no hope or direction for the future.

Process for Preparing the Leadership Team to Lead The Way

After being President for about five months, the new President sought agreement with the Leadership Team to bring in an outside consultant to work with the team and an outside firm to help the organization grow and succeed. The proposal was met with mixed acceptance but was finally agreed to. The consultant and firm coordinated their activities to make sure they were synchronized with a common purpose.

The process that was agreed upon for developing the Leadership Team is shown in *Figure 1*. **It should be kept in mind that team building processes need to be designed to fit the unique needs, resources, and desires of a team and the internal or external expertise available to guide the process.** The fundamentals for developing high performance teams provide a framework for designing the process but each situation may have differing variables that drive the design.

It should also be noticed that the process chosen is an action oriented rather than an experiential oriented design. Team building methodology has often focused on experiential activities such as trust walks, trust falls, and outings that create an awareness of the importance of teamwork and are assumed to therefore improve teamwork and team performance. While these activities can be helpful in building camaraderie and insights about teams and teamwork, there is little evidence to support the assumption that they actually make teams more effective (Robbins and Finley, 2000). There is, however, evidence to show that action oriented team building can significantly improve teams (Anderson, 2012, Larson and LaFasto, 1989, Wheelan, 2005, Leading Teams published by the Harvard Business School Press, 2006).

Figure 1: **Developing The Leadership Team Process: August, September,**

Purpose When leaders lead and are united around a common purpose, great things are possible! Unfortunately, even the leaders who are committed to building exceptional organizations rarely commit the time and resources it takes to build a leadership team capable of leading the way to accomplishing this worthy goal. The purpose of this program is to develop a leadership team that is prepared to function as a united, focused, high performance team committed to building a special, successful, organization. It is a positive approach to change and uses the book Positive Leadership as a philosophical guide in preparing the leaders to be high impact, positive leaders.

Step 1:
Assessing Reality (August)

Step one includes a day that begins with an hour meeting with the Leadership Team to dialog about the program and what it is designed to accomplish followed by 45 minute interviews with each of the team members. The Leadership Team members will also be asked to complete an anonymous survey. The interviews and survey will focus on two parts. Part I includes an evaluation of the Leadership Team that will clearly identify the major Strengths and Opportunities for Improvement of the Leadership Team and what the Leadership Team will need to do to succeed. Part II provides an evaluation of the organization that will identify the major Strengths and Opportunities for Improvement of The organization and what it will need to do to succeed. If you know reality you can almost always do something about it.

Step 2:
Training And Preparing The Leadership Team For Change: Half Day (August)

Step two is designed to build strong commitment to the program, train the Leadership Team in the fundamentals of being a high performance top leadership team, and review and utilize the results of the assessment. This session will provide opportunities to discuss and agree on what it will take for the team to be a high performance top leadership team. A few specific actions will be identified that will need to be accomplished before the next meeting.

Step 3:
Designing The Leadership Team For Success (September)

Step three will include a review of follow-up assignments from the previous meeting and a step-by-step process to design the Leadership Team for success. Participants will be involved in establishing the vision, mission, and responsibilities of the team, team standards the team is committed to operating by, and agreeing on how the team will function and what the team needs to do to be considered highly successful. There will be follow-up responsibilities to refine what was accomplished and present it in the next meeting.

October, November

Program Design The program design includes progressive activities that are designed to move from assessing reality, to training and preparing the Leadership Team for success, to preparing the Leadership Team to lead and build a special the organization. It includes an assessment of the Leadership Team and organization and five half day sessions approximately every other week over a period of 4 months (a total of six activities) and makes it possible to option for a Follow-up Phase. The process is designed to achieve specific actions and measurable changes in the team.

Step 4:
Leadership Team
Goal Setting And
Team Member Role
Clarification (September)
Step four will include a review of follow-up assignments from the previous meeting and engaging in a process to identify a few high impact goals the Leadership Team needs to pursue as a top leadership team. The Leadership Team will also be involved in clarifying the role of each team member and how they can be successful in their job. In addition, the Leadership Team will be involved in planning ways to continue growing and developing as a team. Follow-up responsibilities will be assigned to refine the team goals and individual role descriptions.

Step 5:
Training In Building
A Special, Healthy,
High Performance
Organization (October)
Step 5 will include a review of follow-up assignments from the previous meeting followed by an exciting meeting that provides training in what the best organizations are like and involves the team in developing a model of what it will take to build the organization into a special, successful organization and what it will take to build the desired culture at the organization.

Step 6:
Leading The Way,
Evaluating Progress, And
Preparing For The Future
(November)
Step 6 will include another survey given to team members so an evaluation of progress can be made and a meeting designed to review follow-up assignments from the previous meeting followed by involving the Leadership Team in an evaluation of the survey results and identifying future actions that need to be taken to strengthen the Leadership Team and to build the organization into a successful the organization. Recommendations for engaging the organization at all levels in the change process will also be presented.

Comments About What Actually Took Place

The team building process for the Leadership Team was designed to include a **Team Assessment And Organization Assessment** and **Five Half Day Sessions** that met **Every Other Week** with the whole process taking **Four Months**. It should also be noted that the information provided for purposes of this case is a small fraction of the assessment information that was presented and of what took place. The assessment included interviews of the six team members and ratings by the six team members of both the team and the organization so the latter data could be used by the team to help change the organization. Both before and after assessments were made so progress could be evaluated. While only the highlights of the **team assessments** are shown in *Figure 2*, the actual assessment reports included:

- The Overall Average Score
- Highest And Lowest Ratings
- The Overall Average Score For Each Category Measured
- A Summary Of Major Strengths And Opportunities For Improvement Based On The Survey Results, Open Ended Questions And Interviews With The Team Members
- The Results For Each Item
- Representative Open Ended Comments For Each Open Ended Question Asked

Chapters from the book **Positive Leadership** (Cameron, 2008) were discussed by the team in the first four sessions. This book was selected because it focuses on the concept of positive leadership and how to build a positive culture, positive relationships, and use positive communications. The concepts are supported by a substantial amount of research. The book does not discourage dealing with reality and conflict but encourages doing so in a positive rather than negative way. Using the book helped the team to quickly change leadership, relationship, and communications patterns. The book along with training in leadership, team building, and interpersonal relations was helpful in learning how to dialog about sensitive issues and make difficult decisions that needed to be addressed.

Assessment information can be invaluable in quickly establishing and building a common view of reality, identifying and resolving issues, establishing goals, and providing a strong incentive for change. This was certainly the case with the Leadership Team as the data presented in the first session united the team around a strong incentive to be a united leadership team and make needed changes.

A follow-up group was assigned after each session to synthesize the information generated during the session and report back in the next session on their recommendations...what it will take for the Leadership Team to be a High Performance Team, team standards, team improvements, the team vision, mission, responsibilities, and goals, the role of the team leader and each team member, criteria for building a successful organization and successful organization culture etc. The recommendations of the follow-up groups were discussed and refined by the total team. A pattern was also established where at the beginning of each session each team member was asked to respond to the question, **what have you done to help unite and build a high performance Leadership Team and what have you seen others do?**

There are many keys to successful team building. However, the major key is the commitment and behavior of the team leader. Fortunately, the team leader was very clear and straightforward about what he wanted to accomplish. He also encouraged open dialog, was very supportive of the team members, and was willing to address difficult and sometimes controversial issues. This clearly accelerated the team building process.

Figure 2: **Leadership Team Assessment**

Leadership Team Structure	OA Aug*	OA Nov*
1. The Leadership Team Leader provides the Vision, Direction, and Inspiration needed to keep the team focused and united.	3.7	5.2
2. The Leadership Team has a clear mission.	3.3	6.0
3. The responsibilities of the Leadership Team and each Leadership Team Member are clear.	3.5	5.8
4. The Leadership Team has clear goals.	3.2	5.8
5. The Leadership Team is effectively organized to achieve the best possible results.	4.2	5.0
6. The Leadership Team does the necessary planning to be effective.	3.0	4.8
7. The Leadership Team is effective at following through on goals, projects, and commitments.	3.3	4.8
8. The Leadership Team has the necessary resources, support, and control to be successful.	3.7	4.8
9. The Leadership Team operates with minimal red tape and bureaucracy.	4.5	5.0
10. The potential of the Leadership Team and each Leadership Team Member is fully utilized.	3.0	5.2
11. The Leadership Team quickly adapts and responds to opportunities and needed changes.	3.2	5.3

*Overall Average By All Members Of Leadership Team – August   **OA AUG**
*Overall Average By All Members Of Leadership Team – November   **OA NOV**

1.0 – 1.9	2.0 – 2.9	3.0 – 3.9	4.0	4.1 – 5.0	5.1 – 6.0	6.1 – 7.0
Poor	Low	Below Average	Average	Above Average	High	Outstanding

Figure 2: **Leadership Team Assessment** continued

Leadership Team Processes	OA Aug*	OA Nov*
12. The Leadership Team Leader encourages participation and involvement.	4.8	6.0
13. All Leadership Team Members have a strong commitment to the success of the Leadership Team.	5.0	6.0
14. All Leadership Team Members are skilled and committed team players.	5.0	6.0
15. Leadership Team Members feel free to be candid and communicate openly with the Leadership Team Leader.	4.8	5.5
16. Leadership Team Members feel free to be candid and communicate openly with one another.	4.8	5.7
17. All Leadership Team Members use a style that encourages effective problem solving.	3.8	6.0
18. Problems and conflicts are openly discussed and resolved.	4.3	6.0
19. Leadership Team Members may disagree but are united once decisions are made.	4.3	6.0
20. The Leadership Team has an excellent relationship with Departments it works with.	3.8	5.0
21. Time is taken periodically to evaluate and improve the Leadership Team.	3.7	6.2

Leadership Team Culture	OA Aug*	OA Nov*
22. The Leadership Team has a sense of vitality, enthusiasm, and team spirit.	3.3	5.2
23. The Leadership Team has a strong commitment to being a united, high performance team.	4.7	6.2
24. Leadership Team Members work well together and support and encourage each other.	4.5	5.8
25. An atmosphere of trust exists among the Leadership Team Members.	3.3	5.5
26. The Leadership Team has an environment that is warm, friendly, and fun.	3.8	5.5
27. The Leadership Team has an environment that encourages innovative ideas and constant improvement.	4.2	5.2
28. Leadership Team Members feel valued and appreciated for their contributions.	2.8	5.2

Leadership Team Meetings	OA Aug*	OA Nov*
29. Leadership Team meetings are well-designed to be useful and productive.	2.8	5.0
30. The Leadership Team meets the right amount of times to be effective.	2.7	5.0
31. A variety of meetings are held to accomplish different things (share information, set goals, plan, etc).	4.2	5.2

Leadership Team Results	OA Aug*	OA Nov*
32. The Leadership Team is successful at achieving the desired results.	3.7	5.0
33. Leadership Team morale is high.	3.5	5.2
34. The Leadership Team excels at being customer-driven and service-oriented.	4.3	5.5
35. The Leadership Team produces high quality work.	4.5	5.3

*Overall Average By All Members Of Leadership Team – August   **OA AUG**
*Overall Average By All Members Of Leadership Team – November   **OA NOV**

Figure 2: **Leadership Team Assessment** continued

	August	November
Overall Average Of All Items	3.9	5.5
Number Of Respondents	6	6

The Results

As shown in *Figure 2*, over the four month period the Overall Average for the Leadership Team improved from a 3.9 to a 5.5 with 7.0 being the highest rating possible. All items on the questionnaire showed improvement. The item, The Leadership Team has a strong commitment to being a united, high performance team increased from a 4.7 to a 6.2. Success at achieving the desired results improved from a 3.7 to a 5.0 and team morale improved from a 3.5 to a 5.2. Representative words and phrases used to describe the Leadership Team in the first assessment included "unfocused," "dysfunctional," "political," "unorganized," "ineffective," "not a team," "lack of trust," "reactive," "uncertain about role," and "the Leadership Team does not engage in collective executive decision-making". Representative words and phrases used in the second assessment included "developing a clear vision and leadership skills," "striving for excellence," "creating trust and open communications," "high performance," "dedicated and committed," "coming together," "continuous improvement," "more cohesive and focused," "involved," "competent leaders," "candid," and "honest."

Conclusion

High performance teams don't happen by chance. It takes change leaders committed to building high performance teams and implementing a number of fundamentals and continuous work to build a high performance team. The process is different for different teams and there are many ways to build a high performance team. However, the fundamentals are learnable and can be applied to on-going teams, temporary project teams, and virtual teams. The team in this case has gone from a dysfunctional team to a high performing team but there is still considerable room for improvement and there is no guarantee that the team will stay a high performing team. Team building is an on-going and highly important process that every leader should be skilled at.

Discussion

1. In getting a sense of reality regarding the need for high performance teams and teamwork verses the reality of what organizations actually do to develop high performance teams and teamwork, answer the four questions on page one of the case.

2. Based on what you read in the case and the assessment results shown in *Figure 2*, discuss the major strengths and opportunities for improvement of the Leadership Team before the team building process.

3. Discuss each of the fundamentals of building high performance teams and why they are important.

4. Evaluate the Leadership Team Development Process that was used *(see Figure 1)* and then discuss anything you would do different.

5. Discuss your perspective on experiential oriented verses action oriented team building.

6. Based on the information included under the sub-heading titled Results near the end of the case and the results of the follow-up assessment shown in *Figure 2*, discuss the improvements in the Leadership Team and the next steps you believe they need to take to sustain their gains and continue improving.

Key Lessons In Leading Change

1. Leaders need to understand the importance of developing high performance teams and teamwork within and between teams and to provide planned opportunities to continuously improve and make needed changes in teams and teamwork.

2. Building high performance teams will only occur when leaders are committed to building a high performing team and lead and support the process it takes to continuously develop the team.

3. Experiential oriented team building can be helpful in developing camaraderie and presenting concepts but it is action oriented team building that actually changes teams.

4. Leaders need to recognize when they need internal or external professional help in developing a team.

5. Gains made in developing a high performance team can be quickly lost if there isn't planned follow-up.

References

Anderson, Donald (2012). Organization Development: The process of leading organizational change (2nd ed.). Los Angeles: Sage, 219-220.

Cameron, Kim S. (2008). Positive leadership. San Francisco: Berrett-Koehler Publishers.

Hellriegel, Don and Slocum, John W. Jr. (2011). Organizational Behavior (13th ed.). Mason Ohio: South-Western, 362-377.

Katzenbach, Jon R. and Smith, Douglas K. (1993). The wisdom of teams. Boston Mass: Harvard Business School Press.

Larson, Carl E. and LaFasto, Frank (1989). Team work. Thousand Oaks CA: Sage Publications.

LaFasto, Frank and Larson, Carl E. (2001). When Teams Work Best. Thousand Oaks CA: Sage Publications.

Leading Teams (2006). Boston: Harvard Business School Publishing, 12-13.

Levi, Daniel (2011). Group dynamics for teams (3rd ed). Los Angeles: Sage, 27-30.

McShane, Steven L. and Von Glinow, Mary Ann (2010). Organizational behavior (5th ed.). Boston: McGraw-Hill/Irwin, 236-237.

Robbins, Harvey And Finley, Michael (2000). Why teams don't work: What goes wrong and how to make it right. San Francisco: Berrett-Koehler Publishers Inc., 195-199.

Tuckman, B. and Jensen, M. (1977). Stages of small group development revisited. Group and Organization Studies, 2, 419-527.

Wheelan, S.A. (2005). Creating effective teams: A guide for members and their leaders (2nd ed.). Thousand Oaks, CA: Sage, 39-51.

BIOGRAPHY

Dr. Don Warrick is an award winning educator, consultant, and author who specializes in coaching and developing leaders and in organization development, change, and transformation. He is a Professor of Management and Organization Change at the University of Colorado Springs where he holds the life time title of President's Teaching Scholar and has received the Outstanding Teacher Award at the university, many Outstanding Teacher Awards in the College of Business, and has received the University's highest award, the Chancellor's Award. He has received many awards for his contributions to his areas of expertise including being named the Outstanding Organization Development Practitioner of the Year, the Outstanding Human Resources Professional of the Year, and the Outstanding Educator of the Year. He was recently named the Best Professor in Organisational Development.

Dr. D.D. (Don) Warrick
1370 Rangely Dr., Colorado Springs, Colorado 80921
Phone: 719-488-2240 · E-Mail: ddwarrick@aol.com

22

Re-writing the script for Change: Transforming the Human Resources Function at a Major Film Studio

Robert B. Morris II

Major Focus Of The Case

Perhaps more than ever, companies are learning that success doesn't always breed success. It is no secret that industries frequently experience radical technological change, and those that respond flexibly tend to flourish while those that do not tend to perish. In fact, some have argued that equilibrium, the condition of "no change," is the precursor to death for organizations (Tushman & Romanelli, 1985). Studies of the airline and trucking industries found evidence that a paradox of success is that it breeds complacency in the form of strategic persistence, defined as the tendency to stick with past strategies that have worked rather than adapting to the changing demands of the environment (Audia, Locke, & Smith, 2000). This dysfunctional persistence may begin with the person in charge, but it is also rooted in the culture of the organization (Gagliardi, 1986). The lavish and hi-tech movie industry is one in which continuous change is simply the nature of the business; however, as one major film studio has learned, people often adapt at a much slower pace than the business environment demands. The primary purpose of this case is to examine how one Human Resources Director (HRD) at a major film studio addressed this challenge while transforming the HR function.

Introduction

A major reason that change leaders struggle is because they have to navigate and transform the organization's culture. To affect significant organization change entails fundamentally modifying "the way we do things" (Burke, 2011) or creating new "rules of the game" (Gersick, 1988). These rules and attitudes are largely implicit and deeply embedded in the culture of the organization, increasing the complexity and level of difficulty for leaders who attempt to change them. Culture forms over time, and it is embedded and dispersed throughout an organization through stories, myths shared experiences (Schein, 1992), and especially shared success (Gagliardi, 1986). This helps stabilize the culture in the absence of concerted efforts to change it. Inherently, many change leaders face the challenge of changing something that people believe directly correlates with their past success.

It has been argued that many change efforts fail because leaders cannot mobilize others or generate enough momentum for the change. Therefore, a critical first step in leading change involves disrupting the status quo and generating some energy for the change effort. This is a delicate process that leaders need to manage carefully, because simply applying pressure to change (i.e., directing or demanding it) often generates resistance in the form of counter-pressure to remain the same (See Figure 1). In general, the change process consists of unfreezing the existing equilibrium, then moving to a new desired level, and finally re-freezing at the new level to create stability and resist further change.

Figure 1: **Kurt Lewin's** (1943) **change process**

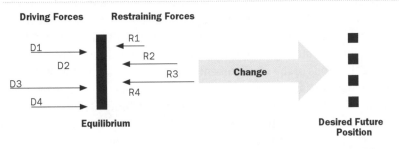

Driving Forces   Restraining Forces

D1 D2 D3 D4   R1 R2 R3 R4   Change   ▪ ▪ ▪ ▪

Equilibrium   Desired Future Position

Phase 1: **Unfreezing the status quo:**   Phase 2: **Movement:**   Phase 3: **Re-Freezing:**

Establishing the conditions for change   Executing the change plan   Ensuring the cange becomes permanent

This framework is helpful for planned organization change initiatives because it requires a leader to first diagnose what enables the organization's stability in the current state. Following this careful diagnosis, a plan or approach that can mitigate or transform these restraining forces into positive driving forces for change can then be formed. Such transformations often begin and end with the person in charge, placing a premium on the skills and characteristics of competent change leaders. Specifically, they need to be capable of anticipating barriers to change and they need to be resilient in the face of any resistance.

Background of Studio A

Our case concerns an international film production company, Studio A (not the real name of the studio), that changed its business model to remain competitive amidst a rapidly changing technological landscape. Although the global economic downturn of the late 2000's affected its top-line revenue, the studio's overall business remained healthy during the global economic crisis, even though industries and businesses all around it faltered. Consistent with its strategy to produce and distribute content on a worldwide platform, the studio's leadership team sought to leverage trends in globalization and the rapid expansion of digital production by opening and expanding movie distribution channels around the world. This would enable the studio to reach a broader audience with more movie platforms than simply theatres and DVDs. To execute this strategy effectively and efficiently, the studio needed a global restructure of its people and processes, which would lean heavily on its previously marginalized Human Resources (HR) function.

The Business Case for Change

Although there were many issues at hand, the film industry as a whole was wrestling with the following two primary issues:

1. *DVD sales were a declining business and Box Office attendance was flat.* Home video sales dropped from $15.9B to $14.5B in one year. The forecast of DVD sales was estimated to drop another 16%, even with the emerging Blu-Ray sales which accounted for 5% of overall DVD sales. This increase was not enough to offset the decline in DVD sales, which was the foundation of the studios' business model (in Studio A and in other studios as well).

2. *The Next Gen platforms were estimated to take over DVD sales in the next 2-4 years.* Improvements in home computer hardware and software made it easier to download and watch movies at home. Similar to the music industry, consumers sought ways to obtain their entertainment cheaper and faster, which could lead to a loss in revenue from increased pirating and illegal sharing of films. Companies like Netflix, which had already influenced the demise of Blockbuster, were trying to stream movies directly into living rooms through television sets and computers by partnering with companies such as Starz Television. This meant that, in addition to addressing illegal competition, film studios would face even more legitimate competitors than ever before.

These challenges plagued every film studio, but few were taking action to address the issues directly. Although Studio A's business was healthy, its forward-looking executive team decided that the trends pointed to a need for change, which would begin with an internal overhaul of its structure and management practices.

According to one executive, "The myth in the film industry is that success depends solely on a studio's ability to sign the best creative talent. In fact, the best studios not only have big name talent, but they also manage their operations and business effectively." To better integrate and manage its business, Studio A introduced a range of initiatives to improve the effectiveness and contribution of its HR function. Historically, the studio's HR function served a 'policing' role for the business, servicing and enforcing employee contracts and managing employee relations. In the new order, the function would need to enable change in the business by aligning talent strategies with the new business model, coaching and aligning business unit teams around the new strategy, and monitoring both progress and effectiveness of the change. This marked a sea change for the business, because there were many stories and beliefs within the studio that served to relegate the HR function to its service role. Few people, including the HR team members themselves, saw a pressing need for the HR function to change.

To lead this transformation, a new Human Resources Director (HRD) was hired from outside the studio. This move was significant, because people within the film industry placed a premium on studio experience, mainly due to the relational nature of the industry. In hiring an outsider, the studio's leadership made a statement that they wanted someone (and something) significantly different than the status quo. This was their first move toward unfreezing the current state of affairs.

There were approximately 80 people in the HR function globally, but most of them were seated in Hollywood. The new HRD began by educating himself on the business of making films, while at the same time indicating to his team that change was imminent. Six months into his role, he was clear that there was a compelling case for change, but he saw little to no energy for change, especially in the HR function.

The Sources of Resistance

On a rational-logical level, the business case would seem to be a strong driving force for change, but it was at best a weak force for Studio A. The specific issue for the HRD was that the business case, although persuasive in its rationality, did not create sufficient dissatisfaction among the HR employees to warrant change. From their perspective, the studio was successful and the new HRD was an outsider who did not understand their industry (or, therefore, the sources of their success). Consider the statement below, which came from a senior HR leader:

> If I had a magic wand, I would do something to make the most senior management of this organization understand how they have failed the HR function and the employees by this change in the HR head. It is embarrassing and absolutely terrible. It is hard to believe that this organization's senior executives could possibly think it is appropriate to switch to an unknown HR head...It is disruptive and distracting and now we are left with no real leader and a department and senior team that are truly splitting at the seams.

The HRD launched an organizational survey within the HR function to determine the team's overall level of employee engagement. One major finding of this survey was that the HR employees did not believe they had the resources (i.e., the structure, systems, or skills) to effect the change they were tasked with, which negatively influenced their overall level of engagement and commitment to the studio (i.e., less engaged employees were significantly less committed to staying with the studio).

The survey also provided insight into the studio's culture, specifically into the source of motivation behind employee engagement. The majority of the HR team reported low to medium levels of engagement in their work, and correspondingly low levels of commitment to the studio (i.e., they intended to leave the studio within the next two years). Interestingly, the employees with low engagement levels also placed a higher value on financial rewards. In essence, the few people who were engaged with their work were also motivated by this more than they were financial reward.

The HRD concluded that his team was not emotionally on board with the change and, in some cases, with him personally. He also knew that he neither had the resources nor the desire to motivate people with pay, as this was not the culture that he wanted in the function. Committed to the success of the change effort and of his people, he decided instead to invest in developing his people by giving them the requisite leadership and change management skills.

The Way Forward

In consultation with a team of organization development (OD) professionals, the HRD launched a Change Leadership Program (CLP) with the mission to support the HR leaders in developing the skills to engage in and lead a fundamental change process such as this. The program's objective was to help the HR team transition from focusing on film performance as the key driver to success to focusing on strong management and leadership as the key driver to success. Success was defined as Studio A becoming a better organized and managed organization, and the HR team would be responsible for facilitating this change.

Over the course of the next year, the top twenty-five HR leaders in the studio embarked on an education and training program that included a personal leadership assessment conducted by a business psychology consultancy, followed by attending professional conferences, select executive education programs, and a series of organization change skills training sessions. After being benchmarked against a global HR and OD capability model, the HR leaders attended learning workshops targeting their skills and experience gaps.

Along with this, each person participated in or led a stream of work that focused on an area of change for the business. These work groups were responsible for researching, designing, and implementing change in areas such as talent management, employee engagement, and reward. The workgroups took their learning and plans back to the business for input and, ultimately, they drove the execution of those plans. In essence, the HR employees were given a voice through their involvement in the change effort and they were given the knowledge and skills to be successful.

The Initial Outcomes

A year into the change effort, the HRD followed up with a second organizational survey to measure the level of employee engagement in the HR function. The major difference in the second survey results was that the majority of the HR employees valued the transformation initiatives, especially as they lead to more effective cooperation with the business and a stronger focus on staff development. Although there were a few individuals who remained negative about the change effort, the majority viewed such negativity as holding the function back. Consider the following:

- Despite undergoing significant organization change, employees reported higher levels of engagement - 20% of the HR team reported high engagement in their work, which represented a 10% increase from the first survey.

- Those same people who experienced more engagement in their work also reported more long-term commitment to the studio, i.e., they intended to stay at Studio A more than two years.

- Overall, motivation by financial rewards significantly decreased among the HR employees, indicating that others sources of motivation accounted for the increased commitment.

Although the change effort was still in the early phases, the HRD had accomplished two important goals. First, he involved and developed his people, which increased their engagement and buy-in for the change. Second, in doing this, he managed to transform the culture from one in which financial reward drove commitment, to one in which engagement in one's role predicted his or her commitment to the studio.

References

Audia, P. G., Locke, E. A., & Smith, K. G. (2000). The paradox of success: An archival and a laboratory study of strategic persistence following radical environmental change. Academy of Management Journal, 43, 837-853.

Burke, W. W. (2011). Organization change: Theory and practice (3 ed.). Thousand Oaks, CA: Sage Publications.

Gagliardi, P. (1986). The creation and change of organizational cultures: A conceptual framework. Organization Studies, 7, 117-134.

Gersick, C. J. (1988). Time and transition in work teams: Toward a new model of group development. Academy of Management Journal, 31, 9-41.

Kotter, J. P. & Heskett, J. L. (1992). Corporate culture and performance. New York: Free Press.

Lewin, K. (1943). Defining "The field at a given time". Psychological Review, 50, 292 310.

Schein, E. (1992). Organizational culture and leadership (2nd Ed). San Francisco: Jossey-Bass.

Tushman, M. L., & Romanelli, E. (1985). Organizational evolution: A metamorphosis model of of convergence and reorientation. In W. W. Burke, D. G. Lake & J. W. Paine (Eds.), (2009). Organization change: A comprehensive reader (pp. 174-225). San Francisco, CA: Jossey-Bass.

Discussion

1. Discuss the three stages of Lewin's model for change and why it is important to think of change from this perspective. Since the model was developed in 1943 and times have changed, would you re-name any of the three stages of change?

2. Using Figure 1 discuss the driving and restraining forces for change in the case. What could the HRD do to increase the driving forces and reduce or eliminate the restraining forces against change?

3. Why was the business case for change, which clearly showed that the current business model was unsustainable, insufficient by itself for unfreezing the status quo at Studio A? What strategies did the HRD use to engage both the hearts and minds of the HR personnel in the change process? What are some other alternatives he could have used?

4. What was the HRD's vision for change, and what is the appropriate amount of involvement of others (i.e., how many of the HR employees should have been included) in developing this? What are the benefits and limitations of more/less involvement?

5. Make a list of the skills and personal characteristics that the HRD used in this case.

6. What skills and personal characteristics would you bring to leading change? What skills and qualities do you need to develop in order to be a more successful change leader?

7. Do you think this change could have been successful without the engagement of an outside organization development professional or team? Discuss your reasons.

Key Lessons In Leading Change

1. The paradox of success is that it can actually serve as a source of resistance to change, especially when people believe that past strategies will be effective in the future, even when current results show this not to be true.

2. The business case for change is not always a strong enough driving force for change, regardless of how logical and rational it may be. You must engage the heart as well as the mind.

3. Pressure to change, even from legitimate sources, is likely to prompt resistance. Successful change leaders need to be skilled at using various influence tactics and strategies.

4. Resistance to change can be difficult and it is often directed at the change leader, requiring his or her patience, persistence, and resilience.

5. Change leaders must ensure that their people have the knowledge, skills, and abilities to do what they are asked in order to sustain their engagement and commitment throughout the change effort.

6. It takes time to understand deeply the culture of an organization, and leaders don't always have the resources or patience to assess the dynamics that create stability in the first place. After all, change leaders tend to think about the future and are not necessarily entrenched in the present themselves. Regardless, if the change recipients are not invested in and equipped for the change, it will be hard to win them over.

BIOGRAPHY

Rob Morris is an organizational consultant specializing in leadership and organization development. Rob graduated with a degree in leadership psychology from the United States Military Academy, West Point in 1994. He served for twelve years as an Infantry Officer in the United States Army, and he spent four of those years designing leadership development programs and teaching leadership at West Point. He is a General Manager of a team of business psychology consultants in New York City, where he consults to several large, global companies in the areas of leader selection, development, and organization change. He is passionate about executive coaching; especially when he can help his clients unlock their true potential. He holds an MS in counseling and leadership development from Long Island University and a PhD in Social-Organizational Psychology from Columbia University.

Robert B. Morris II
Director and General Manager at YSC, Ltd.
295 Madison Avenue
19th Floor
New York, NY 10019
+1 212 661 9888/rob.morris@ysc.com

23

Building A High Impact HR Department
In A Progressive Chinese Company:
Learning Through Observation

Joanne C. Preston & Kenneth W. Wall

Major Focus Of The Case

HR Departments can be the hero or the goat of their organizations. The progressive departments can provide valuable services that play an important role in helping their organizations compete, attract and retain talented employees. However, many HR Departments have dated paradigms and practices that have not adapted to a rapidly changing organization world. They, at best, play a maintenance rather than proactive role that does little to help their organizations succeed. This case is about a visionary HR Director in a Chinese Company who is committed to building a high impact HR Department. The case also focuses on the win/win value of having students evaluate, help, and learn from what goes on in organizations. In this case nine doctoral student's were involved with the HR Department and evaluated four action research projects to compare the leadership practices in the company with the leadership practices and commitments proposed by Kouzes and Posner (2002).

Introduction

We discovered a very unique and exciting gift in a progressive Chinese company in Beijing – an HR department that moved beyond tradition. Doctoral students from the CTU, Colorado Technical University participated in a collaborative research project in a Chinese medium sized sporting goods company. This case compares the performance of the HR leadership units to the leadership practices and commitments proposed by Kouzes & Posner (2002) during the team interventions. We observed great progress in HR through dynamic leadership and reorganization. This leadership significantly advanced the goals and profit objectives of the organization. The company developed new capabilities improving their operations using internal consultants and expect to meet international growth objectives with these highly trained resources. Organizationally, the company leaders instituted a structure conducive to encouraging young managers to lead in talent development, organization development and change, process consulting, and business unit development. Simultaneously, the CTU students and professors learned many lessons by working with this successful Chinese company and grown in ability to conduct cross-cultural studies. Continued future collaboration appears beneficial for both the company and CTU as both organizations gain in leadership in their respective endeavors.

Background

Human Resources (HR) are the building blocks of any company. Leadership knows that providing the right people and maintaining the right people helps to fulfill the mission, vision and strategy of an organization. Without HR to provide the right people to carry out these important organization functions, the organization falters. As consultants, we feel like a broken record and yet in the United States, HR continues to carry out the traditional wage and benefits tracking and is not seated where it belongs – at the strategy table managing the all important human potential.

The company with whom the doctoral students worked is a Chinese medium sized sporting goods company which was rated by CCTV (China Central Television) as one of the top 20 Best Employers in China. When we arrived at the company, we could understand why. What a find! The human resource department interfaced with marketing, sales, strategy and all other departments as active leaders in the decision making process. Four human resources units: Organization Development, Business Unit Human Resources, Talent Development, and Performance Consulting worked directly with the chiefs of all major functional areas to ensure HR concerns were considered in all significant decisions. So how did this develop?

The Chief Human Resource Director (HRD) leads her young group (average age 31) of unit chiefs into areas where traditional human resource departments often fear to tread. Through her influence with the Chief Executive Officer and Chief Financial Officer, she has her mentees involved in all aspects of the company from marketing, sales, and supply chain management, to developing long term strategy for international expansion. While responsible for the traditional HR functions, she has reorganized the department to emphasize the need for involvement in the profit producing core functions. During this project, all unit chiefs exhibited a high degree of professionalism, skill level, and knowledge that moves the company towards approved goals. The HR department personnel exhibited exemplary leadership practices (Kouzes & Posner, 2002).

After completing studies in Chinese history, culture, government, and the selected company's background, the CTU action research team (Reason & Bradbury, 2008), 2 professors and 9 students, traveled to Beijing, China. Since we were not experts in either China nor in the sporting goods industry, we reviewed process consulting (Schein, 1999) concepts. After a couple of days touring the Beijing cultural sites, which gave the team some time for jet lag cure and observing the rich history of China, it was off to the company headquarters to begin the work.

How to improve profitability and to continue to deliver quality products to customers was the main goal of the interaction of the CTU team with their counterparts. Prior to arrival at the company, the HR Department provided a "wish list" to support these goals. On arrival, we received further explanation of the planned strategies meeting those objectives giving the students clearer insight. Four human resource units lead much of the effort to assist in company development and played important roles with the assistance of CTU team in making positive change.

The HR department personnel exhibited strong leadership practices and characteristics which were: model the way, inspire a shared vision, challenge the process, enable others to act, and encourage the heart (Kouzes and Posner, 2002, p.13). To accomplish these practices, the leader must make ten commitments (p.22):

Find your voice by clarifying your personal values.

Set the example by aligning actions with shared values.

Envision the future by imagining exciting and ennobling possibilities.

Enlist others in a common vision by appealing to shared aspirations.

Search for opportunities by seeking innovative ways to change, grow, and improve.

Experiment and take risks by constantly generating small wins and learning from mistakes.

Foster collaboration by promoting cooperative goals and building trust.

Strengthen others by sharing power and discretion.

Recognize contributions by showing appreciation for individual excellence.

Celebrate the values and victories by creating a spirit of community.

Let's look at the roles and practices that each unit played in this leadership case and how some of these specific commitments were observed.

The Organization Development Unit

The role of the Organization Development (OD) unit attempts to improve performance through structural reorganizations. This unit searched for innovative ways to grow (Kouzes and Posner, 2002) that led to a project using process change methods to gather product data resulting in optimizing the supply chain. The OD department working with the sales personnel constructed a very impressive understanding of the entire supply chain. This led to a structure for improved performance built on collaboration between groups which meant a change in company culture. Presently, silos within the company tend to impair the communications since members protect their part of the organization at the expense of meeting overall company goals. One solution presented by the doctoral students was the development of a network organization (Chisholm, 1998) to span the silos. The students discovered the problem and recommended the networking solution in this way.

The company OD members provided an excellent overview of company operations and included a description of the organizational structure. The presentation allowed the student team to ask questions about the company's products, partnerships, and industry challenges. The OD unit noticed that the company supply chain had two major issues: a lack of accurate customer data and no automated demand planning system. These factors created challenges since thirty wholesalers place product orders several times a year to serve over 7,500 retail stores who serve customers directly. Orders are received from the company wholesalers, which are then sent to the manufacturing facilities for production. It is very difficult to make changes to the orders once they are placed with the manufacturing facilities. Lack of flexibility inhibits timely response to customers and causes company sales to fall short of growth targets. The company's goal is to integrate the supply chain using data collected on product sales at all supply chain levels. To make these changes, these areas must collaborate as well as develop an upgraded computer/software system. During this discussion, the students discovered the silos and suggested a matrix or cross-functional intervention (Cummings & Worley, 2009) for project management. There was resistance to both but the networking concept of an umbrella group (Chisholm, 1998) seemed acceptable. This umbrella would consist of 2-3 key members from appropriate functional areas coached by an OD member to increase cooperation. This structure provides training for management heads while avoiding matrix problems and provides relationship building and collaboration.

The OD team needs to continue building networks (Chisholm, 1998) as part of their change plans bridging the silos to succeed internationally. What the organization did unknowingly is establish independent parallel organizations within one organization generating what is essentially a trans-organizational problem (J.C. Preston, Nov. 2009, Personal Communication). The OD unit asked the students to provide additional organizational structure models used by competitors that might help them.

Because the OD Unit has little formal training in organization development, the CTU professors presented them with a copy of Cummings & Worley (2009) *Organization Development and Change* (9th ed.) as a reference to help build collaboration and networks. Not only did the OD unit find the silos troublesome, the Business Unit Human Resources (BUHR) had similar experiences.

The Business Unit HR Group (BUHR)

Within the HR Department, a separate group called BUHR directly interfaced between the major functional areas and the HRD. This group also fostered collaboration by promoting cooperation and building trust (Kouzes and Posner, 2002, p.22). The functional areas, such as marketing are not business units in the traditional sense; they are not separate profit centers but are functional departments in the traditional sense. Upon CTU team arrival, each of the BUHRs did other areas of HR for the business functional areas. For example, one BUHR unit chief was interviewing manager candidates for one of the functional areas. The team felt that the duty should have been within the hiring area of HR. During the HR reorganization, the BUHR team took on the role of liaisons. They no longer performed the jobs assigned other HR units but act as a liaison between HR and the business units (functional areas) to increase communication amongst all functional areas.

This major HR reorganization established the BUHR as liaisons but the concept was not completely developed or accepted. Prior to this reorganization, the personnel in this unit had a recruiting role but now expected to improve performance, efficiency, and profit in company. In a transition period, much confusion concerning their roles and responsibilities created governance issues. The BUHR lacked the specific job-descriptions and up-dated policy and procedures required for goal setting. Team members worried about resistance to the BUHR in its new role as an inter-unit information liaison or point of contact (POC). During the visit, the roles and responsibilities were reviewed by the HRD, which resulted in a redefinition of the workload of all members of the BUHR unit. This redistribution of responsibilities encourages better ways to plan activities to assist their respective units within HR. The BUHR unit needed to embed its members within the other HR units to build synergistic relationships allowing a deeper understanding of all unit needs.

The BUHR unit members and the CTU students identified areas for future collaboration. One intervention is experiential as well as operational. This is strategic training to build synergy in their roles as liaisons to the various functional areas. Another is the development of appropriate job descriptions across all HR units to support the strategic goals of the organization, the correct policies, and what "effective use" means for the BUHR unit.

The Talent Development Unit

The third unit is the Talent Development (TD) group that focuses on increasing the required core competencies of the high performance (HIPO) employees by supervising the talent pool required for successful expansion of the company. The group was responsible to "strengthen others by sharing power and discretion" (Kouzes and Posner, 2002, p.22). While participating with the CTU students, the TD unit created a framework for meeting significant goals, which included a system for identification of best practices and a system to develop successful methodologies for processing applications, mentoring programs, coaching, and various core competency models.

The TD team focuses on developing the methodology and best practices throughout Company. They create opportunities for on-the-job training (OJT), mentoring, job coaching, and shadowing within the Company. These experiences enhance the overall effective development of the HIPO employees. TD wanted the students to benchmark cases for succession planning, procedures to effectively evaluate and analyze HIPO candidate competences, develop a workable mentoring system, best practices for job rotation processes, and a system for balancing promotion from within versus external recruitment.

The joint team developed a cohesive framework and model for growth and development. Using action research methodology (Reason and Bradbury, 2001), the CTU team conducted interviews with stakeholders focusing on the hurdles that HIPOs have with their development plans. The CTU members conducted a very successful workshop to examine the HIPO issues. In the workshop, the TD unit developed a rank order for the thirteen HIPO core competencies. The company HR members then participated in role playing to develop a mentoring scenario and a job shadowing process. At first, the Chinese resisted role playing but once underway the company members became actively engaged. Through the role play, it was discovered that the assigned mentors met only once a month on average with their mentees. Mentors were assigned rather than having any matching process. When the TD team realized the limitations of this process, they agreed mentors should be voluntarily chosen and personality styles should be matched. Upon completion of the workshop, all agreed that a mentoring training project was needed. Mentors and mentees now meet weekly with a variety of topics not limited to work related issues.

One important issue for the TD team was recognition of HIPOs. Together with the CTU members, they found a number of ideas to enhance the status and recognition of HIPO achievements at all levels. This recognition allows company employees/learners to attain core competencies in non-traditional settings in both formal and informal contexts. The HIPO development should allow individuals to quickly progress, where they are especially capable. The system should allow HIPOs to pursue attainable, credible achievements, which are challenging for them and are matched to their needs while providing the skills and knowledge required for the next level. Other ideas for HIPO recruitment should consider e-learning and assessment tools, the reward system for both vocational and academic activities, encourage after-hours initiatives, and develop scalable programs with an accreditation strategy.

The Performance Consulting Unit

The last HR unit involved in this project is Performance Consulting (PC), which faced many challenging problems and led the effort to "Envision the future by imagining exciting and ennobling possibilities" (Kouzes and Posner, 2002, p.22). As a new unit, duties needed clarification. Working with the CTU students, the PC group found the duties included process consulting (Schein, 1999) to establish their authority and responsibilities. They developed a competency and evaluation model for assessing the performance of consultants. The joint team articulated the skills and required actions needed for successful performance consulting such as tools for problem diagnosis. During the visit, the PC unit participated in an exercise to improve performance and profit for a subordinate profit center by surveying the company customers to determine their likes and dislikes. The PC unit now encourages internal trainers throughout the company to focus on the improvement of performance and profit.

This unit's role also changed as a result of the HR reorganization, which was training before the change. Their focus was only on the technical skills and focused on individual departments. The unit focus is now on a holistic approach to diagnose "bottlenecks." After an issue is diagnosed, the PC unit is responsible for designing interventions such as internal workshops, retaining external consultants or trainers, and involving other HR departments as appropriate.

Diagnosis of performance issues takes time and are often quite complex and the resolution of issues require extensive cooperation with the units under review. The PC unit needed to identify their roles and responsibilities along with associated authority. Their first priority was to learn their core competencies as consultants, evaluation of their performance and understand the diagnosis tools for performance consultants. The PC unit must overcome resistance as they interface with all company functional areas, not unlike external performance consulting while building support and trust so the functional areas will share bottlenecks that lead to joint solutions.

The PC unit facilitated a "consumer insight" workshop to assist in product development for a company subunit. As a result of the PC unit leadership, the company Product Development Manager (PDM), wanted the PC unit to facilitate the process with PDM being responsible for the content of the workshop. The General Manager (GM) for the subunit came to the workshop and was very impressed and indicated this workshop should be conducted annually. The PC unit's capabilities in this instance helped ensure future consulting assignments within the company functional areas.

From this experience, the PC team decided to conduct the following additional actions. The team will present articles for the Company's internal magazine as part of an evaluation process conducted after a project. They will also develop email procedures to discuss the role the PC unit can perform with those who wish PC unit support. To increase visibility, the PC unit needs to continue to train the company internal trainers within the organization using their learned process consulting methods and tools to improve performance and profit. The teams jointly agreed that additional cooperation between Company and CTU was needed to refine the role of the PC unit members and develop a competency model and an assessment tool.

Conclusion

Through dynamic leadership and reorganization in the HR Department, we have observed great progress in advancing the ability of the company to meet their goals and profit objectives. The company has developed new capabilities to improve their operations using internal consultants and can expect to meet company international growth objectives with these highly trained resources. Simultaneously, the CTU students and professors learned many lessons by working with this successful Chinese company and the authors have grown in their ability to conduct cross-cultural studies and greatly appreciate the opportunity given to us.

References

Chisholm, R.F. (1998) Developing network organizations: Learning from practice and theory, Reading, MA: Addison Wesley.

Cummings, T. G., & Worley, C. G. (2009). Organization Development and Change (9th ed.). Mason, OH: South-Western College Publishers.

Kouzes, J. M., & Posner, B. Z. (2002). The Leadership Challenge (3rd ed.). San Francisco: Jossey-Bass.

Reason, P., & Bradbury, H. (Eds.). (2008). The Sage Handbook of Action Research, Participative Inquiry & Practice (2nd ed.). London: Sage Publications.

Schein, E. (1999). Process Consultation Revisited: Building the Helping Relationship. Reading, MA: Addison-Wesley Publishing Company, Inc.

Discussion

1. The HR Department was a major contributor to the success of the organization and unique to the Chinese culture. How did the department differ from typical HR Departments?

2. The leader of the HR Department took the risk to build a special, high impact department. What does a leader need to do to build something special like the HR Department in this case?

3. Evaluate the HR Department using the leadership practices and commitments presented by Kouzes and Posner (2002).

4. What are the advantages and disadvantages for a company of bringing in an outside group like the nine doctoral students and two professors to study the group and make recommendations? What were the benefits to the students, professors, and HR Department?

5. What kind of coaching is apparent from the professors who were leading the project? Is there anything they could have done different to maximize the learning experience of the students?

Key Lessons In Leading Change

1. It takes visionary and courageous leaders to build high impact organizations.

2. Leadership can be exhibited by a group as well as individuals.

3. Kouzes and Posner (2002) pose a list of important characteristics and practices with commitments that are relevant in organizations around the world.

4. Dynamic, creative leadership helps produce successful organizations competing to be international leaders.

5. Leaders can benefit by having outside groups come in to evaluate their organizations.

6. Coaches must consistently lead clients in directions that enhance organization abilities to achieve goals.

BIOGRAPHY

Dr. Joanne C. Preston has a Ph.D. in both
Developmental Psychology and Organization
Psychology and has conducted OD process consulting
domestically and internationally. She has extensive
experience consulting in Africa and communist
Poland. She is currently a partner in the Global
Exchange Group and editor of the *Organiztion
Development Journal*.

Joanne C. Preston, Ph.D.
Partner, Global Exchange Group
Tel.: 504-723-6192
Email: jpreston@globalexchgroup.com

Dr. Kenneth Wall has a Doctor of Management
Degree and conducts research in Chinese business
cultural change as the country transitions from a
planned to a market economy. He is a former Air
Force military commander, entrepreneur, and real
estate investor. Currently he is the President of the
Global Exchange Group.

Kenneth W. Wall, DM
President Global Exchange Group
Tel 303-883-4106
Email: kwall@globalexchgroup.com

24

Building a Leadership Community

Philip H. Mirvis

Major Focus Of The Case

What comes to mind when you hear the word leadership? Most often the image is of a heroic individual, often charismatic, whose formal power, intellectual strength, and persuasive gifts motivate and guide followers. But this is not necessarily the best model in large global organizations, where different leadership ideals are in play and shared leadership is needed to address complex, interlocking problems. The case for building a community of leaders hinges on a simple proposition: *none of us is as smart as all of us.* Now some companies enlist collective brainpower through mul ti-level and cross-functional team building. This case focuses on the more inclusive and egalitarian idea of building a community of leaders who share responsibility and truly work together.

Introduction

Community building adds something new to the practice of leadership in group and organization development. Drawing on elements from human relations training, spiritual traditions, twelve step programs, and large group intervention, community building efforts aim to increase a leadership group's capacity to function as a *single intelligence.* The generic model of group development, based on studies of 8-12 person groups, involves stages of forming, storming, norming, and performing (Tuckman, 1965). Community building programs, which can engage between fifty and two hundred plus people, have analogous phases but different developmental processes.

For instance, small groups typically develop by "working through" issues (membership, authority, control, trust) that are posed at each stage. The intent in community building, by contrast, is not to confront these dynamics directly. Instead, the community building process has people "empty" themselves of barriers to others by sharing reflections on their own lives and listening deeply to others' stories. The result of this emptying and empathizing is the emergence of group consciousness, whereby a group begins to think, feel, and operate as one.

In addition, most group development workshops encourage group members to give one another feedback. By contrast, participants in community building programs are urged to self-reflect, and be aware of their filtering and judgments. Here the group serves as a "container"– to hold issues and conflicts up for ongoing reflection. This keeps potentially hot conversation cooled sufficiently that people can see the "whole" of the group mind.

The process of building a leadership community involves deep dialogue among organization members arrayed in a circle. Programs can run from intensive 2-3 days workshops to periodic dialogues extending over weeks and months. The foundation is for individuals to understand *"who I am"* and make a conscious choice to lead with others. Conversation that deepens person-to-person relationships, in turn, creates a sense of trust and unity that is needed to bring a collection of individuals into community. Thoughtful, if sometimes heated, reflection on "who we are" yields a collective identity and oneness that, at the same time, preserves individuality and diversity in the community.

The next layers of community building engage collective consciousness and apply it to complex business problems in such a way that every individual thinks and acts mindful of the "whole"– themselves, fellow leaders and employees, the enterprise, and, of course, customers, shareholders, and other stakeholders. Much of the writing and practice regarding community building in business to date concerns its applications to problem solving, visioning, organization learning and culture change (c.f., Peck, 1993; Kofman and Senge, 1993; Gozdz, 1996). The case here is unique in that it shows its use to aid business leaders in not only developing their internal processes but also inquiring into their very purpose for being together.

Background on Unilever Asia

To build a sustainable, profitable foods-and-beverage business in Asia, Unilever Food's Asia Chairman Tex Gunning worked with the author to build a leadership community among 250 managers spread across seventeen countries in the Asia Pacific. We first met based on our interest in the work of M. Scott Peck (1987) – who pioneered an approach to community-building that emphasizes group consciousness to open up a sense of wonder about human purpose and the presence of a higher power. The practical intent is for the assembled group to develop deeper connections and ultimately find common ground. Tex had used these methods, along with other group development and learning tools, to join together 180 business team leaders and turn around Unilever's foods business in Holland – going from years of losses to double-digit growth (Mirvis, Ayas, and Roth, 2003). He brought this philosophy with him to Asia when he took charge of the foods-and-beverage business.

But it is one thing to unite people from a single country with a relatively egalitarian culture; quite another to bond leaders of so many different nationalities, and in many cases from ethnic cultures that favor hierarchy and social distance. Furthermore, the Unilever Asia leaders were based in historically independent country business units and, to this point, had progressed through single-country career paths. Tex's operating model called for the creation of pan-Asian business models and management practices. Behind this was his desire to build the capacity of this entire leadership body to think, feel, and work together, that is, to operate as a community of leaders. Could the Asian leaders find common cause and learn to work together?

Community Building in Business

There are obvious parallels between the development of small groups and large ones (or communities). To begin, the theories behind community building, which has people in a large forum open up about their lives and speak from their heart about coming together with others present, certainly incorporate group dynamics but also reference trans-personal psychology and spirituality. Dialogue, a community-building practice, has individuals speak to the "group as a whole" about matters of interest and simultaneously scan their feelings, assumptions, and reactions to the experience, also reflects ideas about the interconnection of human thought and energy (Isaacs, 1999; Scharmer, 2004). A look at their conceptual foundations highlights similarities and some key differences between stages of development in small groups, dialogue groups, and community building forums (see Figure 1).

Figure 1: **Stages of Development in Groups, Dialogue, and Communities**

	Forming	Storming	Norming	Performing
Group Development Tuckman	Forming	Storming	Norming	Performing
Group Dialogue Isaacson, Scharmer	Talking Nice	Talking Tough	Reflective Dialogue	Generative Dialogue
Community Building Peck	Pseudo-community	Chaos	Emptiness	Community

1. Pseudo-Community

In the formative phase, individuals in a group have to deal with their purpose in coming together and form relationships with one another and with formal leaders. This raises issues of "inclusion" and begets questions about how much a person wants to be included and is inclined to include others. Peck labels this phase "pseudo-community." Here, a new group often adopts a culturally comfortable form and rhythm that allows each individual to bring forth his or her needs, style, and ideas. In dialogue, this has people "talking nice." The drive is to incorporate everyone, blur individual differences, and establish a common, familiar baseline of relating.

Coming together for the first time as a leadership circle from fifteen different countries in Asia Pacific, the leaders of the food's business struggled with the process of opening up, talking together deeply, and making space for and including divergent points of view. A facilitator intoned: "This is an effort to build a leadership community where everyone thinks and acts mindful of the whole. It is one based on shared understanding among people and deep communication, a community that values personal reflection, deep listening, and authentic conversation." Sitting in a circle, the two hundred fifty leaders present are asked to take a moment of silence, attend to their feelings and any discomfort, and heed when they are "moved to speak;" they are encouraged to speak up when they were so moved.

There is a long, awkward silence. The leaders sit on little benches, thinking and squirming, as a huge fire throws sparks into the blackness. The chairman finally begins to talk, by way of example. A few more speak up, with long stretches of nothing in between. There are genuine attempts at dialogue, but the bulk of the talk takes the form of stand-up speeches, filled with logical reasons to come together and occasional references to ancient wisdom or poetry on such matters, followed by polite applause. Most of speakers are from central Asia – India and Pakistan – or with origins in Europe, all fluent in English. One Chinese leader finally speaks directly to the chairman, "It's hard to have a conversation with two hundred people at a time."

The talk winds down and the gathering ends in silence. Some leaders talk quietly in clusters of two or three. Most walk wordlessly away. One participant reflected:

> The evening dialogue was very frustrating, despite my own pitiful
> efforts at involvement. The exercise left a sour taste in my mouth,
> and some anger as well, for forcing such an uncomfortable and
> culturally insensitive situation on us all. I felt so much empathy
> for my South Asian colleagues. I also come from a more publicly

conservative culture, unlike our (European and Central Asian leaders). I went to bed feeling very upset.

Not everyone shares the same anguish and anger: "There are moments that things happen and moments when they don't," says a Pakistani leader. "I did feel a little let down when we failed to dialogue with each other but then I quickly used that opportunity to question my beliefs, the status quo, the easy and comfortable solutions." says another. Others continue to reflect and question more deeply why it was such a struggle:

Why was I not open and honest during that night when we tried to start-up up a dialogue? I believe there was a barrier of judgment...of my mind not letting me reach my heart. I was hiding myself in that darkness behind self-centered and mind-driven judgment, resulting in neither giving or receiving, though my heart was forcing me to share.

2. Chaos

In the next phase of group development, individual differences come to the fore and a group faces conflict and constraints – and begins to "storm." Group members have to deal with issues of control – how much to exert and how much to accept from others. This conflictual phase is called "chaos" in community building language and in dialogue has people "talking tough." Throughout this phase, boundaries are being set and a collective culture begins to take shape. One common collective issue concerns a leadership crisis – who is in charge? Can a community lead itself?

The next day's dialogue begins in chaos among the Asians. One leader challenges the chairman for seeming to question him about speaking up. At issue is the strength of his leadership. Several speak of their disgust with having "rules" for talking together and with the inefficiency of a whole group conversation. In some respects, this is akin to the "revolt" found in encounter groups where members turn against their leaders and the group begins to establish its own independent identity. A revolution is forestalled here when a young female leader from Thailand spoke up and told a personal story of experiencing fear. More stories then follow in sequence about personal adversities, trials, and even triumphs. In the community building vernacular, people begin to "empty."

I sat there wondering why it was so easy for us to put our messages across but so difficult to listen to others' points and build on them. I was not sure if this was arranged intentionally, but it really pushed my colleagues and me to the border of discomfort, so much that we exploded implicitly afterwards and explicitly the next day."

3. Emptying

In group dynamics, confrontation segues a group into "norming" and has it finding its own direction, setting rules and getting "organized." In practical settings, like team building, this is sometimes sped up through techniques like role negotiation, structured problem solving, goal setting, or conflict resolution interventions – common tools in a group facilitator's regimen. On a larger scale, it involves setting direction and defining rules for collective behavior.

Methods for setting norms and addressing conflict take a different form in large groups involved in building community. In groups intending to form a learning community, for instance, conversation is directed not toward negotiation or problem solving but to what learning theorists characterize as collective "inquiry" (Argryis, 1982). The group might, for example, be urged to ponder how it is conversing. And people are encouraged to talk personally about what's keeping them from connecting to the group. This entails personal vulnerability and the surrender of formal roles, agendas, and even goals. By "emptying" themselves, as in meditation or prayer or as one would in self-help groups or Quaker meeting, people open up to others present and comprehend their own lives and circumstances afresh. As this phase unfolds, self-awareness increases and feelings of empathy with others often emerge. A sense of community is born as people start then to see themselves in another and another in themselves (Mirvis, 2002).

Among the Asians, a Filipino said, "I know now that the experience drove me and a colleague with whom I had never had a discussion with before to open up. We shared deeply our thoughts and difficulties and experience." "Whilst there were differences in our appearance, speech and food yet we were bonded by feeling of friendship and caring." said an Indian manager, "Sharing inner most feelings and fears so openly bonded us emotionally." Said another, "We all have different backgrounds, so I have to look into that deeply and I have to open my mind up and be big enough to accept each one of you in my heart. Then we can have some sort of understanding and then become more united together."

What makes the second day's dialogue fascinating is that nearly all the speakers are South Asian leaders (from Indonesia, Thailand, Malaysia, Vietnam, and China) who to this point have not spoken to the group as a whole. The more expressive English speakers from India and Pakistanis have seemingly emptied themselves of their needs to speak. They are giving space to and welcoming the diversity of other voices. There is no applause. No speeches. People are standing up one at a time, as they are moved to speak, not competing for airtime but attentively listening and building on what is said. This is a glimmer of what true dialogue can be. Now that it has begun, what will the leaders talk about?

4. Community

In solo, in small groups, and as a community, the Asians probed deeply into existential questions of Who am I? Who are we? and, finally, What are we here for? The result of their collective inquiry was a shared aspiration to make their work more relevant to the communities they serve in Asia. Said one, "I started getting the feeling that my work need not be confined to producing and selling as efficiently as possible but has a higher purpose of community service to the people of Asia. Maybe I can call it (a shift) from a mercenary to missionary view (of our business)."

Ongoing dialogue brought them closer to the conclusion that organizations have to be driven by their missions rather than by numbers and processes. "We should be able to serve the larger community by being relevant for them – not by just being providers of products," said one. An imperative emerged: the leaders needed to puts flesh into these caring aspirations and translate them into a mission and a way of life that would emphasize the healthy, nourishing aspects of food. Hear one of the statements:

We want to be responsible partners with the people of Asia, to provide health, vitality and the development of the children and families through better food and beverage. We can do this by earning the trust of people everywhere, having authentic standards for what is right food. We can do this by being at the leading edge of nutrition science and technology. We need to be actively involved in communities, to understand all their needs, especially the needs of the economically underprivileged, and children. We need to do so with humility, truth, and authenticity. That means we have to do what we say.

An emerging sense of community

In its mature or performing phase, a group of whatever size dedicates more of its time and resources to its tasks – whatever they may be.[37] The interpersonal agenda has people asking how much to give of themselves to the task and how open and intimate to be to one another. A dialogue group asks "generative" questions about its tasks and about itself. And, in community building vernacular, the mature group organizes in line with an "unseen" order that is both generative and healing. This transcendental state goes by many names. Spiritualists liken it to a state of grace (Peck, 1993) and learning theorists describe it as "presencing" (Senge et al., 2004).

On these matters, two Asian leaders reflected:

I realized that words like emotions, feeling, moods may not sound businesslike, however, once used in their best and sincere form have real consequences for getting work done. I began to understand that building a resonant culture, one where all of us can bring out the best in us, would bring us to greatness.

I feel very close to the Asia group. There was some weird sense of bonding that developed even though I didn't know more than half of the people. I really can't explain it well but it was a sense of oneness or being together. It is strange because I felt this when weren't even talking. It was a nice feeling. For the first time I experienced it outside my family. Maybe this is what we call community feeling.

A sense of community grew easily as the Asian leaders strove to speak authentically, build on comments, challenge gracefully, and help new thoughts and intentions to emerge. The process was maturing to the point of collective thinking. Said one, "Initially it was hard, it was painful to talk so openly as we are so new to each other. Now it was great to see that words just poured out from everyone. We are starting to see the connections with each other." "I was struggling with the concept of community in a business corporation such as ours but the layers unpeeled over the days slowly," said another. "It is a very powerful thought and I am still trying to soak it in. I saw a deeper meaning of life in all this...understanding, belonging, affiliation, caring, working together in a responsible and dedicated fashion

---

37 Some key points about development of groups: First, progress through stages is by no means smooth or inevitable. On the contrary, groups often seemingly get "stuck" at one or another phase and either do not face or fail to master more complex developmental challenges. Second, rather than a sequence, developmental stages might be better depicted as a spiral. Changes in setting and circumstances mean that groups must continuously cycle through activities involving forming, storming, norming, and performing. In the ideal, new challenges can be managed more quickly and effectively by "mature" groups. In practice, however, many other factors can either increase progress or lead to regression.

like a family, a sense of fulfillment and so on. While family is so central to me in personal life, I feel that similar core thoughts need to be internalized and become a way of life in work life."

Fine words and uplifting sentiments, but the challenge facing the company going forward is how to transform them into a way of life. In sharing their final thoughts and feelings on the challenge, some found the prospect to be daunting: "What still concerns me is how I will make this transition with my own selfish interests – of career growth, financial security, being in good books of my bosses, saying the politically acceptable things, taking short-cuts, putting myself ahead of others, etc.?" Said another: "This mission cannot co-exist with bad business performance or the absence of immediate action to bring it alive."

References

Argyris, C. (1982). *Reasoning, learning, and action*. San Francisco: Jossey-Bass.

Isaacs, W. (1999). *Dialogue and the art of thinking together: A pioneering approach to communicating in business and life*. New York: Doubleday.

Gozdz, K. (Ed.), (1996). *Community Building in Business*. San Francisco: New Leaders Press.

Kofman, F. and Senge, P. (1993). "Communities of Commitment: The Heart of the Learning Organization," *Organization Dynamics*, Fall.

Mirvis, P. H. (2002). Community building in business. *Reflections* 3, 45–51.

Mirvis, P. H., Ayas, K. and Roth, G. *To the Desert and Back: The Story of One of the Most Dramatic Business Transformations on Record*, San Francisco: Jossey-Bass, 2003.

Peck, M.S. (1987). *The different drum: Community making and peace*. New York: Simon and Schuster.

Peck, M.S. (1993). *A world waiting to be born: Civility rediscovered*. New York: Doubleday.

Scharmer, C. O. (2004). Theory U: Leading from the emerging future. www.ottoscharmer.com.

Senge, P. (1990). *The fifth discipline*. New York: Doubleday.

Senge, P., Scharmer, P. O., Jaworski, J. and Flowers, B. S. (2004). *Presence: Human purpose and the field of the future*. Cambridge: Society for Organizational Learning.

Discussion

1. What do you think of the idea of exercising collective leadership in business? Is it possible for large numbers of people to operate as a "single intelligence?"

2. Can "community building" work in every culture? Many countries in Asia, for example, emphasize the group. America, by comparison, is a more individualistic culture. Would these methods have "worked" in a U.S. business?

3. Evaluate the possible strengths and weaknesses of the kind of approach used in the case.

4. In figure 1, consider how the three models emphasize different practices for developing collective capabilities. What are the strengths, weaknesses, and relevance of the models for development?

5. The case shows the Unilever managers aspiring to develop a very community-oriented approach to leading their business. What would this look like in terms of stakeholder engagement, products and services, and social responsibility/sustainability? Generate some ideas then check-out the Unilever.com website to see what the company has accomplished.

Key Leadership Lessons

1. Communication is integral to building community– not surprisingly, as the two words have the same root word, communus – to share. To build a sense of community, leaders in the region would be asked to open up about their life experiences, values, and dreams, talk frankly about their own leadership, national culture, and business, and listen thoughtfully to one another in search of commonality and differences. It would take time to create an environment of candor and trust. "If we as leaders live in denial about our fears, doubts, and anxieties, and about the differences of opinions amongst ourselves," Tex said when the top 250 leaders first met together. "We will never get convergence; we will never get the sense of a powerful group pushing in the right direction."

2. Unilever Foods adopted the mantra "leadership is a choice" and encouraged its leaders to inquire into their motives, ambitions, personal strengths and weaknesses. Like many companies, Unilever uses personality tests, 360-degree feedback, coaching, and the like to enhance self-awareness. And, while these have their place in personal development programs, there are more timeless means to promote self-awareness in the full community of leaders. In Asia, self-reflection and storytelling are part of every leader's work. In a future leader's forum, for example, younger execs have written and shared their life stories with one another. "It's like a surgery of the soul, you begin to see the roots and patterns," says one young leader about this self-reflection, "and you understand what truly moves you."

3. What helped a sense of community to emerge so strongly? In this case, more time together and familiarity were no doubt factors. So were practice with dialogue, experience in sharing personal stories and expressing vulnerability, and a degree of psychological safety established from past encounters. Furthermore, some of the norms of building community in a circle – speaking personally, listening thoughtfully, raising difficult issues, and talking from the heart – while originally "foreign" to these Asian leaders were proving agreeable.

4. Passion. Purpose. Community. Fine words and uplifting sentiments, but what meaning do they have in business? Says an Asian country manager: "We had put together aspirations for our country and where we want to go. But we found out, actually, it was very superficial. We were not truly listening nor truly talking from our heart. So this morning, we started to be truly open. Of course we know that there will be stormy periods. We will have debates and arguments. But at least it has started. It's just the beginning of our journey."

BIOGRAPHY

Philip Mirvis is an organizational psychologist on the faculty of the Leadership for Change program at Boston College. His studies and private practice concerns large-scale organizational change, the character of the workforce and workplace, and business leadership in society. An advisor to businesses and NGOs in five continents, he has authored ten books on his studies including The Cynical Americans (social trends), Building the Competitive Workforce (human capital), To the Desert and Back (a business transformation case), and Beyond Good Company: Next Generation Corporate Citizenship. Mitchell Marks and Mirvis have recently authored their 2nd edition of Joining Forces (on mergers and acquisitions). Mirvis has a B.A. from Yale University and a Ph.D. in Organizational Psychology from the University of Michigan.

Philip H. Mirvis
Organizational Psychologist
28 Water St., Ipswich, MA 01938
Tel.: 978-356-8742 · Email: pmirv@aol.com

25

Using Complexity Theory To Manage Changes Among Diverse Groups

Gary Mangiofico & Ann E. Feyerherm

Major Focus Of The Case

The primary subject area is that of leadership and complexity theory as demonstrated through a case involving a start-up of a quasi-governmental organization. One of the perpetual leadership questions: "What do we need to do to fundamentally secure the future of our organization's essence?" can be best understood by using a complexity theory perspective. Since organizations today are embedded in a complex and constantly changing environment, leadership is a function of anticipating, scanning, reflecting and acting. This case will highlight leadership in a start up, quasi-government organization, and how a complexity theory perspective informed its formation, the structure, and how the ongoing challenges were faced. Lessons for leaders are elicited from the case, highlighting the skills needed to deal with start-ups, resource constrained environments, and the ever-changing landscape that confronts most organizations today.

Introduction

Leadership in any environment is a challenging, albeit rewarding role. In complex environments, from small to large, the challenges are multiplied and require different actions from leaders if they are to achieve something extraordinary. The following is just such a case where the task of managing in a non-profit in a large metropolitan area carried demands that no one could have anticipated and thus the leaders were leading in the "unknown" as complexity theorists would call it.

The whole science of emergence, self-organizing systems and complex adaptive systems is based in complexity sciences and applied as a metaphor to the behavior of organizations. A complex environment is generally defined as one wherein the unpredictability of occurring and emergent dynamics operating in a rapid, potentially volatile environment precludes knowing future forms of phenomenon. As Stacey, Griffin, & Shaw (2000, p. 5) put it, "The future is recognizable when it arrives but in many important respects not predictable before it does." This places the leader in a position of relating with perpetually developing dynamics and processes and the emergent phenomenon that occurs rather than a knowable system.

Main Principles Of Complexity Theory As Applied To Social Systems

The purpose of this case is not to extensively review complexity theory, but there are a few key principles that are worth mentioning to set the context. These five principles are important in this case:

- Order and disorder exist simultaneously (Wheatley, 1999)
- Comprised non-linear forms of feedback and relationships (Briggs & Peat, 1989)
- Paradox is inherent (Stacey, Griffin, & Shaw, 2000)
- Emergent conditions result from perpetual dynamics (Byrne, 1998)
- Organization at any time arises "spontaneously and is adaptive" (Frederick, 1998).

As the principles cited above suggest, the leader is involved in a world of "complex responsive processes" (Stacey, 2001). In other words, the leader in complex environments must learn to navigate the processes that emerge from the occurring dynamics at any given time, in real time. This means being able to make sense out of these dynamics as they occur, regardless of developed strategic business plans, determining what is important to attend to and how (Griffin, 2001). Griffin argues that the leaders must understand the dynamics of their complex environment as a "local communicative interaction in the living present" and understand themselves as an "...emergent person in social interaction" (p. 25). Thus, understanding of what one needs to address to move the organization forward must come from the anticipation of what is possible given the intent/goals of the organization in the environment in which it is emerging, requiring spontaneity of being able to respond to what emerges as it occurs. This unpredictable emergent coherence requires ability by the leader to engage in dialogue with the involved actors (stakeholders) to make and take meaningful action towards the collective intent (Shaw, 2002). Similarly any design features of organizations must also take into account the possibility of spontaneous development emerging from the conversations of the participating stakeholders.

Leadership Skills In Complex Environments

There are four skills that leaders must posses and are highlighted in this case. The first is the perpetual scanning of the "ecology" in which their organizations exist and the network of relationships that are present or could develop (Goldstein, Hazy and Lichtenstein, 2010). Since diversity of perspectives, resources, and purposes all bring about the perturbations necessary for innovation, there must be scanning and discernment of the diversity which exists and will cause disruption and hence the possibility for emergence. The second is a skill of dialogue. One of the hallmarks of a complex system is the web of interactions between the actors – both "internal and external" to the boundaries of the organization that provide resources and information. In fact, innovation often emerges from the richness of the flow of information. Continuous effort is needed "to strengthen, widen and deepen the capacity of the relationships..." (Goldstein, Hazy and Lichtenstein, 2010, p. 31).

Helping make sense – creating coherence out of the various conversations, experiments and directions that occur is the third skill of a leader in an organization that is in a complex environment. As new information and changes come forth, they need meaning-making to make the new "attractors" (patterns of interactions that an organization adopts because of norms and assumptions that are operational). Therefore, leaders work at the level of meaning and assumptions. And the final skill that a leader needs is to support the emergence of innovation that occurs, assuming that it is creating value. This may be providing stabilizing feedback.

The dynamics of leadership in a complex environment are highlighted in the case provided.

Setting The Context

In 1998, the voters of a large western state approved a $0.50 tax per package of cigarettes that provided support for early learning services across the state. To appropriately allocate the funds to each of the 58 county commissions, a state commission was formed in 1999 and charged with providing services to children. This case covers one of those counties and how the service delivery was structured and the challenges that faced leadership in this political and turbulent environment.

In 2000, a major metropolitan area in the state formed their commission and started determining how to organize the delivery agency. There were a couple of options available to the commission, 1. Deliver the services directly themselves, 2. Outsource services to existing organizations, or

3. Issue grants to organizations who submitted proposals. Other counties had utilized different variations of these approaches, but on a much smaller scale. However, this large county decided to create a networked organization. With a substantial amount of reserves committed, a board was established,

The Board of the Non-Profit (hereafter referred to as NP) endeavored to create an innovative early learning system in a major metropolitan area by the founding and launch of a newly formed not-for-profit organization. The intent was to establish an organization that could be innovative and cutting-edge in the development and implementation of an early learning network of preschool programs without the bureaucracy found in typical state or federal programs. The vision was to provide high quality preschool services to four year-olds from economically disadvantaged neighborhoods to ensure school readiness by the time they started kindergarten. Approximately 25% of the children would be monolingual in a language other than English when they started the program and came from many ethnically diverse backgrounds.

The governance structure sat within the overall state commission and also one of the 58 county commissions. The "Commission" was comprised of political appointees made by the County Board of Supervisors (BOS) who were from around the county and with different professional backgrounds, along with designated professional role appointees. A similar approach was taken with NP's Board of Directors, with a mix of political appointees and professional staff. With ten political appointees between them, along with one of the BOS members serving as Chair of the Commission, there were significant political dynamics that had to be considered by NP's leadership team. Additionally, day-to-day oversight for political issues was delegated to the BOS's child welfare deputies. Furthermore, the Commission's organization itself was run by an Executive Director appointed by the Commission. Collectively, this meant that on any given day, 30-35 professionals had a say in the development, implementation and operations for NP that NP's leadership team had to respond to.

The ensuing challenge was the complex web of relationships that existed among these stakeholders. Their interests, the critical nature of their roles (tied to funding), the volatility of the politics and differing professional opinions combined to create innumerable dynamics that had to be addressed daily. At any given time, any one of these stakeholders could call in to question any dimension of NP's operation, external relations, network management, or financial management. These blended dynamics were blind to the functional structure and required NP's management to watch for and interpret patterns within these dynamics and be responsive with its processes.

To create market opportunity for these programs in the least costly manner, it was decided that a network structure would be the most effective and efficient organizational structure. This meant developing partnerships with over 200+ separate entities to develop the 300+ programs. These partners ranged from school districts, large not-for-profits, to small individual proprietors. Each partner had its own governing body to interact with. This meant having a "start up" team that essentially started each program individually. This could entail the actual building of a preschool center, to renovations, to outfitting an individual proprietor's home to create a home-based preschool program. Once programs began to mature after six months, they were transferred to a group of coaches who would work with the program on its quality, further development, and financial management.

Given that NP was a start-up and its innovative organizational design was without precedent, virtually every process from business development, early learning programs, bi-lingual programs, finance, payment structures, contract structures, continuous quality improvement initiatives had to be developed from scratch. This effort took over 18 months to achieve and automate through the development of a customized enterprise operating system for NP.

The launch and development of NP was actually quite successful. Within 5 years NP had built and/or developed over 300+ high quality preschool programs and had serviced over 50,000 children and their families. And, while everyone involved recognized both the importance and quality of these services, the five years referenced above were fraught with difficult dynamics that had to be overcome.

Challenges and Dynamics

As the CEO of the non-profit was at the nexus of the political and governance dynamics which determined future funding and the operational details it is in his eyes that this case will be viewed. After the organization had been operating for 3 years, and had been given several awards for quality, the political and economic landscape shifted. While this is about a case in the public domain, it is not too unlike a business organization that has multiple constituents and a changing and volatile economic and political environment.

As the political and economic environmental context shifted, the powers that controlled funding began challenging the need for the non-profit's structure and costs, despite its repeated successes and high performance, even as they acknowledged such success and performance. Citing that "times have changed", the Commission began a challenge to the continued funding of the non-profit at its current levels if not altogether, again regardless of its document effectiveness. Personal preferences as to how the Commission's monies should be spent replaced documented performance and goal achievement as measures of success. This created an ambiguous future for the non-profit as all rational bases for defending itself where replaced by the emerging dynamics of this new debate.

On the one hand, performance criteria were established for maintaining funding, even as the non-profit's actual performance was disregarded. Dealing with the Commission as a whole resulted in many public meetings which devolved in to hostile debates as experienced by the non-profit staff and Board of Directors over this paradox. While typically only a couple of the Commissioners held this adverse view, they were dominant in the meetings, and other Commissioners being silent were seen as having acquiesced to these dominant players suggesting then that this was the view of the entire Commission. This repetitive pattern essentially made dealing with the Commission as a whole and the public meeting environments a less than productive space in which to address the non-profit's future. To cope with this pattern of interaction the leader chose to disaggregate the conversation by holding individual meetings with the various Commissioners and other stakeholders involved over the course of 16 months. The choice to disaggregate the conversations resulted from the leader's ability to be reflective and understand that the dynamics of certain individuals along with the politics of the collective whole made it nearly impossible for some Commissioners to feel able to express their views. This required the leader to set aside any defensive attitude and ego that when combined with the Commission's dynamics usually resulted in perpetuating the arguments versus reaching any solutions. Furthermore, the leader had to continually research and determine the position of each individual stakeholder involved and determine the most effective way in which to interact and what conversation to hold. And, through analysis of past performance and modeling of potential future benefits establish an alternative paradigm wherein each Commissioner felt able to express their support of the non-profit.

Through dialogue, or conversations, the leader and others were able to create sense out of emerging dynamics as they occurred, even as paradoxes were occurring. Take for instance that when given an individual opportunity to hold a conversation about these issues, the majority of the Commissioners in fact did support the non-profit's mission, performance, and continued funding regardless of how they appeared in public meetings. The individual CEO/Commissioner interactions were able to coalesce into a coherent defense of the non-profit resulting in its ability to retain its funding and stratify that funding over a longer period of time, a result the CEO and Board of Directors considered a successful outcome.

The "conversations" with Commissioners made it possible to establish a common value that reflected the original intent of everyone involved, and that was to help children. Using this values-based approach changed the previous dialogue from one over preferential use of funding to what in the long run would leverage current funding to benefit children. The change in dialogue as a bifurcation point allowed a new dialogue to emerge where common ground could be found.

References

Briggs, J. & Peat, F. D. (1989). *Turbulent mirror: an illustrated guide to chaos theory and the science of wholeness.* New York: Harper & Row.

Byrne, D. (1998). Complexity theory and the social sciences: an introduction. London: Routledge.

Frederick, W. (1998). Creatures, corporations, communities, chaos, complexity. *Business & Society, 37,* 4, 358-389.

Goldstein, J., Hazy, J.K., Lichtenstein, B.B. (2010). *Complexity and the nexus of leadership.* New York: Palgrave Macmillan.

Griffin, D. (2001). The emergence of leadership: Linking self-organization and ethics. London: Routledge.

Shaw, P. (2002) *Changing conversations in organizations: A complexity approach to change.* New York: Routledge.

Stacey, R. D., Griffin, D., & Shaw, P. (2000). *Complexity and management: fad or radical challenge to systems thinking?* London: Routledge.

Wheatley, M. J. (1999). *Leadership and the new science: discovering order in a chaotic world.* San Francisco: Berrett-Koehler.

Discussion

1. Describe the elements of complexity that were evident in this case, using the principles listed.

2. Discuss the four complexity skills needed to lead in a complex environment and give examples of how each was used in the case.

3. Discuss how complexity theory can inform what leaders might do in building healthy, high performance, and innovative organizations?

4. The CEO had to manage change and build a successful organization while working with diverse groups with different private and public agendas. How did he use complexity theory to accomplish this?

5. Organizational politics often play a role in leading changes. What are some of the realities change leaders need to consider when faced with organizational politics?

6. If the board hired you to be the CEO that replaced the CEO, what you do different?

Key Lessons In Leading Change

1. A Complexity theory perspective can be used to understand leadership actions and skills necessary for building innovative, high performance, sustainable organizations in times of unpredictable change and complex work environments.

2. Change leaders need to be skilled at building collaboration and teamwork with diverse groups that may have different goals and agendas.

3. Change leaders need to be students of the people and groups they lead and in touch with the realities they face if they are going to be able to build organizations that can perform at a high level and adapt quickly to change.

4. It is very important for leaders to be aware of their own leadership skills that are required for managing a complex, changeable situation. The skills mentioned in the case are; perpetual scanning; ability to dialogue; provide meaning making and helping to support emergence. There are others that the complexity literature would suggest and that may be gleaned from the case and those are: the ability to press for innovation yet constraining for costs; tolerating the ambiguity of paradox; addressing the present while anticipating the future (manage for today, lead for tomorrow); and being self-aware and reflective.

BIOGRAPHY

Dr. Mangiofico is currently the Associate Dean of Programs at the Graziadio School. He has held a variety of leadership positions in health care and education. These include being a vice president for Johnson & Johnson Health Care Services; COO and senior vice president for Pathmakers; senior vice president for Apria Healthcare Group; and chief executive officer for CPC Alhambra Hospital, and most recently, the CEO of Los Angeles Unified Preschool. He holds a B.A. and M.A. in psychology from Chapman University in Orange, Calif., and a Ph.D. in Organizational Psychology from the California School of Professional Psychology (Alameda/Berkeley). He has been delivering consulting services to corporations, private business, and non-profits since 1989. An active member of the Academy of Management, the American Psychological Association, and the American College of Healthcare Executives, he has conducted over 300 workshops and keynote presentations in healthcare, community health, and healthcare economics.

Gary Mangiofico
Associate Dean of Programs
Graziadio School of Business and Management
Pepperdine University
6100 Center Drive, Los Angeles, CA 90045
Tel.: (310) 568-5500 · Email: gary.mangiofico@pepperdine.edu

BIOGRAPHY

Dr. Feyerherm is currently the Chair of the Applied Behavior Science and Organization Theory and Management Department, and Professor of Organization Theory and Management at Pepperdine University since 1993. In 2009, she received the Howard White award for teaching excellence. Before earning her doctorate, Dr. Feyerherm spent 11 years in various management positions at Procter & Gamble, She also consults on projects such as improving multifunctional teams, creating learning organizations, negotiating effectively, leadership development and managing change. Her work has been published in the *Leadership Quarterly, Journal of Applied Behavioral Sciences, Organization Dynamics, The Graziadio Business Report* and several book chapters. She regularly presents at the Academy of Management and Western Academy of Management. Dr. Feyerherm just completed a five-year leadership position of the Organization Development and Change Division of the Academy of Management.

Ann E. Feyerherm
Professor of Organization Theory and Management
Graziadio School of Business and Management
Pepperdine University
18111 Von Karman, Irvine, CA 92612
Tel.: 949-223-2534 · Email: afeyerhe@pepperdine.edu

CHAPTER SIX

26

Leadership Challenges In Merging Three Sports Medicine Organizations

Owen P. Hall, Jr. & Charles P. Leo

Major Focus Of The Case

Sports related injuries have been on the rise over the past few years. The executive management committee of Alanta Financial, a venture capital firm, has approved funding for the merger of three existing sports medicine firms into one unified business organization called SportsSynergy. The merger of the three companies, all located in the Orange County area, will result in a firm with approximately 250 employees. Sales for the first year are estimated at $30 million. The primary reasons for the merger are to increase revenues, cut costs, and increase access to emerging technologies. This case summarizes some of the leadership, cultural, and technical challenges associated with the merger of three small to mid-size enterprises.

Case Overview

The primary topic at a recent meeting of Alanta Financial's executive management committee was the proposed merger of three existing medical service firms into one unified business organization to be called SportsSynergy. The proposed merger of the three companies will result in a firm with approximately 250 employees. The first years' sales are estimated at $30 million. Each of the companies has been in business in the Orange County area for over 15 years, and has developed a fairly strong base of patients and suppliers. The primary reasons for the merger are to increase revenues, cut costs and increase access to emerging technologies. Alanta's management team sees considerable opportunities for economies of scale associated with the merger which should help control costs.

The sports medicine industry has seen many mergers and acquisitions over the past few years which are being driven by rising competition. Based on an upward trend in sports related injuries especially among baby boomers the business plan calls for SportsSynergy to expand into the greater Southern California area. The current proposal calls for Alanta to loan SportsSynergy upwards of $3 million to facilitate the merger and growth of the new company. The loan will be in the form of a convertible warrant that is a security that can be converted to equity at a future date. While ownership will remain in private hands for the present time Alanta plans to take SportsSynergy public with an IPO within three years.

The President of the Acquiring Company will be the New CEO

In terms of the corporate governance, the president of the largest of the three firms will become the CEO of SportsSynergy. The presidents of the other two firms will become executive vice presidents. The new board will consist of seven members including two representatives from Alanta. This means that the new organization will need to eliminate eight directors from their current total number of 13 directors. Several of the directors have had long term and close personal relationships. This obviously complicates the board selection process. One of Alanta's board members will serve as the board chairman for the first year. A regional accounting firm will be retained to oversee record keeping and conduct audits.

Characteristics of the Acquired Companies

The *smallest* of the three organizations is strictly a "physical therapy" business that specializes in the treatment of sports-related injuries. They currently have five facilities located throughout the greater Orange County area. Some of their employees work part-time, and others are full-time employees in a non-union environment similar to the other two firms.

The *second largest* firm currently produces a complete line of custom orthotics. Most of the components are manufactured in China. The third and by far the largest company specializes in orthopedic surgery, arthroscopic surgery, and pain management. The "physical therapy" firm is currently a family-run and owned business. The other two organizations have a more traditional business management environment.

The Major Challenges Facing the New CEO

Two major challenges facing SportsSynergy management in this regard are significant technological and cultural differences between the three firms. How these two risks (cultural and technological) are managed will most likely determine the ultimate viability of the new firm. SportsSynergy's future CEO was present at the executive management committee meeting for the purpose of presenting the overall business model and financial projections. Specifically, he presented the following mission and vision statements.

MISSION STATEMENT

SportsSynergy's goal is to provide for the evaluation and immediate care of athletic injuries. SportsSynergy will offer a comprehensive sports medicine program that utilizes a multidisciplinary approach for supporting the needs of the local community using a team of committed professionals.

VISION STATEMENT

SportsSynergy's vision is to become a regional leader in sports medicine and rehabilitation. SportsSynergy will retain consumer loyalty through innovation, integrity and service. SportsSynergy will educate the general public, through an outreach program, on the importance of immediate injury assessment and rehabilitation.

The future CEO indicated that in addition to the potential for economies of scale there would also be opportunities for economies of sameness (combining similar operations) and fitness (combining complementary operations). He also stated that it was his opinion that the integration of complementary operations will provide for greater synergy than the combining of similar operations and that higher performance levels could be achieved via a moderate level of diversification such as providing a full range of treatment programs. After a lengthy discussion the executive committee approved the requisite funding based on the presented business plan. As the meeting was concluding the chairman of the executive committee directed the future CEO to undertake the necessary steps to implement the merger according to the business plan.

The date for the merger of the three organizations has been set for early February. SportsSynergy's new management team is presently in the process of finalizing the legal, corporate, and accounting aspects of the merger. Currently, each of the companies have their own (and different) health insurance and 401-K plans. Additionally, each has their own payroll system, vacation and holiday schedule, and differing HR policies and procedures. Another challenge is the current incompatibility between the three firm's information systems. The new CIO estimates that it will take four to six months to completely integrate the three information systems into a seamless and single compatible system. He reported that a project team, which includes an outside consultant, has been established to help facilitate the necessary changes. The leadership and managerial styles are also quite different for each of these organizations. As an example, in the smallest of the current businesses, the managerial style is best characterized as a "close-knit family", informal collaborative environment. The other two organizations have more formal styles of reporting relationships and a more formal organizational structure. In other words, the companies currently have significant cultural differences, leadership differences, personnel policy and procedures differences; and different compensation and benefits structures.

Clearly, one of the major leadership challenges facing SportsSynergy is the cultural differences between the three firms. The management team is also concerned about the impact of the recently passed health care bill by the United States Congress. The incoming CEO stated that he was particularly troubled that the co-pay for services could double and that some services may not be covered as a result of the new legislation. Another concern expressed by the CEO is the marketing and advertising implications given the differing range of services that will now be offered by the new firm. The CEO believes that it is imperative that the strategic vision and objectives of SportsSynergy be communicated throughout the organization as quickly as possible. Furthermore, he wishes to maintain effective customer relations and to harmonize management compensation and incentive systems during the transition phase. The CEO knows that many mergers fail because one or more of these issues is not adequately addressed. The CEO also wishes that the new firm reach a state of technological equilibrium as quickly as possible. He is aware that incompatible information systems can leaded to both supplier and customer satisfaction issues. The CEO knows that one of his most important roles during the transition is to serve as a head coach. He has inherited three disparate firms that he needs to unify into one winning-oriented organization. The CEO, through effective leadership and coaching, needs to ensure that each team member is developed to their full potential and that the entire team keeps their eyes on the ball.

References

Macpherson, A.; Jones, O.; Zhang, M. 2005. Virtual reality and innovation networks: opportunity exploitation in dynamic SMEs. *International Journal of Technology Management;* 30(1/2), 49.

Maguire, S.; Koh, S.; Magrys, A. 2007. The adoption of e-business and knowledge management in SMEs. *Benchmarking,* 14(1), 37.

McAdam, R.; et.al. 2010. Developing a model of innovation implementation for UK SMEs: A path analysis and explanatory case analysis. *International Small Business Journal,* 28(3), 195.

Harland, C.; Cadwell, N. 2007. Powell, P.; Zang, J. 2007. Barriers to supply chain information integration: SMEs adrift of eland. *Journal of Operations Management,* 25 (6), 1234.

Hartman, R. 2011. Mergers and Acquisitions of Small Businesses in a Troubled Economy. *Journal of Finance and Accountancy,* 5,1.

Lee, W. 2007. Strategic alliances influence on small and medium firm performance. *Journal of Business Research,* 60(7), 731.

Discussion

1. Discuss the critical role of top level leaders in planning and implementing successful mergers and acquisitions and why many mergers fail.

2. In regards to this case, discuss and list the major challenges the leaders will need to be aware of and have a plan for addressing.

3. Comment on the appropriateness of the mission and vision statements and any changes, if any, you would recommend.

4. Identify five to ten items that leaders need to consider in planning successful mergers and acquisitions.

5. Assume that an outside consultant who specializes in Change Management has been retrained to work with a transition team. What are some things the team could recommend to engage and involve employees in the transition?

6. What specific coaching characteristics does the new CEO need to demonstrate to insure a successful merger? Comment on the importance of effective coaching to achieve the larger strategic objectives associated with the merger.

7. What can the CEO do to make sure he is in touch with the realities of the change process and how successful the process is in achieving the desired objectives so any needed adjustments can be made?

Key Lessons In Leading Change

1. Leaders need to appreciate the complex challenges associated with successfully orchestrating mergers and acquisitions.

2. Leaders need to understand the importance of culture and what is required to integrate different cultures into one new culture.

3. It is important for leaders to have the wisdom to utilize internal or external help or both in accomplishing goals that they have little expertise in such as successfully merging organizations or achieving other major changes. Mergers require expertise in creating a new organization that integrates vision, mission, leadership styles, cultures, systems, and processes. Furthermore, the management needs to understand how to leverage economies from the merger (scale, scope, fitness, sameness).

4. Using transition teams that have access to professional expertise can be an effective way to guide major changes.

5. The role that coaching plays in successfully merging disparate organizations comprises the following:

   a. An emphasis on collaborative working relationships.

   b. Assisting people in adequately adapting to organizational change.

   c. Bringing individuals and the newly merged organization into alignment.

   d. Providing effective guidance to staff in a "tutor" role.

   e. Foster skill-development and knowledge necessary for a successful merger process.

   f. Keeping the focus clearly on required strategic change resulting from the merger.

   g. In terms of "culture", successful coaching should foster a newly formed positive work culture throughout the organization.

   h. The emphasis given to developing effective teamwork, throughout the coaching process, is critical.

6. There are some basic principles and characteristics that define successful coaches. The Pyramid of Success developed by Coach John Wooden is usually a good starting point. Some appropriate Coach Wooden quotes include*:

a. "A leader's most powerful ally is his or her own example."

b. "Be slow to correct and quick to commend"

c. "There is no substitute for work. Worthwhile results come from hard work and careful planning."

d. "Keep your priorities both clear and straight."

e. "Some of the greatest pleasures come from finding ways to overcome obstacles."

f. "If we fail to adapt, we fail to move forward."

* The above quotations were taken from *"The Life Wisdom from Coach Wooden"*, Copyright, 2008 Hallmark Licensing, Inc.

BIOGRAPHY

Dr. Hall holds the Julian Virtue Professorship and is a Professor of Decision Sciences at the George L. Graziadio School of Business and Management, Pepperdine University. He is the recipient of both the Charles Luckman and Howard A. White teaching excellence awards. Dr. Hall has over 35 years of academic and industry experience. He is a registered professional engineer, State of California. Dr. Hall is the author of several textbooks on computer based decision-making. He has also authored numerous technical papers on business management, cloud computing and Internet based learning. Dr. Hall is a member of the Beta Gamma Sigma and Delta Mu Delta Honor Societies. He is the former Editor-in-Chief of the Graziadio Business Report. Dr. Hall received his Ph.D. from the University of Southern California and undertook post-doctoral studies at the Center for Futures Research.

Owen P. Hall, Jr., P.E., Ph.D.
Professor of Decision Sciences
Pepperdine University
Tel.: 310-541-5797 · Email: ohall@pepperdine.edu

BIOGRAPHY

Dr. Leo has over 25 years of executive-level management experience in the areas of human resources management, employment law and policies, strategic planning, and organizational development. In addition to his diverse and extensive corporate business experience, for over 25 years he has also simultaneously served as an adjunct professor at the Graziadio School of Business and Management. Dr. Leo writes primarily in the areas of Human Resource Management, Employment Laws & Regulations; and Organizational Development & Leadership. He is a member of PIHRA (Professionals in Human Resources Association), the APA (American Psychological Association), and the CPA (California Psychological Association). Dr. Leo received his MBA Degree in Labor Economics and his Ph.D. Degree in Organizational Psychology from the University of California at Los Angeles.

Charles P. Leo, Ph.D.
Practitioner Faculty of Applied Behavioral Science
Pepperdine University
Tel.: (714) 742-4239 · Email: charles.leo@pepperdine.edu

27

Changing a School District
Through Appreciative Inquiry

Gervase R. Bushe

Overview

The case follows the first two years of a cultural change process in a large diversified urban school district. The same organizational change process was used at 8 sites (three were single high schools, two were combined elementary and high school sites, one was an adult learning centre, and two combined all three types of institutions in common geographical areas). There was a large variation in results: half showed transformational outcomes, a quarter showed incremental changes and a quarter showed no change at all. Comparing the experiences at the different sites leads to conclusions about situational conditions and elements of the change process that supports transformational change.

Introduction

A new superintendent and a new school board at the Metropolitan School District wanted to find a way to change the organization's dominant discourse that emphasized labor discord, teacher-employer conflict, and a government that was strongly focused on measuring student achievement. They wanted, instead, to emphasize collaborative learning communities and make the experience of the individual learner the centre of the discourse. The Superintendent facilitated a consensus inside the "District Planning Group" (approximately 40 people representing all stakeholder groups) to involve everyone in the District in an inquiry into "What Do We Know About Learning". Though he had no experience with appreciative inquiry (AI), the Superintendent suspected it was the right method for his organizational change objectives. His initial image of AI was that of conventional action research with a positive focus. A senior District Level administrator was given responsibility for a $720,000 budget, and two teachers were appointed to be District AI Consultants. All three attended one of my two-day courses on AI. After the course I was asked to consult on the project. We designed an AI that eventually involved 21 schools in eight sites in the first three phases of the 4-D model between January and April 2006, including two-day AI Summits for each site.

A Brief Description of Appreciative Inquiry

Appreciative Inquiry emerged out of the Department of Organizational Behavior at Case Western Reserve University in the 1980's as a response to the limitations of the action research model for organizational change. Rather than focus on problems and problem-solving, AI focuses attention on what people want more of. The concept's originator, David Cooperrider, for many years resisted defining "how to do" appreciative inquiry, preferring to focus on the "know why" and let others innovate with "know how". As a result many different forms of appreciative inquiry practice have, and continue to be, developed and it is inaccurate to say there is one way to do it. However, during the late 1990's the "4-D Model" of appreciative inquiry appeared and has come to be strongly associated with it. Prior to this, AI practitioners had relied on the initial set of 4 principles (Cooperrider & Srivastva, 1987) which stated that positively transforming an organization should utilize an inquiry that is **appreciative** and **collaborative** and result in ideas that are **provocative** and **applicable**. The paper called for a collective discovery process using 1) grounded observation to identify the best of what is, 2) vision and logic to identify ideals of what might be, 3) collaborative dialogue and choice to achieve consent about what should be, and 4) collective experimentation to discover what can be. Most early AIs focused on what gave "life" to the group or organization by asking participants to describe the time in their organizational experience they most felt alive, energized, and excited in that organization. These stories were then used to create a platform for participants to identify their ideals and propose "provocative propositions". These were statements about how the organization should be that were intended to be inspirational but not necessarily attainable, more in the spirit of strategic intent (Hamel & Prahalad, 1989) than a strategic plan. As the idea of appreciative inquiry spread and was used by more organizations, many inquiries shifted from looking at the "life giving properties" to focus on specific organizational concerns, like customer service or workplace safety. It wasn't until 1997 that the 4 D model was born which persists to this day (Barrett & Fry, 2005; Cooperrider, Whitney & Stavros, 2008). To understand the change theory behind appreciative inquiry see Bushe (2012), Cooperrider, Barrett and Srivastva (1995) and Cooperrider & Whitney (2001).

During phase 1, Discovery, organizational members interview each other about the best experiences they have ever had related to the focal topic. For example, if the inquiry is about improved customer service, participants might inquire into their best experiences as a customer, or the best experiences of their customers, or study the best customer service organizations they can find. The extent to which the fruits of this inquiry are then analyzed or summarized varies widely by application. During Phase 2, Dream, participants are asked to imagine their group, organization or community at its best and an attempt is made to identify the common aspirations of system members and to symbolize this in some way. The amount of preparation and the degree to which clarity about that common dream are sought vary widely by application. In phase 3, Design, participants are asked to develop proposals for the new organizational state they wish to create. How that is organized varies widely but in most cases participants are asked to make concrete proposals that identify how the system will work when it is achieving its dream. Then in Phase 4, Destiny, people take the steps required to make those proposals happen. How that is managed varies widely as well.

Some practitioners argue that the 4D model omits an important first step in the AI process of identifying the focus of the inquiry itself. The Clergy Leadership Institute in the U.S. suggested "Define" as the first step and some AI models refer to a 5–D model. Cooperrider's dissertation called this the "affirmative topic" and many models have retained that label. How, exactly, that topic is defined has not been well articulated but is generally regarded as essential to the overall success of the effort.

Project Roles

Eighteen secondary schools (grades 8-12), 88 elementary schools, and seven adult learning centers were invited to apply to be part of the learning inquiry. Members of the District Management Team, the elementary and secondary school teachers' unions, and the Internal AI staff chose eight out of 20 or so applications. Some of these were from a single high school. A few were combined elementary and high school submissions. One was an adult learning centre, and two combined all three types of institutions in common geographical areas. At the District level, the Associate Superintendent responsible for the site was the District Sponsor, and a principal at the site was made the Site Sponsor.

Each site had one teacher who was given release time to be the site AI coordinator/ change agent. To support him/her, each site created an AI team that included administrators, teachers, students, and, in some cases, parents and school support staff. The two District AI Consultants, along with their manager, were the District AI team and worked with each site. Money was provided for teacher release time to attend team meetings, for interviews, and for attending the summit.

AI Application

The external consultant spent considerable time at the front end educating the Sponsors and District Ai team about AI and their roles. In particular, he worked to change the normal relationships between the teachers on the District Team and the senior managers in the District utilizing the ODR model of Sponsors-Change Agents-Targets (Conner, 1993). Normally, teachers in head office staff roles, who were members of the teacher's union, did not attend senior management meetings and felt awkward and intimidated acting as consultants to senior managers. Senior managers were educated about the need to think of the AI team as change agents and consultants, not project managers, and about the crucial role they would play in advising the sponsors on the issues and activities the sponsors needed to engage in. He facilitated a number of conversations between the sponsors and change agents about their roles and relationships and over time the District AI team developed effective consulting relationships with key senior managers.

Together with the consultant, the District AI team devised a plan for utilizing AI within the sites that was agreed to by the district management team. It involved creating AI teams at each site, having each team run a separate Discovery phase at each site, followed by a 2 day event where a large number of site members would engage in Dream and Design. Destiny would follow depending on what happened at the event, steered by the site and district sponsors.

Soon after being chosen, AI site teams of 6-10 members were formed, and they attended a two-day training course run by the external consultant. During the training they were taught the philosophy of AI, the design of this inquiry, and their tasks and roles. In addition, they participated in an AI process to develop the two Affirmative Topics that would guide every inquiry in the District. Just before noon of the second day, members of the District Planning Group (DPG) came to the training and, in the midst of site teams busily creating Design Proposals for the affirmative topics, the DPG members were given a short introduction to Appreciative Inquiry.

All proposals were put on the wall and explained, and then everyone (approximately 100 people) used sticky dots to indicate their preferences. The 20 DPG members then fish bowled a decision-making meeting, led by the Superintendent, and chose the two affirmative topics. These were: "what do educators do that create exceptional learning experiences?" and "what choices and options offered in educational settings most enhance learning?". This sponsorship process was widely seen as innovative, transparent, energizing and empowering. The Superintendent later described it as a high-point in his career. The AI process got off the ground with a lot of positive energy and strong sponsorship.

Each site was encouraged to create a local affirmative topic and communicate this to the District AI team who crafted the AI interview guide for each site. For example, one of the multi-site inquiries focused on the transition from elementary to high school around "collaborating to create confident math learners". One of the high schools focused on "creating a healthy community of lifelong learners". Along with the district wide questions, each site created one or two questions specific to their interests that were part of the interview guide used at their site.

Phase 1: Discovery   The purpose of the Discovery phase was to capture people's interest in the inquiry, draw out the best stories about learning and use these to engage people in a process of thinking together about what they did know about learning while building relationships. *Figure 1* shows an example of some interview questions used at all sites.

Figure 1: **Example of Appreciative Interview Questions**

In this next set of questions I want to explore with you what educators do to create exceptional learning experiences. By educators, I mean anyone in a school system who contributes to student learning.

Please tell me about the most exceptional learning experience an educator ever created for you or others, and what that educator did to make the learning experience so exceptional?

- (If the person describes the educator's personality or traits, like they were very caring, ask what they did that seemed caring, or how their caring showed up in their actions).
- Why do you call this an exceptional learning experience?
- What other things did you see this teacher do that you think helped to create such a high quality learning experience?
- What does this story teach us about creating exceptional learning experiences?

2) What do you think are behaviors required for educators to consistently produce exceptional learning experience in students? What is it they have to do?

3) What is the best way to organize schooling to support educators producing exceptional learning experiences? Are there ways to manage and organize the classroom, the school, and/or the district that can help educators act in these ways every day?

Assuming there would be uneven levels of enthusiasm and some cynicism towards the inquiry, the site teams were coached to create a stakeholder map and target high status individuals in each important sub-group to interview. Interviewees were asked for stories of their "best of" learning experiences, and the interviewer would choose the best one to write up and give this to the site coordinator for later use. Each interviewee was asked if they would be willing to interview two other people as well as attend an event where Dream and Design would occur (2 day AI Summit - Ludema, et. al. 2003). It was hoped this "viral interviewing strategy" would generate a large number of stories, create interest and enthusiasm in the AI process, and in itself begin changing the discourse towards the hoped for direction in each site (Bushe, 2001).

Approximately 3 weeks before each AI Summit the site team organized one or more synergenesis meetings, a technique for working with appreciative interview data (Bushe, 1995; 2007). At these meetings small groups would read one story together to catalyze a search for creative answers to the affirmative question. Once the energy ran out, they would read another story and keep going until no more ideas were being generated. The output of these synergenesis sessions was captured, and a "Discovery Document" created that was circulated throughout the site. The effort put into these sessions, and the resulting quality, varied considerably.

The site sponsor together with the AI team decided on whom to invite to the 2 day AI Summit held off-site, away from the school. Schools were given funds to hire substitute teachers to cover for those attending the Summit. With a few exceptions, summit participants had also participated in interviews. Summits, held in March and April, varied considerably in composition. Those with multiple schools tended to be more administrator heavy, and the ratio of teachers varied for a variety of reasons. There was always a fair percentage (approximately 20%) of students. There were a few parents and the occasional board member or union official. The District Sponsors varied in how much time they spent at the summits, though all were on hand for the final half day. The Superintendent made an inspirational speech at each summit. Summit size averaged around 80, with one as small as 50 and some as large as 100.

The external consultant designed the Summit and they were facilitated by the District AI Team. Summit design evolved over the first three summits and from the fourth on the process described here was used. All Summit participants were asked to read the Discovery Documents before attending. Upon entering, people began by milling about and describing what most excited them about their experience during the Discovery phase. Participants were pre-assigned to small groups to maximize a diversity of views. These groups were asked to sit at round tables and discuss what they had learned about the affirmative topic from the Discovery process. Then the large group discussed what had been learned.

Phase 2: Dream About an hour before lunch, participants were taken into the Dream phase using guided imagination. They were asked to relax and close their eyes and imagine they were five years in the future and that their school(s) had attained their highest goals and expectations (related to the affirmative topic) and to imagine what was happening and what had taken place to make that happen.

In the same small groups as in the morning, they described their individual dreams, and the groups pulled out common themes. Over lunch these groups devised skits to act out their common dream elements for the rest of the participants. After lunch the skits were presented, usually with high energy and lots of laughter. Afterward, the large group discussed the main themes coming out of the skits. These were captured and consolidated into 10-14 dream themes. Participants were invited to choose one theme to work on, and people self selected themselves into small groups and given art materials to produce a visual image that captured their part of the collective dream. These were assembled on a large sheet of butcher paper taped to a wall, with an aboriginal "dream catcher" drawn in the centre. Describing each part and assembling the "Collective Dream" ended the first day. Sites were encouraged to take their Dream Mural back to their schools and post them in a conspicuous place after the Summit.

Phase 3: Design Once participants were gone for the day, the District AI team and external consultant met with the site team to devise the "organizing model" that would be used on the next day for Design. The "organizing model" was 8 to 12 categories that captured all the key elements required for a design appropriate to the affirmative topic. For example, the "BHS" site, which combined all 3 types of institutions, had the affirmative topic "Site Collaboration to Enrich Success through Relationships and Engagement".

Their organizing model included the following elements: grade 7/8 transition, secondary/adult transition, education partnerships, physical facilities, school schedules and organization, diversity of programming and instruction, community/parent engagement, connections and partnerships, experiential learning, and celebrating varieties of success. After a quick check in, the second day began with the site team laying out the organizing model, explaining their rationale for it, and adjusting it according to comments from participants. Very few adjustments were made.

Participants were then asked to go to the element of the organizing model they wanted to build a design statement for. Design statements were described using the metaphor of blueprints for building a house: each design statement described, in as much detail as possible and in the present tense, what a room looks like in the ideal house. The first drafts of Design Statements were posted and participants milled around, reading the design statements and writing feedback on what they liked and what they wanted changed on post-it notes they left by the Design Statement. The teams reviewed the feedback and then rewrote their Design Statements and all of them were then read out. An example of a final Design Statement at BHS is shown in *Figure 2*.

Figure 2: **Design Statement for the design element**
"Diversity of Programming and Instruction"

At BHS, in addition to strong academic programs, we believe in training and teaching essential skills in fields students are interested in. We promote and provide a variety of programs suiting our student' diverse needs, wants and abilities. Adding on to our existing options at BHS we have developed several new programs. These include 1) a sports academy emphasizing high performance training, 2) a media arts program including film/television, magazine publishing and digital arts program, 3) a partnership with post secondary trades in food, businesses and automotives 4) aestheticians program with business partnerships, 5) visual arts programs, 6) a junior program emphasizing common leadership, experiential education and academics. These new and diverse programs have flexibility in time tabling and include work to school and apprenticeship training while recognizing the different potential and multiple intelligences of our students as well as providing the opportunity to bring forth community and school unity through a multitude of activities.

Phase 4: Destiny The Destiny phase commenced by describing *improvisational style* used in this AI (Bushe, in press; Bushe & Kassam, 2005), contrasting that with the typical *implementation style* of change. They were told that upon returning to school, it was up to them to make their dreams come true. There wouldn't be any action teams formed or plans made by managers. They were not to wait for permission, and just do what they thought was right. Participants were asked to go to the Design Statement they wanted to contribute to making a reality. The resulting groups were asked to discuss and note what needed to happen for each design to come into being, and then each person was given 5X7" cards and asked to write down what they were personally willing to do to make something happen. A "Roadmap to the Future" made of butcher paper was taped to a wall and people attached their 5X7" cards at the point in time where they aimed to complete their commitments. Participants milled around and read the cards on the roadmap, and the Summit ended with the variety of sponsors in the room (usually 3-5) each describing their experience of the summit and what they were personally committing to do in the coming months. The expectation was that the Design Statements would be taken back to the school and put on display and that the Roadmap would be typed up and distributed.

At the end of the school year each site was asked to submit proposals for funding change initiatives related to their Design Statements (most were funded). Over the following year the District AI team organized three events for the coordinating teams of each school to meet and describe what they were doing and learning. Another round of proposals and funding took place. District level sponsors continued to work with school principals and follow up on the design statements with varying degrees of motivation.

Outcomes at the End of the School Year

In most sites the process engendered a heightened sense of community, empowerment and informal, distributed leadership. Five key themes emerged from all the inquiries and became the answer to the initial question of "what do we know about learning", published in a report prepared by the District Ai Team: create caring, supportive relationships; demonstrate passion in teaching; offer experiential and out of classroom learning opportunities; address diverse learning styles; and provide flexibility and choice. A variety of projects and processes were proposed at the change sites. The process was widely seen as successful. During the summer the District committed approximately $150,000 in its budget to support these initiatives and almost $400,000 for new Appreciative Inquiries into learning. Later revenue shortfalls reduced the money for new inquiries.

As part of a study of this process, structured observations and surveys were completed at each summit. Survey ratings indicate the summits created high levels of optimism and hope across sites. Table 1 shows some of the items from the survey and the lowest average score at any site was 4.07 out of 5. In most sites, teachers and administrators commented on the important contribution that students' voices made to the summit. A common observation was that the students kept the adults honest. Some opened doors that the adults might have left closed. A few students had powerful ideas. Increased opportunities for student leadership were developed at many of the sites.

Table 1: **Average Ratings from all Summit Participants**

I am confident that good things are going to happen as a result of this Summit.	4.24
I am excited by all of the potential and opportunity that I see to make positive changes	4.26
At this stage, I feel positive about the future because of my participation in the Appreciative Inquiry process	4.30

(5 = strongly agree)

Most of the design statements were long run in nature and few could be implemented by the time the summer recess began. The uneven levels of leadership, site engagement, and site team competence led me and others to expect not all sites would be successful. I expected the two month summer break to reduce momentum for change considerably. At the end of the school year predictions were made about the level of success expected at each site. None were expected to be transformational.

One Year Later [38]

Follow up interviews in the spring of the following school year found that half (4)of the 8 sites showed convincing evidence of transformational change in areas related to student learning. Examples of transformation include redefining the role of teachers in the lives of students, breaking down boundaries between elementary and secondary schools to the point where they were coordinating curriculum, a complete revamping of the structure of grade eight, revolutionary changes in the use of technology in an elementary school and a complete change in the encouragement of student leadership throughout all grades in a secondary school.

38 A fuller report exploring these findings in more detail, with a review of the actual data and statistical analysis, is available in Bushe, 2010.

Two sites showed evidence of positive incremental change. These were sites where changes were less dramatic, and were best described as a continuation of changes that were already in progress. Two sites showed not much change at all. Finding a 50% transformational success rate was way beyond expectations. This distribution of outcomes allowed for some interesting findings in sorting out what contributes to transformational effects of appreciative inquiry.

Transformational sites had passionate leadership from either administrators or respected teachers and a widely shared concern or issue that the Appreciative Inquiry addressed. In both incremental sites, there were respected leaders but the majority of participants were happy with how things were prior to the summit. There were no pressing issues requiring resolution. In the six change sites there were informal leaders who played significant roles in the success of the effort, and these were absent in the no change sites. As well, there was a relationship between the degree of change and the legitimacy of site coordinators who were change agents. In both the no change sites there were problems with how the leaders of the effort (site sponsors and/or site coordinators) were perceived by teachers, causing a lack of engagement. This seemed to be the common difference in the no change sites. In one of the no change sites, the focus of the inquiry appeared to be too narrow to engage most of the staff while in the other there didn't seem to be a widely shared, agreed on problem that needed attention.

There was little difference in summit outcomes (all were very positive) and few summit variables seem to account for degree of change. All transformational sites had affirmative topics that focused on students and learning. Three of the other four sites, on the other hand, had topics that were more general, vague or focused on other ideals. How well the Discovery process was managed appeared to make a difference. In particular, the quality of insights generated and communicated seemed tied to transformational change. There is some indication that the level of understanding of the AI process created in the school before the summit, and the degree of support for design statements, might have been related to degree of change.

Appreciative Inquiry was effective at building relationships between groups if the outcome of the summit supported the emergence of a common identity. This latter finding is consistent with the pre-identity, post-identity hypothesis about the effects of appreciative inquiry (Bushe, 2002). In sites where participants came from a variety of groups that did not identify with each other, the transformational effects came from developing a common identity and increased collaboration amongst those groups. In those sites were participants already indentified with each other, changes were directed entirely toward the effectiveness of the schools.

One result that was important to the School District was the emergence of a number of informal leaders in the various sites who continue to champion change and the AI process. It was noted that this was very different from a culture of seniority, where leadership tends to come with age and tenure. During the AI process some younger, energetic teachers emerged as leaders for specific initiatives.

This fit in well with the philosophy of "distributed leadership" that school district leadership had embraced and wanted more of. Two things seem to account for increased motivation to offer leadership. Consistent with AI theory, some felt encouraged to act on their dreams, so they engage creatively. For others it was the appreciative philosophy itself that animated their new or renewed effort to engage.

The Appreciative Inquiry process had transformational effects beyond the sites themselves. There are numerous instances of the District, and individual schools throughout the District, taking an appreciative approach to issues since the initial Learning Inquiry. One of the most transformational is in the engagement of teachers in school planning processes. Prior to the Appreciative Inquiry, the teachers' unions in this district were against the government mandated school planning process and in most schools teachers did not participate. Subsequently, many schools adopted appreciative approaches to school planning and the union endorsed teacher participation in those processes. Another impact has been the five key learnings that emerged from the inquiry, described above. They became central to the District's mission and strategy and are used as a template for all District planning and reporting.

Questions for Discussion

1. In most change processes a small group of experts interviews organizational members and then feeds back what they have learned but in AI everyone is both an interviewer and interviewee. What differences do you think that makes?

2. In this case, the approach to Discovery focused more on identifying new, creative ideas than on analyzing how things currently are. What do you think the effect of that was on the change process?

3. To what extent could the way this Dream process was managed really result in a "shared dream"? How important would it be for a large group to find complete agreement on a "dream"?

4. What do you think the effect of posting the Dream Mural and the Design Statements in the schools was? How could they best be used to enhance the effectiveness of the change process?

5. At many points in the Summit people self-selected the part of the change initiative they wanted to work on. What do you think the plusses and minuses are to this approach?

6. When would an improvisational approach to the action stage of a change process be most likely to work and when would it most likely not work?

Key Leadership Lessons

1. Generativity of a change effort may be the most important determinant of transformational change. Generativity could be defined as the creation of new ideas (new to the people creating them) that are highly motivating to act on. In a generative change process, instead of new ideas being brought from the outside, new ideas emerge from inside the target group.

2. In this case the level of "positive energy" during the inquiry was not a predictor of the level of change. Since all sites showed high levels of positive beliefs and feelings at the completion of the summits, it might be that positive energy isn't really important, or is a necessary but not sufficient condition for transformational change.

3. AI is widely described as opposed to problem-solving and to focus "on the positive" – strengths, possibilities, opportunities. But how much energy and commitment are people willing to put into change efforts if there isn't some pain? Transformational change probably requires that there is a widely shared problem to be addressed, but instead of using problem-solving, AI approaches it through generativity.

4. Forcing people to attend an AI Summit is at odds with the philosophy of equality and engagement inherent in AI, so some way of making people want to attend is required. The viral interviewing strategy accomplished the three objectives (generate a large number of stories, create interest and enthusiasm in the AI process, and begin changing the discourse in the sites) where it was competently executed.

5. The personal stories were extremely powerful in capturing people's attention and in generating positive dialogue among and between various stakeholders. The story telling process supports full engagement as it levels the playing field: everyone has a story to tell and sometimes the most powerful stories come from the least powerful people in the system. It also helps build relationships, particularly between groups of people that don't know or trust each other.

6. Using an "improvisation" as opposed to "implementation" Destiny phase and encouraging individual action, was highly energizing for both followers and leaders. For leaders, it took the burden off their shoulders and put the onus for action on those who have to make the changes. For participants it was empowering to know they could act without waiting for a plan or permission.

References

Barrett, F.J. & Fry, R.E. (2005) *Appreciative Inquiry: A Positive Approach to Building Cooperative Capacity*. Chagrin Falls, OH: Taos Institute.

Bushe, G.R. (in press) Generativity and the transformational potential of appreciative inquiry. In Zandee, D. Cooperrider, D.L. & Avital, M. (eds) *Generative Organization: Advances in Appreciative Inquiry, Vol.4* . Bingley, England: Emerald Publishing..

Bushe, G.R. (2012) Appreciative inquiry: Theory and critique. In Boje, D., Burnes, B. and Hassard, J. (eds.) *The Routledge Companion To Organizational Change* (pp. 87-103). Oxford, UK: Routledge.

Bushe, G.R. (2010) A comparative case study of appreciative inquiries in one organization: Implications for practice. *Revista de Cercetare si Interventie Sociala / Review of Research and Social Intervention*, (Special Issue on Appreciative Inquiry) 29: 7-24.

Bushe, G.R. (2007) Appreciative inquiry is not (just) about the positive. *Organization Development Practitioner*, 39:4, 30-35.

Bushe, G.R. (2002) Meaning making in teams: Appreciative inquiry in preidentity and postidentity groups. In Fry, R., Barrett, F., Seiling, J. & Whitney, D. (eds.) *Appreciative Inquiry and Organizational Transformation: Reports from the Field* (39-63). Westport, CT: Quorum.

Bushe, G.R. (2001) Five theories of change embedded in appreciative inquiry. In Cooperrider, D. L., Sorenson, P., Whitney, D. & Yeager, T. (eds.) *Appreciative Inquiry: An Emerging Direction for Organization Development* (117-127). Champaign, IL: Stipes.

Bushe, G.R. (1995) Advances in appreciative inquiry as an organization development intervention. *Organization Development Journal*, 13:3, 14-22.

Bushe, G.R. & Kassam, A. (2005) When is appreciative inquiry transformational? A meta-case analysis. *Journal of Applied Behavioral Science*, 41:2, 161-181.

Conner, D.R. (1993) *Managing at the Speed of Change*. NY: Random House.

Cooperrider, D. L., Barrett, F. & Srivastva, S. (1995). Social construction and appreciative inquiry: A journey in organizational theory. In Hosking, D., Dachler, P. & Gergen, K. (eds.) *Management and Organization: Relational Alternatives to Individualism* (157-200). Aldershot, UK: Avebury.

Cooperrider, D.L. & Srivastva, S. (1987) Appreciative inquiry in organizational life. In Woodman, R. W. & Pasmore, W.A. (eds) *Research In Organizational Change And Development*, Vol. 1 (129-169). Stamford, CT: JAI Press.

Cooperrider, D.L. & Whitney, D (2001) A positive revolution in change. In Cooperrider, D. L. Sorenson, P., Whitney, D. & Yeager, T. (eds.) *Appreciative Inquiry: An Emerging Direction for Organization Development* (9-29). Champaign, IL: Stipes.

Cooperrider, D.L., Whitney, D. & Stavros, J.M. (2008) *Appreciative Inquiry Handbook* (2nd Ed.) Brunswick, OH: Crown Custom Publishing.

Hamel, G. & Prahalad, C. K. (1989) Strategic intent. Harvard Business Review, 67:3, 63-78.

Ludema, J.D., Whitney, D., Mohr, B.J. & Griffen, T.J. (2003) *The Appreciative Inquiry Summit*. San Francisco: Berret-Koehler.

BIOGRAPHY

Gervase R. Bushe is Professor of Leadership and Organization Development at the Beedie School of Business, Simon Fraser University in Vancouver, Canada. He received his Ph.D. in Organizational Behavior from Case Western Reserve University and his research and writing on organizational change, group dynamics and leadership has won numerous awards. He has been an OD consultant for over 30 years and has worked with leaders in business, education, government and health care to change their organizational cultures and improve their personal, team and organizational effectiveness. Through his company, Clear Learning Ltd, he licenses others in his leadership development processes worldwide. He lives in the rain forest of North Vancouver with his wife and two children, enjoys the outdoors and good food.

For more information and links to download his publications go to
www.gervasebushe.ca
Email: bushe@sfu.ca

28

Leading Company Turnaround Within The Luxury Industry During A Downturn Economy

Abraham B. (Rami) Shani, Massimo S. Brunelli,
Stefano Cirella & Marco Guerci

The Focus of The Case

This case is about leading company transformation. The challenge of leading turnaround in an organization is not new to most leaders. Successful leadership in the Apparel & Fashion Industry is contingent upon the ability of leaders to design and manage a work environment that enhances ongoing creativity, provide high quality product and service. Coupling the industry nature with increased competitive business environment in a downturn economy, with the need to transform a company from a family owned and managed company for over 100 years into a professionally run company, turned out to be a major challenge. The leadership team at Mantero has been engaged in leading the company turnaround during the past three years. The transformation effort kept the company successful, while continuing to address the challenging task of nurturing creativity, during one of the most difficult economic eras of our times. This case captures the leadership challenges of managing transformation.

Introduction

Massimo Brunelli, the newly appointed CEO of Mantero Seta Spa, was driving from his home at Milan on Monday morning, the 4th of December, 2006, at 6:00AM on his way to Como, Mantero Seta Spa headquarters. As he was enjoying the majestic views of the Italian Alps and Lake Como, he began to reflect on his decision to join the company as the first outsider Chief Executive Officer. This was not a decision that was taken lightly and was the outcome of thorough studies and dialogue with many over the past several weeks. Yet, mixed emotions were surfacing: The feeling of pride – to join a company with such rich traditions and culture, history, and distinctly creative products; the feeling of overwhelming challenge:

How to turn around ten years of financial losses (to the staggering tune of €80 million); How to develop knowledge depth of products, material, managing creative people, designing and managing the creative process, the manufacturing process, and; How to lead four members of the Mantero family working in the company while being part owners of the company. Brunelli arrived at company headquarters at 6:45AM, parked the car, took a deep breath and walked towards his office. The only other person at the building was the guard on duty.

The textiles and fashion industry, or the luxury goods industry as it is known today. The industry is a $180 billion business that produces and sells clothes, leather goods, shoes, silk, scarves and neckties, watches, jewelry, perfume and cosmetics. Thirty three major brands control 65 percent of the business and many smaller companies account for the rest. Several of the companies, such as Chanel, Christian Dior, Giorgio Armani, Gucci, Hermes, Louis Vuitton and Prada have annual revenues in excess of $1 billion. Many of the companies that we know today were started a century ago as simple one person shops that sold beautiful handcrafted pieces. Most of these companies today still carry the name of the founders and, for the most part, are owned and run by CEOs that have turned them into multibillion dollar conglomerates with global brands during the past decade.

Each customer, such as Prada, presents four complete collections per year for each different age group, men and women, each of which is likely to include a wide variation of possible components from the shirt to the handbag to the wallet to the glass case to the shoes and, in some cases, to the perfume. As such, the companies must provide new ideas and proposals in four clusters – known in the industry as the new seasonal collection. The expectation in the industry is that each collection is to be distinctly different from the previous one and from the previous years. The leadership challenges that most of the industry leaders face center on designing and managing for continuous creativity.

Companies in the industry can be classified into one of two types, "convertors" or "holistic". The convertors are companies that develop and sell the product but do not produce or manufacture the product. They subcontract the printing and/or weaving due to the highly specialized technology, skills and knowledge that are required. The holistic companies are vertically integrated and have their own mills that print and/or weave the product.

The Como District. The Como district was fertile ground for the industrial revolution developments, beginning in the second half of the nineteenth century. Even though the official recognition of the district is fairly recent (1993), its origins date back to the sixteenth century, when artisans started diversifying their wool production. Craftsmen covered the whole supply chain, from the breeding of silkworms to the pulling and twisting of the silk threads. The plethora of water streams in the districts provided the energy necessary to run the first steam-powered machines that were appearing in the many small shops. Later on, the first industrial entrepreneurs, with their factories, lead the Como district to produce, just before World War I, 85% of the national silk production, which, in turn, constituted one of the main items of national Italian exports.

The crisis between the two wars and later the rising competition – of both international players and development of new fabrics, such as nylon and polyester – changed the nature of the district: focus shifted from the retail of fabrics to the making of clothing, and employment decreased due to the specialization of roles. Creative designs, product quality and productivity through process technology have since been the drivers of the district's success. Such technologies constituted the main field of innovation in the sector. New conglomerates that followed acquisition growth strategy (such as Louis Vuitton or Prada) began to increase their presence and drive competition in the district.

Located in Northern Italy, at the border with Switzerland and famous all over the world for its lake, Como and the surrounding area is one of the wealthiest areas of Italy. With approximately 580.000 inhabitants, the Como District is a composite of small-medium sized firms, that operate in the textile, chemical and pharmaceutical, furniture and machine tools sectors; tourism is another major economic activity of the area. The textiles and fashion industry is one of the main branches of activity in the district, where about 30% of manufacturing manpower is employed in the textiles and fashion sector. While the top five companies in the industry are located in the district, no single company has a dominant position.

Background on Mantero Seta Spa

Located in the Como district, by Lake Como, Mantero was founded in 1902 by Riccardo Mantero. Since its establishment, Mantero has grown into one of the market leaders of silk fabrics and accessories design and manufacturing. The company has always been a privately held and family owned company that had been managed by a family member. Three generations of the Mantero family have led the company since its establishment, and a fourth is now part of the company's management team. As of December 2006, the company had a seven member board of directors that included four members of the Mantero family. The evolution of Mantero through December 2006 could be summarized into four periods or phases:

- **1902-1929**: The company was established in 1902 by Riccardo Mantero. He launched his business when he moved to Como. He was a young trader from Novi Ligure, a famous location for silk production in the Liguria region of Italy, where he developed a special appreciation for silk and its potential application. He began to trade silk, and after twenty years of increasing success he decided to expand the business. He purchased land in Como within the Roman walls of the city and built the first company building, what is known today as the Mantero headquarters, located in the Como town center.

- **1930-1969**: The company growth slowed down during this period due to the Great Depression and the economic sanctions against Italy resulting from the invasion of Abyssinia. While the first years of war were favorable to Mantero, because silk fabrics were in great demand to manufacture parachutes, after the German occupation of Italy, Mantero's activity almost ceased. In 1942 Riccardo had acquired the first weaving plant and had added his children to the leadership positions of the enterprise. The rising demand pushed them to adopt an integrated production cycle and expand the company's manufacturing capabilities into silk printing. The Grandate factory began operations in 1964 as one of the largest silk printing mills in the world, with state of the art production lines, from flat and rolling printing tables to rolling machines, from washing to finishing plants .The plant is still operational today and serves as the main production hub. Here the phases of dyeing, printing and finishing were designed, optimized and integrated with the rest of the production process. During this period, the company started the production and distribution of ties, scarves and other silk accessories. Mantero's relationship with the most prominent fashion houses worldwide was established and nurtured. The company gained the reputation as a producer of creative designs, quality products, and as a reliable manufacturer.

- **1970-2002**: During the seventies, Mantero strengthened its international presence by opening commercial offices in New York, Paris, while the Hong Kong office came in 2004. In the nineties, the organization was restructured from a traditional function-based design to a geographic-based design that was served by an operation/manufacturing unit at Como. To complement the Mantero family, a few middle level professional managers were hired to help lead the company's expansion. In the early 1990s, an office was opened in the Zhejiang Province, China, in order to increase control over raw materials. The company invested heavily in providing advanced technology and technological knowhow in order to bring both the quality and reliability of products up to acceptable standards. These changes were followed by investment in new IT systems for the logistical and commercial department, and the development of website Mantero.com. Financial losses during 1999-2001 were attributed mostly to the investment in technologies and increased global competition. The management crafted a strategic business development plan that centered on improving customer service.

- **2002-2006**: The end of the 2000 fiscal year recorded the first significant net financial losses to the sum of 3.0 million Euros due to increasing challenges in the Chinese operations and an overall negative trend in turnover. This losing trend lasted for the following eight years. Attempts to combat the continuous financial losses have not yielded major successes. At the most basic level, many people in the company seemed to have accepted the fact that operations would continue even though the financial losses were mounting. People believed that the most important dimension was the creative designs and the craftsmanship. "Our designs are the most creative in the industry, just look at our library and who buys our products" was a common belief during this period.

During the past two decades, the company size was reduced from 1200 to 732 employees due to changing business financial situation, business model and business context. During the same period, the company operated three to six different manufacturing sites. As the financial pressures increased, management accelerated efforts to improve efficiency and reduced the number of employees by closing down two of the manufacturing sites. While some marginal financial recovery occurred, the downward slope began to increase again in 2005. In 2006 the company recorded a €19 million loss. Total losses since 2000 mounted to €80 million. By December 2006, the company had a workforce of 732. The employee profile included: Two percent with a university degree; average age of 42; and an average seniority of 17 years.

By the end of 2006, the company was organized as a modified function-based design: Sales division – organized by geography; Operations division – responsible for the manufacturing, purchasing, production programming, inventories, quality assurance; Atelier division – development and design activities (not at all connected to the sales); Administration led by chief financial officer was also responsible for human resources. Since 2000, the company had lost almost 50% of its revenues. Yet, the company's 100 year reputation for creative designs and distinct products seem to have stayed constant. In December 2006 the board hired an outsider executive to be the CEO.

The Long and Painful Company Transformation

During his first day on the job, Massimo met with the CFO and realized that the company had two months of cash available; the company had no money to pay suppliers; current cash provided for two to three more months of wages for employees; and when he asked the Company's CFO about the previous month accounts, he was told: "we are in a business that doesn't require to close the books every month, we only have quarterly PL's". Nobody had a sense of the coming financial crash, let alone a sense of urgency in dealing with it. Massimo was not surprised that the company had lost € 80 million in the period of 1999 – 2006, of which € 40.5 million was owed to the banks. Massimo reminded himself that Moritz Mantero hired him because of his competencies in finance and his past successes and experience in leading company turnarounds. Yet, where does one begin?

Massimo realized that for the company to survive, the management team must tackle the challenges on multiple fronts and, in all likelihood, simultaneously and within a relatively short timeframe: First, it would be critical to get a handle on the financial situation and come up with a recovery plan (both short term and long term) that would include a buy in from all the relevant constituencies; Second, it would be necessary to revisit the company vision and mission, revise them and align the organization design and management systems with the mission; Third, he would need to become familiar with and transform the company culture while at the same time protect and even enhance the creativity process and output, Mantero's competitive edge. Massimo believed that an agreement with the union on the required changes and the beginning of a dialogue with the banks around the development of a recovery plan were critical.

Getting a handle on the financial situation and introducing cost cutting measures. The first goal Massimo had to face was to achieve the financial survival of the company. The financial state of the company required drastic measures. The challenge was how to stop the bleeding and at the same time preserve the company core. Cash and cost cutting became the real drivers of management decisions in the first months of Massimo's tenure.

In the discussion with the union leadership, Massimo's message was simple: "If you trust me, I will fix the company, yet I cannot do it without you. I would like you to help in the process such that we can save the company together. I am here to stay and risk my career because I believe in the potential and deeply rooted tradition of this company." During the company transformation thus far the union viewed itself as a partner to the recovery process and even though the company downsized during the past three years by 25%, no strikes took place. Union leaders understood the gravity of the situation and knew that labor unrest would likely result in major damage from which the company may not be able to recover.

The message to the banks' CEOs was the same, with one additional request, "I need you to avoid the financial collapse of the company and grant me a grace period for my financial obligations to you such that I can embark on the development of a financial recovery plan. Otherwise in less than two months I'll have to take the books to the tribunal (the Italian jargon for filing for bankruptcy)".

The workforce was reduced, money losing product lines were closed, G&A expenses, capital expenditure and inventory were drastically reduced. A major disposal plan of non operating assets was implemented and the long term debt was renegotiated with the lenders and its repayment rescheduled. Once the emergency period was over, the management drive became efficiency: better management of manufacturing and product development in order to increase margins and reduce the cost of non quality.

Management tools to support the restructuring and recovery process were based on a monthly reporting process and the implementation of divisional accounting procedure. Managers were held accountable based on performance data. The executive team for the first time had a clear understanding of where the company was making or losing money. A new information system was implemented to support the reengineering of the company and, particularly, its drive for reducing the cost of its non quality. The outcome was an increased operating profitability, in spite of declining revenues, an increased revenue per head and, an improved debt to equity ratio. Some of the proceeds from the assets disposal were invested to upgrade plants machinery and the management information system.

Developing a shared company strategy. The company vision and mission in December 2006 stated: "Weaving emotions. Mantero pursues a role of leadership in the silk industry and related value added services". The mission was beautifully drafted, but was not business oriented. The mission was interpreted by many in the company to suggest that their jobs were to craft works of art and not necessarily to make products to be sold at a profit.

The changing market conditions, the need to refocus the company energy and increased competition led to the need to revise the mission. The top management team developed the statement and in a semi-participative process led the rollover process to create a buy-in by the entire organization. The latest revised (September 2010) mission states: "Mantero's mission is to grow with profit at the service of our customers. We endeavor to guarantee excellence and leadership in textiles and accessories thanks to the quality of our unique and innovative creations." The revised mission reflects and emphasizes the combined drive for both profitability and high quality service to clients. It also magnifies the commitment to continuous creativity, innovative design, and product quality. The revised mission provided a clear message: Emotions don't pay the mortgage, we are in the business of making money, not only crafting art or poetry.

Re-structuring the company based on the emerging business strategy. The 2006 company structure was driven by a sales organization that was geographically-based. The sales division would bring in orders to the design and manufacturing units and serve as the main contact with the customer, regardless of its size or versatility in terms of possible product interest. The prevailing view was that the company was a supplier of raw material to the big fashion companies. The sales organization had limited knowledge of design and/or manufacturing capacity or about the ability to deliver the ordered material in the requested timeframe. Design units and manufacturing units had very limited or no direct interactions with the clients.

In 2010, a hybrid of "convertor" and "holistic" (vertically integrated company) orientation was crafted. Four divisions – women, men, fashion & licensing – with all the resources to be "convertors" and two manufacturing divisions along with quality control and logistics – printing and weaving - were established in order to serve its clients best. An additional administrative unit composed of human resources, information technology, finance and, purchasing and procurement was established to work in close collaboration and support of the four divisions: Women's Wear – fabrics and accessories for the luxury clients; Fashion – women's wear and beachwear fabrics for the fast fashion segment; Men's Wear – accessories (fabrics and finished products), and; License and Distributions – distribution of women and men's accessories made under license agreements. The business divisions are responsible for their own sales, creation design and development, purchasing and sourcing. They source their products both internally (from the manufacturing divisions) and externally.

The rationale for the changes made in the organization was twofold. *First*, the marketing orientation – product, and not geography, was the key variable for the sales efforts to be effective. Customers who buy both scarves/fabrics and ties have different buyers and purchasing decision makers whether they purchase the former or the latter, and the product and sales skills required to service the menswear and womenswear segments are different. One sales person cannot service both. There must be one taking care of menswear and another taking care of the womenswear sales. *Second*, management accountability - functional organizations and their heads were always in the position of blaming someone else for their poor performance. Sales people were blaming designers or manufacturing, because they were not delivering products on time or to the customer satisfaction; manufacturing was blaming the commercial organization because they usually oversold – products not yet sufficiently tested or delivery dates that were practically unattainable. Conversely, under the new organization, division heads had control over the whole development, sourcing and sales process, and were free to choose their suppliers. The relationship between the various divisions entertained was at an arm's length: The products divisions were free to choose where to have their products manufactured; the manufacturing divisions were free to set their prices and to decide whether or not to take an order from the products divisions. Management had to convert to a "no excuse" culture and approach.

The structure of the "external governance" was also changed. The structure and composition of the *board of directors* changed from having four family members and three outsiders that were family friends to three outsiders with a variety of managerial expertise and knowledge depth of the industry. The new board became a proactive body that would both challenge the management team and provide a wide array of expertise to help support and guide the company. The *statutory audit committee* (linked to the Italian regulations that mandate for the socalled "collegio sindacale"), composed of three individuals that by law must audit the company practices and reports (law and tax periodic assessments) periodically, was revitalized with new two highly skilled and knowledgeable members, one of whom is the head of the committee.

Transforming the company culture. A company culture and subculture reflect the common experiences of organizational members within their working units. Company culture arises through shared experiences of successes and failures. At the most generic level, company vision, mission, strategy and structure set the context for human experiences that lead to the emergence of units' subcultures and company culture. At Mantero, following a critical analysis of the company culture during the first part of 2007, the following cultural features were identified: The geography-based design of the sales force and the way the company was organized created a context in which personal accountability for product design and delivery was lacking.

The assumptions that emerged in the sales organization included, amongst others, that the success of the company depends on their ability to bring in sale contracts; it was up to others in the company to design, manufacturing and delivery to supply the product according to the specification of the contract. If the product was not delivered within the expected specifications, quality or timeframe, it was not the sales organization responsibility. The assumptions that emerged in the product design organization included that, the success of the company is based on the continuous demonstrated ability to design and develop creative products, that the creative process is a craft and thus can not be completed within unrealistic time frame. Conversely, the assumptions that were made by the manufacturing organization, included the notion that no one knows better then the people in the manufacturing organization their production capacity, that the sales organization has no clue about the complexity of the manufacturing process and many time, production schedule were set without any consultation with manufacturing people's input. The overall norm that emerged was the view that no one saw themselves as the responsible party.

At the same time, employees of Mantero were proud to be a part of the company. Over 100 years of success resulted in what some would classified as arrogant behavior. Different variations of the comments, "we are Mantero, we are 100 years old", "we have created the most beautiful designs and products, and most people do not know and do not understand the beauty of our products" were common. The norm that emerged over the years focused more on the elegant designs and creative products, and less on finance or profit. Some even claimed that they are about creating a magnificent artifact regardless of cost or who would pay for its design and/or production. Furthermore, "if the client is not interested, regardless of its size and potential volume of sales, it is his loss". The organization's prevailing norm was of a passive attitude towards goals, clients, sales and results. "If things are not OK... this is life".. "if people are not performing or holding up to a commitment.... things eventually will work out"... "as long as I do my job, even if others do not, it is not my responsibility anymore".. "as long as I cc you (as my supervisor) on the email that I send, you are in the know, and it is not my responsibility".. "we always have done it this way, so why do it any differently?".. Last, since the company lost money in the previous eight years, people thought that losing money was "normal" and the emerging common feeling was that "someone will pay the bill".

Critical reflective summation of the culture that emerged at Mantero by December 2006 suggested that four distinct subcultures emerged over time: The printing and weaving subculture, the sales organization subculture, the design or craftsmanship subculture and the administrative/management subculture. The subcultures, while distinctly different, seem to have lacked basic alignment.

Massimo set out to transform the culture by getting to know people by valuing their experience and knowledge, by building a professional leadership team, by fostering the notion of ownership, by facilitating accountability-based practice by every member of the organization, and by beginning a dialogue with their major clients about past, present experience and future opportunities. During the month of December 2006, he met with most of the employees, one-on-one with most managers, and had group meetings with individuals that were part of the different areas, such as sales, designers, men and women units, license unit, and those in the weaving and printing mills. Following the dialogue at the different levels and units of the organization, a new vision and structure were crafted by the top management team. By mid February 2007 (two and one half months after Massimo's arrival), the company was downsized from 700 to 550 employees, half of whom were in the four 'converter" divisions and the rest in the production divisions.

Internally, a new management team was established that bought into the new vision and the importance of the development of a professional management culture. Most of the top management team (with one exception) was replaced by new managers that were promoted from the inside.

'Leading by example as professional managers' became the mantra. The focus shifted to performance indicators such as quality measures, reliability measures, budget planning and management, developing people and enhancing creativity. Performance and professionalism became key criteria for managerial success, promotion and retention. Managers were expected to create a professional culture in their own units by sharing information, communication, involvement, and creating high performance teams.

Massimo believed that "... if we change the way we work – by becoming more professional, more scientific, and more rigorous – we can change dramatically". Managerial practice must be embedded in data that is collected regularly in a scientific and rigorous way, interpreted and acted upon. As work units began to collect, share and interpret data, the degree of professionalism increased. This drive also led to two more tangible major results: The company became more cost effective, and the company increased its competitiveness.

Enhancing creativity was viewed by Massimo as a key element in the company's transformation. Creativity was one of the anchors that led to the success of the company over the century. As such, product design and development units were established within each of the four divisions. Having the product design and development capability within each division allowed for closer proximity to the customer which, in turn, enhanced creative solutions. A new VP for the Product Design and Development position was created to lead, coordinate, and enhance the overall emphasis on creativity. Last, the company launched a collaborative research project with researchers from the Politecnico di Milano to study the phenomenon of collective creativity and to experiment with alternative ways of designing learning mechanisms that can enhance or trigger collective creativity.

Communication was viewed as critical to the transformation process and the establishment of a professional culture. A number of communication mechanisms were institutionalized. Once a quarter, a communication forum was convened by Massimo in which he meets with a group of 50 people coming from all across the organization. During the meeting, Massimo shares company and units' results, goals, and key emerging issues. During the meetings, individuals are invited to share their interpretations, views, and insights. The executive management team is expected to lead similar sessions and discussions with their units. Performance data is distributed, discussed, and interpreted quarterly in different management forums, while daily sales data are made public and available to all employees. According to Massimo, "communication is a crucial element of leadership and its practice by managers at different levels is essential in leading company transformation."

The word about Mantero's transformation began to take hold in the industry. The company was able to attract new talent, old customers began to increase their orders and, old customers that dropped the company began to discuss opening new accounts. Customers knew about the transformation effort and as a result sales began to increase overall.

Reflection on Current State of the Company's Transformation

Massimo is proud of the company, its tradition, its people, and of the recovery process to date. He speaks very passionately about where they have been, where they are today, and where they can be in the future. "We have reclaimed the number one place in a few of the product lines but can do so in other areas as well." Even though last year's global economy was the worst in recent history, the company has done OK and is on target with the recovery plan. 2009 was the first year of a positive net profit and 2010 will be a "close call" in terms of profitability. Massimo believes that the company needs a new phase to complete the cultural transformation of the company.

Some of the challenges ahead include: The continuous integration of the company culture into a more unified professional culture (vs. a few subcultures that are still not fully aligned); finding ways to design and sell complete products with a variety of appropriate accessories directly to customers with higher marginal profits; and continue to explore alternative ways to design for and manage creativity while sustaining profitability, accountability, quality, and service orientation.

Discussion

1. Summarize the challenges that the new CEO (Massimo Brunelli) faced when he took over.

2. What did the new CEO do to prepare the company and the company stakeholders for change?

3. What are the steps that the new CEO took to transform the company?

4. Describe the major company culture and the distinct subcultures prior to the new CEOs arrival, what Massimo did step by step to change the culture, and what the new emergent new culture is designed to be like.

5. What would you consider to be the major qualities of a successful transformational leader?

6. Discuss (1) what the new CEO did to build a new top management team; (2) the role of the team; (3) any additional roles you think they should have; and (4) the importance of a top management team in the transformation process.

7. What advice would you give the CEO as he begins to plan the continuous transformation of the company over the next three years? What will likely be his biggest challenges? What should the transformation process look like?

Key Lessons In Leading Change

1. Transformational leaders develop the capability and emphasize the need to address simultaneously financial performance of the firm, company culture and company growth.

2. Transformational leaders inspire followers to commit to a shared company vision and goals.

3. Transformational leaders motivate others to do more than they originally intended and often even more than they thought possible. They tend to set more challenging expectations and typically achieve higher performance.

4. Transformational leaders empower followers and pay attention to their individual needs and personal development, helping them develop their leadership potential. They tend to develop followers' leadership capacity via coaching and mentoring.

5. Transformational leaders view continuous organizational change as the key to company survival and success.

6. Transformational leaders create an organizational culture that values and enhances creativity and innovative solutions.

BIOGRAPHY

Abraham B. (Rami) Shani (Ph.D., Case Western Reserve University) is a professor of management at the Orfalea College of Business, California Polytechnic State University, San Luis Obispo, California and a research professor at Politecnico di Milano, Milan, Italy. He is an author, co-author or co-editor of 20 books, some of which include *Organizing for Sustainable Effectiveness, Creating Sustainable Work Systems, Behavior in Organizations (in its 9th edition), The Handbook of Collaborative Management Research, Learning By Design: Building Sustainable Organizations, Fundamental of Organization Development (4 edited volumes), Research in Organization Change and Development, and Collaborative Research in Organizations: Foundations for Learning, Change and Theoretical Development.* His most recent activity centers in co-leading the development of an international community that focuses on the challenges of organizing for sustainable effectiveness. He splits his time between the Central Coast of California and Milan, Italy.

Abraham B. (Rami) Shani Research Professor
Politecnico di Milano, School of Management,
Department of Management, Economics and Industrial Engineering,and
Management Area, Orfalea College of Business,
California Polytechnic State University, San Luis Obispo, CA 93407, USA
Tel: + 1 805 756 1756. Email: ashani@calpoly.edu

Stefano Cirella (Ph.D., and MSc, Politecnico di Milano) is a researcher at the Politecnico di Milano. His research areas focus on collective creativity, learning mechanisms, experiential learning and collaborative research methodologies. He leads seminars and training courses in the area of Organizational Behavior and Human Resource Management, and Organizational Systems.

Stefano Cirella
School of Management, Department of Management, Economics and Industrial Engineering, Politecnico di Milano, Via Lambruschini 4/B, 20156 Milano, Italy.
Tel: +39 02 2399 3958. Email: stefano.cirella@polimi.it

BIOGRAPHY

Massimo S. Brunelli (BA, University of Bologna; MSc, MIT) is the CEO of Mantero Seta Spa, Como, Italy. Prior to Mantero he was the CFO of EBPA, a Cleveland based company publicly traded on the NYSE; CFO of ENEL, the second largest electric utility in the world; CFO of Telecom Italia, one of the largest European telecoms. Subsequently, as a turnaround specialist he had assignments in industries such as fashion, motorcycles, tourism, IT, construction. He is the chairman of Synergo, a private equity fund. He lectured in International Finance at LUISS, Rome and is currently a lecturer in International Planning and Management Control at Bocconi University, Milan.

Massimo Brunelli
Mantero Seta SpA
Via Volta 74, 22100 Como, Italy
Tel: +39 031 321 321. Email: massimo.brunelli@mantero.com

Marco Guerci (Ph.D., Politecnico di Milano and Università degli Studi di Milano) is assistant professor of Organizational Behavior and Human Resource Management. His research areas focus on Training Evaluation Systems and sustainable human resource management practices and system development. He teaches courses and leads training programs in Human Resource Management, Training & Development, Organization Behavior.

Marco Guerci
School of Management,
Department of Management, Economics and Industrial Engineering,
Politecnico di Milano,
Via Lambruschini 4/B, 20156 Milano, Italy.
Tel: +39 02 2399 3967. Email: guerci@mip.polimi.it

29

Change Lessons in Whole System Transformation™

Susan Donnan & Roland Sullivan

Whole System Transformation (WST) is the methodology chosen to drive transformation in the Information and Communication Technology (ICT) function of an anonymous global corporation, a large manufacturer with 55,000 employees worldwide. WST has been institutionalized to develop ICT into an agile organization capable of adapting to any external and/or internal drivers for change.

An agile organization changes on a dime to respond to arising internal and external customer needs. It is a resilient system that has the capacity to handle disruptions or new business demands and to re-organize itself while preserving its core values and its essential historical identity.

Each successive cycle of change has four phases: (1) Yearly retreat to align or transform the executive leadership team; (2) Yearly assessments of next changes as part of strategy update; (3) Large group interactive event to align or transform a critical mass; and (4) Implementation of planned change projects as defined by the event participants.

One key element of WST is the use of large group interactive event to generate excitement, enthusiasm and energy for change. However, when participants leave the bubble of the event and get back to their daily life, reality tends to take over very quickly. The focus of this case is on how ICT has learned to sustain the momentum for change between cycles of change.

Figure 1: **Whole System Transformation**

1 Yearly Executive Team Retreat

Align and/or Transform Leadership

2 Yearly assessment as part of ICT Strategy update taking into account the Company Strategy

An agile ICT capable of adapting to any external and/or internal drivers for change

4 Between cycles of change, improvements are managed as projects with quarterly review by the Executive Team and supported by core domain and local change agent networks

Implement & Sustain Change

Assess & Plan Change

3 Large group meetings with different configurations and durations to celebrate progress and to define next set of improvement opportunities

Align and/or Transform Critical Mass

The Case Study

This case describes the continual application of Whole System Transformation (WST) in the Information and Communication Technology (ICT) function of an anonymous global corporation, a large manufacturer with 55,000 employees worldwide. WST allows leaders to engage all parts of an organization in a paradigm shift to accelerate sustainable positive results.

Our story began with the appointment of a new Chief Information Office (CIO) who inherited a function with 1,200 staff. In his first year, the CIO worked with his new executive leadership team and a core group of middle managers to define its new vision, mission, and customer-facing transnational organization. However, he knew that these changes were only the beginning. It could take months, or even years, to formulate and implement the necessary changes.

In his second year, he chose to use WST to drive the transformation. A summit was held with 300 participants, a carefully-selected microcosm of ICT. They represented all units, levels, and locations. The outcomes of this first summit were a clear understanding of the rationale for change, vivid pictures of what success would look like, and clear first steps at the individual, unit, and system-wide levels. The summit was followed by immediate engagement of the entire organization and the translation of actions and commitments from the summit into change projects and individual objectives. The ICT Executive Team and the internal change agent regularly reviewed the progress of projects and objectives. In addition to improved communication, greater empowerment, grass roots initiatives and an increased capacity to act, ICT is getting significantly, and measurably, better at delivering on its projects, services and cost promises to its internal customers.

Our story continues with the CIO's third year and the second application of WST. At the last annual ICT Executive Team retreat, the team celebrated a multitude of transformation achievements and explored the next steps for transformation. They decided that the next areas of focus would be cross-unit or transversal breakthroughs and involvement of the entire ICT formal leadership population. A 12-person design team representative the ICT leadership was empowered to design the large group interactive event. A summit with all of the top 200 ICT managers was convened.

A key theme at the summit was "Leading as ONE". The managers explored the current leadership practices that keep ICT stuck and prevent it from further transforming and from implementing its strategy. They then discussed the positive leadership practices that if increased, enhanced, and developed would significantly help ICT transformation and its strategy implementation.

A key module of the summit was "Hot Potatoes". The managers were asked to identify and describe the top undesirable current situations that prevent them from delivering effectively and efficiently as well as from implementing the ICT strategy. The whole room voted on the top 12 undesirable current situations ("Hot Potatoes") that they most want to transform within the next 12 months. This resulted in 12 traversal transformation projects such as: Leadership alignment; Empowerment; Decision making; Cross-unit working; Management of remote teams; Balance between management and leadership; Budgeting; Sourcing etc. The CIO spontaneously allocated a 7-digit budget for the projects.

Following the summit, each of the 12 projects is sponsored by an ICT Executive, led by a project leader, and supported by one or more Design Team member(s). Each and every ICT manager is expected to work on one of the 12 projects. A formal business improvement methodology is used for the projects. Delegation is not allowed until after the milestone where the as-is analysis is completed and the to-be solutions are defined. The internal change agent and the Design Team perform the programme management and steering functions for the 12 projects to ensure that they will deliver concrete results and reach successful conclusions.

The ICT managers are fully engaged in the 12 projects despite having to work on them on top of their operational activities. This is because they were the ones who decided that these were the right issues to address and they are empowered to address them in the way they see fit. An added benefit of the projects is the increased capacity and capability of the mangers to work across organizational and geographical boundaries as well as in virtual settings. A true community is naturally developing.

In working with the managers, the internal change agent observed that all 12 projects are interrelated and they shine the light on a deeper core systemic issue round time, a rare resource that money cannot buy. ICT is part of a global organization that has experienced and continues to experience tremendous growth. In general, people are already overloaded and stressed in keeping today's business running. At the same time, they are also being asked to transform the business for the future. Focusing on the true top priorities and saying no to lesser priorities still remain difficult for the majority of the people in this global manufacturer.

At the time of this writing, the ICT Executive Team is preparing for its next annual retreat. New conversations are being identified. Like the metaphor of putting the oxygen mask on yourself first before helping others, ICT transformation has been focused mostly, although not exclusively, internally for the last two years. It is now ready to focus outward towards customers and suppliers. The third summit is planned and a new design team that represents the participants (potentially including customers and suppliers) will be nominated by the Executive Team.

At recent communication sessions with the ICT Community, the CIO thanked everyone for their contributions in services and project deliveries as well as progress in transformation. He added: "ICT Transformation has been institutionalized and is delivering credible results. Our journey continues."

Conclusion

David Houle said: "We now live in the Shift Age, a time of transformation that will be regarded by future historians as one of the most significant periods in human history." www.davidhoule.com

For organizations to thrive in the new "Shift Age", we have shared with you a new and what we believe a very powerful methodology that is relevant in helping organizations deal with the rapid, surprising and chaotic global transformation that is occurring at an increased pace.

Our dream is that you will take what we have shared and evolve even more effective and powerful system-wide transformation and change processes that will enable organizations to take advantage of the incredible opportunities that exist in our new globalizing world!

1. Discuss the four phases of Whole Systems Transformation and why each is important to the change process.

2. The purpose of change is to improve business results in the triple bottom lines: profit, people and planet. How would you measure progress and results along your transformation journey?

3. Large group events create tremendous excitement, enthusiasm and energy for change. However, when participants leave the bubble of the event and get back to their daily life, reality tends to take over very quickly. How would you make sure that you capitalize on the momentum generated at the event until the next large group event?

4. Organizing change teams is a critical part of the success of efforts to make significant and lasting changes. Discuss how the various change teams (Leadership Team, 12 Person Design Team, 12 Project Teams) were structured to plan and implement changes.

5. In an organization struggling with growth, a key challenge is to prioritize one's time and activities in order to focus limited resources on the highest priorities. In reality we know that most organizations are incapable of doing this. They are responding to the customer and feel tremendous anxiety and stress to meet the customer deadlines. How do you help the system to find resources and time to deal with the additional change and organizational transformation work?

6. What are the major insights you gained from this case about how to transform organizations?

Key Lessons In Leading Change

1. Sustaining momentum for change after the large group interactive event

The paradigm shift happens during the carefully designed interactive group events. Yet the real work of transformation occurs between interactive events. The structured follow up approach after the second summit proved to be effective. The definition of the 12 transversal projects with descriptions of the undesirable current situations and the desirable future states; the use of a formal improvement methodology as well as project and program management; the executive sponsorship; the engagement of participants in the projects; and the allocation of sufficient funds; ensure the delivery of concrete results. In practice, a core group of people naturally emerged in each project to lead and drive it. The remaining project team members contributed by reviewing and validating the project deliverables. In additional to these formal projects, individual and local initiatives continued to be encouraged and welcomed.

A significant momentum motivator was the commitment to repeat the 4-phase cycle cited in the beginning of the chapter. All managers know that they must face themselves as a system as new members gather in the third large summit. Current project team members wish to pass on to the next group their results which will motivate effective work on newly arising challenges.

2. Finding the resources and time for transformation

We have no great answers to offer and still have a lot to learn about the important issue of finding resources, especially time, in an organization challenged with growth. A hypothesis we have about this global manufacturer is that managers at different levels of the organization are doing the same level of work. One way to free up resources and time is to help everyone in the system to do the right level of work by improving empowerment, delegation, decision-making, alignment and leadership. Another way is to be realistic with the transformation workload that the system can handle on top of operational activities. ICT has learned that it is better to complete a few priority projects effectively within 12 months then to start many initiatives all at once and not achieve results for a long time.

Additional suggestions for finding resources and time:

- Determine as a whole system to stop current activities that are adding the least value.

- Determine planned changes that will create more efficiency so more time is freed up.
- Delegate or outsource tasks that can be done more economically by purchased services.
- Help individuals and teams manage their time better. Especially find ways to have more effective meetings.
- Do more virtual work so time is saved from traveling from country to country. This assumes that great relationships exist between members of virtual teams.

3. Ensuring a long-term sustained journey

In today's uncertain and complex world, the ability to change and adapt is the only sustainable competitive advantage. The WST process must be repeated regularly to ensure a sustained long-term journey. We have observed that everyone who experienced the WST process, regardless of his/her role in the process (design team, logistics team, executive team or participants), develops greater understanding and competences in leading, driving and making change. A total of 33% of the ICT population have been through the transformation process. Over several years, it is possible to engage 100% of the population.

After transferring the WST competences to the internal change agent, the next challenge is for the internal agent to transfer the same to the organization leaders and members themselves so that they can sustain the journey on their own. When this is achieved, ICT would be a truly agile and resilient organization capable of adapting to any external and/or internal challenges. However, ICT is a system embedded within a larger system. Eventually, other parts of the system must also evolve in order for ICT to evolve. The ICT executives have identified five or more potential areas in the larger organization that could benefit from WST.

Going forward the internal change agent has established a core change facilitation team as well as local change agent networks. Although the best way to learn WST is experientially (i.e. by doing), advanced training in facilitating organizational change is recommended.

4. Lead and lag indicators for measuring progress and results

Following a large group interactive event, the lead indicators of success are team spirit, confidence, commitment, relationships, energy, trust, inclusiveness, transparency and alignment which are difficult to measure but can be felt, observed, and captured in anecdotal stories. This is followed by more tangible indicators such as behavioral changes and the definition of improvement projects. However, it is only when the improvement projects are successfully deployed before improved business results, the lag indictors of success, can be measured. It is important that ICT executives and managers understand that easy-to-measure lag indicators of success will come if they recognize, support and nurture the difficult-to-measure but equally valuable lead indicators of success. To create a change receptive and agile culture takes time and requires incredible patience. People often resist change when it is dictated or imposed from the top. Given the opportunity, people willingly support and embrace change that they help to define and create. They do so because at the core we all want to be included, to have our voices heard, and to have a significant role to play in defining and creating a desirable shared future.

Figure 2:

LEAD AND LAG INDICATORS ALONG TRANSFORMATION JOURNEY

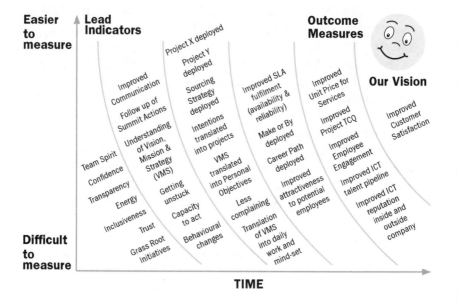

5. WST Differentiators

The synergistic integration of the following elements, applied holistically, are the key differentiators for WST journeys:

- We co-create a compelling purpose with the whole organization.

- We focus on transforming the top leaders and core leadership team before engaging the rest of the organization. The result is a genuinely unified and aligned leadership team on what must change in order to enhance the achievement of business results. Also a commitment to sustaining the journey arises.
- We co-design the entire process with a diverse set of people from within the system (i.e. the design team).
- We take the participants through a real-time experience of dissatisfaction, aspiration, first steps and belief that lead to transformation.
- We build strong committed relationships across, up and down the organization by initiating meaningful dialog on significant issues that are typically not discussed.
- We empower people with critical knowledge at all levels of the organization by creating a safe environment in which to share their truths. The system wide business intelligence ensures the right changes are put into play.

6. Key competencies for change agents and facilitating large groups

The following are the top ten competences that we have identified:

- Knowledge of the business and its language.
- Ability to explain OD and intervention approaches in plain English.
- Ability to intervene from units of one person to small teams ... to the whole system.
- Ability to work with the CEO, executive team, middle managers, and front line employees.
- Good project and programme management skills to drive change implementation.
- Ability to partner with HR.
- Ability to build internal capacities and to know when to get the help of a guru.
- Access to a support network outside of own organization.
- Ability to attract followers and enroll others for a greater cause than themselves (i.e. Level 5 leadership).
- Know thyself, your strengths and your weaknesses.

For more competencies go to: http://x.co/aRqT *(is case sensitive)*

References

Antonymous executive client. (2010). Personal Communication.

Burke, W. (2010). "Warner Burke on Organization Change and Development." A keynote presentation delivered at the 12th Annual "Best of OD Summit" in Chicago, IL.

Cady, S., & Dannemiller, K. (2005). Whole System Transformation. In W. Rothwell, Stavros, J., Sullivan, R., and Sullivan, A. (Eds.). *Practicing Organization Development.* 3rd ed. San Francisco: Pfeiffer.

Dannemiller, K,. (1985). Personal Communication.

Donnan, S., Rothwell, W., Sullivan, R., Dick, T., (2011) Leadership Lessons In Whole System Transformation ™ In Warrick, D., & Mueller, J., (Ed), Lessons in Leadership: Learning from Real World Cases, Colorado Springs, CO: USA Info. Inc.

Haines, S., Aller-Stead, & McKinlay, (2005). *Enterprise-Wide Change: Superior Results Through Systems Thinking.* San Francisco: Pfeiffer.

Rothwell, W., Stavros, J., Sullivan, R., & Sullivan, A. (Eds.). (2009). *Practicing organization development.* 3rd ed. San Francisco: Pfeiffer.

Schein, Ed. (2010). Email communication.

Schein Ed. (1999). Personal communication.

Todd. J., Parker. J., & Sullivan. A.,(2009) Whole system transformation: Becoming dramatically different. In W. Rothwell, J. Stavros, Sullivan, R., and Sullivan, A. (Eds.), *Practicing Organization Development.*3rd ed. San Francisco. Pfeiffer.

Warrick, D., (2009). Valuable insights on OD from contributors. In W. Rothwell, J. Stavros,   R. Sullivan, and A. Sullivan. (Eds.), *Practicing Organization Development.* 3rd ed. San Francisco: Pfeiffer.

Weisbord, M., & Janhoff, S. (2010). *Future Search: An Interview with Marvin and Sandra.* A video available at www.RolandSullivan.com , go to resources then video or www.FutureSearch.net.

BIOGRAPHY

Susan Donnan was initiated into the world of OD with Pat William's MSOD program at Pepperdine University in 1997. She has 30 years of diverse business experience, facilitating complex change in large organizations. She consults cross-culturally in global and trans-national settings. She is currently working in Europe as an internal change agent for a global manufacturer.

Susan can be reached at: sdonnan@metavolution.com

Roland Sullivan was initiated into the world of OD with a Charlie Seashore HR Lab in 1962 at NTL. Roland coined the phrase "Whole System Transformation" in 1974. He is known for "actually" transforming large systems. He has been involved in OD change efforts with over 1,000 organizations in 30 countries. With Rothwell and Pareek, he co-founded the Asian OD Network.

Roland can be reached at: r@rolandsullivan.com

30

Changing A Country Through Transformational Leadership And Teacher Empowerment: Escuela Nueva

Ron Riggio

Major Focus Of The Case

Transformational leadership is one of the most popular theories of leadership today. It combines a leader's charisma with an authentic focus on the followers. Followers are inspired and empowered, and together, leaders and followers are able to transform organizations and systems. This case illustrates transformational leadership through a focus on a leader who inspired elementary educational reform in public schools in a South American nation – a program that has since spread to many other nations. It illustrates how transformational leaders can, through the empowerment of followers, stimulate change in large institutions and on a grand scale.

Introduction

Prior to the 1980s, the scope and quality of education that Colombian children received was very low. Only one out of every five children in Colombia completed five years of basic education, with children in urban areas receiving the greatest amount of schooling. Urban children completed an average of 3.8 years of primary education, but children in the poor rural farming communities averaged only 1.7 years, putting the rural children into the category of being functionally illiterate. Since the 1960s, many attempts had been made to improve education, both by the Colombian government and international agencies such as UNESCO, but nothing seemed to work.

Today, Colombia is one of Latin America's leaders in basic education, with greater numbers of children continually enrolled in school, and improved test scores in language and mathematics. According to UNESCO's First Comparative International Study of Quality Education in 11 countries in 1998, (Laboratorio Latinoamericano de Evaluación de la Calidad de la

Educación) Surpassed only by Cuba, Colombia is the only Latin American country where rural schools outperform their urban counterparts except in large mega cities. In addition, the self-esteem and civic engagement of Colombian school children has soared. What happened to change things?

This amazing transformation is due to the efforts of Escuela Nueva (New School) , which began in the mid-1970s. Vicky Colbert is coauthor of the Escuela Nueva model, jointly with Oscar Mogollon and Beryl Levinger. She is the founder and Director of a Colombian non-profit that continues to innovate and sustain the model, both in Colombia and in many other nations. Vicky is a prototypical transformational leader. As a dynamic leader in the Ministry of Education she rallied exceptional teachers to develop the model that she co-authored. When she became Vice-Minister she continued to build a team of loyal practitioners who took the model to scale, making it national policy. As a Regional Advisor for UNICEF, she motivated her team to apply the model to other countries. Finally, building on the support she had carefully cultivated over time, she began the Fundación Escuela Nueva Volvamos a la Gente to give sustainability to quality education through a civil society organization.

The theory of transformational leadership is rooted in the work of presidential historian and political scientist, James MacGregor Burns (1978) and his distinction between "transactional" and "transforming" leaders. According to Burns, transactional leaders offer exchanges – pay for effort, praise in exchange for employee loyalty, and the like. Transforming leaders, on the other hand, spur followers to higher levels of achievement by focusing on the larger purpose. As a result, both followers and organizations are transformed.

Inspired by Burns, leadership scholar, Bernard Bass (1985), sought to expand on this theory and identified four key components of what he called "transformational leaders." These four components are: *Idealized Influence* which involves the leader being a positive (and moral) role model for followers; *Inspirational Motivation* which is the ability to inspire and motivate followers by providing meaning and challenge. Taken together, Idealized Influence and Inspirational Motivation constitute what is commonly called leader "charisma"; *Individualized Consideration* is the leader's attention to the needs and concerns of each individual follower, spurring their growth through coaching and mentoring; *Intellectual Stimulation* is the transformational leader's emphasis on challenging followers to be innovative, creative, and to "think outside the box." [*see Table 1* for more detailed descriptions of the components of transformational leadership.]

Table 1: **Components of Transformational Leadership and Definitions**

Component of TL	Definition
Idealized Influence	Transformational leaders serve as positive role models for their followers. They emphasize the collective mission of the group or organization and demonstrate high standards of ethical conduct.
Inspirational Motivation	Transformational leaders are able to inspire and motivate followers through their display of enthusiasm, optimism and the articulation of attractive future outcomes.
Individualized Consideration	Transformational leaders pay particular attention to each follower's needs, concerns, and personal development and growth. The leader encourages the personalized development of each one through mentoring and coaching.
Intellectual Stimulation	Transformational leaders challenge followers in an effort to stimulate their creativity and innovation by questioning assumptions, reframing problems, and encouraging followers to take risks and try new approaches.

Research on transformational leadership has sought to better understand the process by which leaders transform followers and organizations. Evidence suggests that transformational leaders enhance followers' sense of self-efficacy, so that they believe in their capacity to perform their tasks (Bass & Riggio, 2006). Typically, this is done through empowering followers, whereby the leader encourages followers to take on challenging tasks, and supports and coaches them throughout the process. This not only leads to greater levels of performance on the part of followers, but also the transformational leader builds leadership capacity in followers through the empowerment process.

Background on Escuela Nueva

Vicky Colbert was a young, energetic public servant in the Ministry of Education charged with coordinating projects of rural schools. It was clear that the children in rural schools in remote villages were performing poorly and completing fewer years of elementary education than their urban counterparts. Vicky began visiting these rural schools and she discovered teachers in remote areas who were applying innovations in the Unitary School Program, promoted by UNESCO worldwide since the 1960s. Vicky met Oscar Moggollon, one of the outstanding teachers at a UNESCO demonstration school and together, with Beryl Levinger, a USAID professional, they designed and coauthored the new model, which they named Escuela Nueva. Vicky worked hard to combine best practices and to form a team of practitioners who gradually created a national consensus to implement the model. They were successful because they created strategies to make the model technically, politically and financially viable. From the outset the design took into consideration the possibility of scaling up to other regions and nations and eventually led to replication on a large scale.

The traditional education system in Colombia at the time consisted of the teacher as a presenter of facts in a single grade classroom. In the small remote rural schools there was just one teacher handling all of the grade levels in the same classroom. This was commonly known as the unitary school, known today worldwide as multi-grade schools where one teacher handles multiple grades in the same room. Although the unitary school gave teachers techniques to handle several grades simultaneously, teachers were characteristically overburdened, and students were not getting age-appropriate attention. In addition, much of the traditional learning was theoretical and irrelevant to rural children. Therefore, compared to students from the cities, rural students were less engaged, performed poorly, and were less likely to continue the following year. There were difficulties in reaching the goal of providing universal primary education for all children. Vicky and her colleagues concentrated on leading the change from the unitary school to the Escuela Nueva model that introduced a more comprehensive and systemic approach to improve quality learning in all schools.

The Escuela Nueva model that Vicky Colbert and her colleagues developed is designed to improve the quality of basic education through the use of proven educational practices that encourage active participation in the learning process, cooperative and self paced learning and enhancement of self-esteem and civic engagement. The curriculum promotes practical examples from the students' local environments and strengthens and promotes participation of parents in the learning process.

Teachers take on the role of guide and learning facilitator rather than the more traditional presenter of information, and teachers are encouraged to engage families and the local community. Instruction is personalized and child-centered, and peer-to-peer learning is also encouraged. Teachers are trained and provided with learning guides and instructional materials that are tailored to the students' needs and their local environment. Follow-up programs are used to support teachers, to keep them engaged, and to provide ongoing training.

Not only has the Escuela Nueva boosted the educational attainment of students in Colombia, but has spread to other countries in Latin America, mainly through governments and to some African and Asian nations, including Vietnam, East Timor and has inspired many innovations in the Philippines. The program is a great success, due largely to the efforts of its leader and primary advocate, Vicky Colbert. By recognizing teachers' abilities and promoting them as leaders and innovators themselves, the model has earned worldwide notoriety.

Transforming the Educational Process:
An Analysis of Vicky Colbert's Transformational Leadership

Vicky Colbert began the Escuela Nueva program within the Colombian Ministry of Education. She realized that it would be a challenge to persuade the government to explore alternatives to existing educational structures and practices, but the poor results in rural schools required trying a different, more systemic approach.

Vicky was a very high-energy professional in the Ministry of Education. It was a combination of her charisma, coupled with her dedication to the vision of implementing a better educational system, which helped her persuade the Ministry of Education and school district officials to try Escuela Nueva.

As Vicky tells it, "I was young, vibrant, and had lots of energy." She realized that part of the problem was that the remote, rural schools were "invisible" to many in the Ministry, so she began bringing successful teachers from the provinces to the national and ministerial level. Simultaneously, she took Ministry officials and other politicians into these remote villages to see for themselves why the traditional education process was not working and why the Escuela Nueva approach was the solution. She started the Escuela Nueva program within the Ministry and organized the first national team from Escuela Nueva. As a variety of teachers were recognized, their loyalty proved to be indispensable. With their help, Vicky set up demonstration schools in some of the rural communities. Vicky continued to promote some of the teachers, who became professionals and moved into different spheres –in the Ministry, in bi-lateral agencies and educational institutions. Many of them make up the core of her team in the Escuela Nueva NGO that she later founded. She was able to make the best practices of successful teachers visible to education officials and others.

Two key components of transformational leadership – Inspirational Motivation and Idealized Influence – represent the leader's charisma.

Vicky Colbert's high energy and inspiring vision for transforming elementary education made her a much-noticed figure in the Education Ministry. Her commitment to the cause was evident and she took every opportunity to inspire those in the Ministry to get behind her educational reform efforts. By taking officials to the remote demonstration schools, Vicky became the "face" of the educational reform movement.

Vicky Colbert also exhibited the two other components of transformational leadership, Individualized Consideration and Intellectual Stimulation. By promoting a child-centered participatory model, she allowed teachers to do what they do best: to engage and encourage children to flourish in school. This required that teachers received peer support, relevant training depending on their specific needs and appropriate materials. Vicky also pushed teachers to take ownership of their classrooms and to involve local communities – extending their influence beyond the classroom. Multiple stakeholders – children, teachers, communities and local school administrators – benefitted when teachers were empowered. It is this concern with the specific needs of followers, and challenging them to expand their horizons and think creatively that are key characteristics of transformational leaders.

The key to success for Escuela Nueva was consistent with the dynamics of transformational leadership theory. In transformational leadership, leaders empower followers, in this case, the teachers, to take ownership of their jobs and their classrooms. They are challenged to be innovative and are provided the needed support in order to improve their work (curriculum) and their teaching. In addition, transformational leaders build followers leadership capacity, and many of the teachers went on to leadership positions in the educational ministry and elsewhere.

The Challenge of Sustainability

Vicky Colbert established the Escuela Nueva program working within Colombia's Education Ministry, but she realized that such an innovative program might get lost in the government bureaucracy. Therefore, she began a non-profit, non-governmental organization (NGO), the Escuela Nueva Volvamos a la Gente in order to ensure the sustainability of the model. A number of her original collaborators accompanied her in this new endeavor and as a team they continue to innovate and apply the model. The program also became highly recognized with other countries wanting to adopt the Escuela Nueva model and materials. The World Bank, UNICEF,

Interamerican Development Bank have supported Escuela Nueva and provided additional funding to expand the program.

During the early nineties, however, dramatic changes in the Colombian government led to decentralization of education programs, resulting in the transfer of many teachers and a loss of funding for the program. As Vicky Colbert explains, "We had to essentially start all over again." With support from international organizations, and from private sector alliances, such as the coffee growers associations, the Escuela Nueva program was revived. As Vicky tells it, "the teachers kept it going. The program is decentralized and is continuing to thrive and expand." The teachers are the main force of change and, in essence, continue to innovate and apply the model and to lead educational reforms, fulfilling the transformational leadership concept of developing followers into leaders.

Discussion

1. Visionary, transformational leaders can accomplish great things. Vicky Colbert was a young employee in the Columbia Ministry of Education with a commitment to improving education in Columbia. Describe the educational situation in Columbia before she pursued her vision, what her vision for the future was, and what she was able to accomplish.

2. To motivate significant change, it is important to have a compelling and understandable plan and to reach the hearts and minds of influential leaders. What did Vicky Colbert do to prepare herself, organize a vision and easy to understand plan, and convince the Ministry of Education to fund her project?

3. Discuss the four major components of Transformational Leadership shown in Table 1 and how Vicky Colbert practiced each one.

4. Who were the various stakeholders Vicky Colbert identified and how did she engage and involve them in the change process?

5. Changes often regress and unravel if there is not a plan for sustaining them. What did Vicky Colbert do to sustain the program she developed with Oscar Mogollon and Beryl Levinger so the program would not be dependent on political and economic conditions in Columbia?

6. Are there present or future possibilities, large or small, where you could be a transformational leader?

Key Lessons In Leading Change

1. Transformational leaders who understand how to lead, manage, and sustain changes can accomplish far more change that most think would be possible.

2. Although a leader's enthusiasm, zeal, and charisma helps get others' attention, and can be a source of inspiration and motivation, transformational leadership theory goes beyond charisma and examines how leaders AND followers can work together to create organizational and societal transformation.

3. Some of the elements of transformational leadership involve empowering followers, challenging them to be creative, innovative, and to take ownership of their work. Transformational leaders also understand individual follower's needs, desires, and their strengths, providing the support that each follower needs in order to thrive and grow.

4. Transformational leadership is a relationship-centered approach to leadership, involving leaders and followers collaborating to lead the group or organization.

5. Vicky and her team were able to reframe the problems of rural basic education in Colombia and provide new solutions based on best practices. This has been a dynamic process that includes continuous input and innovation from multiple team members. A key to transformational leadership is providing opportunities for innovation and for the continued development of followers' leadership capacity.

References

Bass, B.M. (1985). *Leadership and performance beyond expectations.* New York: Free Press.

Bass, B.M., & Riggio, R.E. (2006). *Transformational leadership* (2nd ed.). Mahwah, NJ: Lawrence Erlbaum.

Burns, J.M. (1978). *Leadership.* New York: Harper & Row.

BIOGRAPHY

Ronald E. Riggio, Ph.D. is the Henry R. Kravis
Professor of Leadership and Organizational
Psychology and former Director of the Kravis
Leadership Institute at Claremont McKenna College.
Professor Riggio is the author of over a dozen
books, and 100 book chapters and research articles
in the areas of leadership, assessment centers,
organizational psychology and social psychology.
Recent books include *The Art of Followership,
The Practice of Leadership* (Jossey-Bass, 2008, 2007),
Transformational Leadership, 2nd ed., coauthored
with Bernard M. Bass (Erlbaum, 2006), and
Leadership Studies: The Dialogue of Disciplines
(Elgar, 2012). He is the leadership blogger for
Psychology Today magazine.

Dr. Roggio can be reached at: Ron.riggio@cmc.edu.

Also available in this Case Book series:

Learning from Real World Cases: **Lessons in Leadership**
High interest cases for leaders, students and teachers that address the essentials of being a high impact leader.

Learning from Real World Cases: **Lessons in Leading Change**
Practical and interesting cases for leaders, students and teachers that address the essentials of leading and guiding changes.

Learning from Real World Cases: **Lessons in Changing Cultures**
Practical and interesting cases for leaders, students and teachers that address the essentials of leading in different corporate cultures.

Lessons from Worldwide Best Practice Cases: **Non-Profit Excellence**
These cases from around the world help make the complex environment of Non-Profit Management transparent and intuitive.

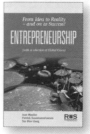

Learning from Best Practices Worldwide: **Human Resource Excellence**
This set of global cases demonstrating highly effective human resource management techniques are a superb resource for learners and HR managers.

Learning from Cases Nationwide: **Canadian Business Excellence**
Look deeply into the best-performing Canadian organizations and learn from the tools leaders use to deliver extraordinary outcomes.

From Idea to Reality – and on to Success! **Entrepreneurship**
Creating successful and sustainable enterprises is not easy. Learn from those who have done it – and review short case examples that illustrate entrepreneurship success.

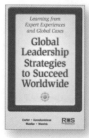

Learning from Expert Experiences and Global Cases: **Global Leadership Strategies to Succeed Worldwide**
No organization can develop today without understanding global markets, competition and cultures. This book is a no-nonsense guide to operating successfully worldwide.

For more Info, Book Sales and Online Downloads visit
RossiSmith www.publicationsales.com